Public and Civil Service in Poland

Ius, Lex et Res Publica
Studies in Law, Philosophy and Political Cultures

Edited by Barbara Janusz-Pohl and Anna Jaron

Volume 37

Tomasz Barankiewicz / Bogusław Przywora (eds.)

Public and Civil Service in Poland

PETER LANG

Berlin - Bruxelles - Chennai - Lausanne - New York - Oxford

Bibliographic Information published by the Deutsche Nationalbibliothek
The Deutsche Nationalbibliothek lists this publication in the Deutsche Nationalbibliografie; detailed bibliographic data is available in the internet at http://dnb.d-nb.de.

Library of Congress Cataloging-in-Publication Data
A CIP catalog record for this book has been applied for at the Library of Congress.

This publication was financially supported
by Jan Dlugosz University in Czestochowa, Poland.

Cover illustration: Courtesy of Benjamin Ben Chaim.

ISSN 2191-3250
ISBN 978-3-631-90564-7 (Print)
E-ISBN 978-3-631-92800-4 (E-Book)
E-ISBN 978-3-631-92833-2 (E-PUB)
DOI 10.3726/b22476

Published by Peter Lang GmbH, Berlin, Deutschland

info@peterlang.com - www.peterlang.com

This publication has been peer reviewed.
www.peterlang.com

Table of Contents

List of Contributors

Tomasz Barankiewicz

The John Paul II Catholic University of Lublin, Poland

https://orcid.org/0000-0002-2454-1456

Anna Budzanowska

University of Silesia in Katowice, Cracow University of Economics, Poland

ORCID: 0000-0002-8662-605X

Jarosław Czerw

Jan Kochanowski University of Kielce

ORCID: 0000-0003-2042-3177

Anna Deryng-Dziuk

Jan Dlugosz University in Czestochowa, Poland

ORCID: 0000-0003-0714-2055

Wojciech Drobny

Institute of Legal Sciences of the Polish Academy of Sciences

ORCID: 0000-0002-7956-4348

Jadwiga Glimińska-Pawlic

Jan Dlugosz Uviversity in Czestochowa

ORCID: 0000-002-2256-4558

Marcin Grzybowski

Cracow University of Economics

ORCID: 0000-0003-1905-8942

Marcin Gubała

WSB Merito University in Gdansk, Poland

ORCID: 0000-0001-8443-3206

Hubert Izdebski

University SWPS, Warsaw

ORCID: 0000-0002-3390-4167

Olgierd Kucharski

Jan Dlugosz University in Czestochowa, Poland

ORCID: 0000-0002-9633-9281

Aleksander Lipinski

Jan Dlugosz University in Czestochowa, Poland

ORCID: 0000-0002-9947-0007

Mariusz Paradowski

Jan Dlugosz University in Czestochowa, Poland

ORCID: 0000-0003-0874-5181

Bogusław Przywora

Jan Długosz University in Czestochowa, Poland

ORCID: 0000-0002-8809-3971

Aleksandra Syryt

Cardinal Stefan Wyszyński in Warsaw, Poland

ORCID: 0000-0002-7501-0786

Adam Wróbel

ORCID: 0000-0002-9315-0213

Jan Dlugosz University in Czestochowa, Poland

Małgorzata Wróblewska

Jan Dlugosz Uniwersity in Czestochowa, Poland

ORCID: 0000-0002-0362-4586

Lidia Zacharko

ORCID: 0000-0002-3799-5502

University of Silesia in Katowice, Poland

Tomasz Barankiewicz, Bogusław Przywora

Introduction

The presented collection of studies by several authors is an attempt at a multi-level analysis of the contemporary and newest issues of "Public and civil service in Poland". This is the result of several years of research conducted at the Faculty of Law and Economics of Jan Dlugosz University in Czestochowa, as well as the Open Scientific Seminar conducted jointly with the Department of Legal Theory and Philosophy of Law at the Faculty of Law, Canon Law, and Administration of KUL in the years 2022–23. The Authors of the monograph endeavoured to present legal and organizational solutions in the field of public and civil service in Poland.

The argument in favour of the choice of particular problems was their social significance and usefulness. The outcome of this work is the formulation of practical *de lege lata* and *de lege ferenda* conclusions. However, due to different ways of thinking and proposed solutions, they may constitute – we hope – an important inspiration for further reflections, research and practical conclusions.

The submitted materials for publication turned out to be difficult to organize. Therefore, we decided to arrange them in alphabetical order according to the authors' last names. The most significant merit of the presented research results is the timeliness of the issues addressed. In this regard, an important stimulus for the discussed topic was the centenary of the first civil service law enacted in Poland in 2022. This occurred just under three years after regaining independence. During this time, the civil service became a significant element in rebuilding Polish statehood. Currently, compiling various viewpoints and experiences into a single monographic study may help the reader gain a broad perspective on the selected research area. The authors point out dimensions and aspects of shaping public service and civil service in Poland that require attention and scholarly debate, proposing the exploration of new ways to solve both known and entirely new problems. However, addressing the timeliness of the issues does not imply a rejection of what constitutes important achievements in the Polish public service and civil service domain.

We hope that the presented monograph will allow readers to deepen their knowledge of the Polish public and civil service, providing a comparative law perspective and thus contributing to further discussions in this field. The work can be a valuable source of knowledge for students, researchers, and practitioners involved in legislative processes.

Editors

Anna Budzanowska, Marcin Gubała

Paradoxes of the Polish Civil Service

1. Historical Background

Immediately after the overthrow of the communist regime in 1989, during political transformation, the question of regulating the status of civil servants was regarded as a priority by pro-democratic decision-makers. Therefore, regulations on the establishment of the civil service were undertaken as one of the first legislative initiatives[1]. The aim was to pave the way for changes to the structure and operation of the public administration. Despite the urgency, the transformation process took several years. The reason for this was great instability of the political scene in the early 1990s[2].

The establishment of a professional, politically neutral civil service was planned as part of the initial phase of reforms carried out by the early independent governments. This was necessary in view of the expectations regarding the organization of the administration in the aftermath of the post-communist period in the Polish People's Republic and in view of the new democratic challenges in the existing political and ideological conditions. In accordance with the adopted concept, the paradigm in use at the time for establishing the civil service was reversed and it now focused on a neo-Weberian model[3]. This was to be guaranteed by statutory norms separating the future administration model from the previous system on its way to contemporary European administration. This resulted from the necessity to provide the reborn public institutions with appropriately prepared and systematically positioned staff understanding the need to introduce new standards for the reconstruction of state structures. The first legislative initiative in this respect brought a glimpse of change and in 1991 it

1 H. Izdebski, *Współczesne modele administracji*, Urząd Rady Ministrów, Pełnomocnik Rządu do spraw. Reformy Administracji Publicznej, Wydawnictwo Urząd Rady Ministrów, Warszawa 1993.

2 B. Springer, *Przesłanki i uwarunkowania tworzenia nowoczesnego korpusu służby cywilnej w Polsce po 1989 roku*, in: *Stulecie polskiej administracji. Doświadczenia i perspektywy*, KSAP, Warsaw 2018, pp. 785–788.

3 See above.

led to the adoption of the Act on the National School of Public Administration[4]. It introduced a new concept of administration, primarily by establishing a dedicated, professional corps of civil servants. However, five years had to pass before further changes began.

It should be emphasized that the first transformational package of laws – the above-mentioned Act on the National School of Public Administration of 1991 and the Civil Service Act of 1996[5], clearly followed the tradition of the interwar legislation. These acts constituted the framework for an institutional system operating mainly in the area of administrative law. It should also be pointed out that these acts established a public law corps of civil servants, selected by way of appointment. The legislator transferred the classically formulated values and legal status of a civil servant in relations with the state as the aims and axioms of the Polish civil service to the provisions of Art. 153 of the 1997 Constitution of the Republic of Poland, i.e. "professional, reliable, impartial and politically neutral performance of state tasks"[6]. This was undoubtedly a constitutive moment for establishing the civil service in the reborn Poland. Therefore, it may be assessed that the above regulations were a success and an important phase in forming a democratic state of law. On the one hand, the act gave hope of depoliticising the administration and, on the other hand, of forming professional staff. However, due to purely political reasons and particular party interests, its legal existence ended in mid-1999, when the amendment to the Civil Service Act passed on 18th December 1998 came into force[7].

This was the first in a series of amendments introduced between 1998 and 2016, the final year analysed in this chapter. In the above period, the adopted amendments were a manifestation of the transformation of the concept and a departure from the original form of the legal status of the civil service as a consequence of the legislator's actions subordinated to party particularisms. Analyses indicate that between 1998 and 2015 amendments were adopted in time sequences corresponding with a regular rhythm of the elections to suit the aims of dynamically changing government coalitions.

4 S. Mazur, M. Możdżeń, M. Oramus, *The instrumental and ideological politicisation of senior positions* in Poland's Civil Service and Its Selected Consequences. The NISPAcee Journal of Public Administration and Policy 11, No. 1 (2018), pp. 63–89.

5 Dz.U. 1996, nr 89, poz. 402./OJ 1996, No. 89, item 402.

6 Constitution of the Republic of Poland of 2nd April 1997 (Journal of Laws, item 483, as amended).

7 Dz.U. 1998, nr 49, poz. 483./OJ 1998, No. 49, item 483.

In the first decade, between 1998 and 2008, changes for the civil service in the area of regulations on civil servants, expanded their axiological principles. The 1998 amendment already reformulated the administrative paradigm adopted in the first period of political transformation, shifting the regulation of relations at work to the area of labour law in terms of establishing a professional corps of civil servants. Labour law tools were introduced by diversifying the employment bases for members of the civil service corps. At that time, first of all, the subjective scope of the corps was changed, as in accordance with the new regulation everyone employed in government administration belonged to it, not only the appointed civil servants which used to be the case before. The civil service corps was divided into two categories: civil servants and civil service staff whose employment relationship was established on the basis of an employment contract. As a result, the number of corps members increased from 104 on 1st January 1999 to 116,613, including 99 civil servants, on 31st December 1999[8]. A category of senior positions was also formally introduced. The act was in force until 2006, when further amendments introducing new public law solutions were passed[9]. A state personnel resource was set up, the creation of which was said to be unconstitutional. As a consequence of the above legislation, a dual system appeared in the public service, i.e. the civil service and the State Personnel Resource – a set of candidates for high state positions[10]. However, the provisions of this amendment remained in force for an extremely short time, as already in 2008, together with a new government coalition, the legislator passed another amendment which partially restored the solutions of the 1998 Act[11]. It should be added here that during the period in question there were plans to regulate the legal status of civil servants, derogating from the provisions of the 1982 Act and subjecting their status to the regime of the Civil Service Act, but the legislator did not address this issue[12]. Instead a decision was made according to which appointment by way of competition in the civil service was to be open

8 See: Sprawozdanie Szefa Służby Cywilnej o stanie służby cywilnej i realizacji zadań tej służby za rok 1999, Kancelaria Prezesa Rady Ministrów, Warszawa 2000, p. 8.

9 Dz.U. 2006, nr 79, poz. 549; Dz.U. 2006, nr 170, poz. 1218;/OJ 2006, No. 79, item 549; OJ 2006, No. 170, item 1218;

10 Dz.U. 2006, nr 170, poz. 1217./OJ 2006, No. 170, item 1217.

11 Dz.U. 2008, nr 227, poz. 1505 z późn. zm./OJ 2008, No. 227, item 1505 as amended.

12 H. Szewczyk, Opinia prawna do rządowego projektu nowelizacji ustawy o zmianie ustawy o służbie cywilnej 15.09.2008, Biuro Analiz Sejmowych./H. Szewczyk, Legal opinion on the government's draft amendment to the Act amending the Civil Service Act 15 Sept. 2008, Sejm Analyses Office.

to persons not belonging to the corps, which was to make civil service more competitive. A profound change in the above-mentioned area also took place after the elections in 2015. An amendment introduced another, third category of members to the civil service corps, i.e. those holding a higher position in the civil service by way of appointment[13]. The above solution caused controversy.

Even such a brief review of the changing concept of regulating the status of civil servants and the current status of the Civil Service Act allows to assume that it is facing another process of changes. The transformations to date, i.e. the abandoning of the vision inscribed in the 1997 Constitution and introducing solutions that are not compatible with one another, lead to reflection on systemic paradoxes, which will be discussed in the subsequent parts of the chapter.

2. The First Paradox – The Incompleteness of the Civil Service

The first paradox refers to the objective and subjective scope of regulations relating to the civil service corps. This paradox is that contrary to clear provisions in the Constitution, the civil service, specified at the statutory level, does not include all the administrative government agencies, which means that the constitutional understanding of the civil service corps has been narrowed down.

It should be pointed out that the Constitution of the Republic of Poland[14] does not contain any exceptions to the principle that the civil service covers the entire government administration. It is also not possible to interpret the provisions of Art. 153 section 1 of the Constitution, assuming that the legislator has the competence to establish exceptions at the statutory level. This regulation is complete (i.e. it does not refer to other statutory regulations) and absolute (i.e. it does not contain exceptions that could be specified in other legal acts). This means that the legislator has fully defined the civil service. Acts may (and should) regulate issues that are derived from this systemic decision, but the statutory matter must fit within the constitutional framework and cannot constitute an exception to it.[15].

---

13 Dz.U. 2016, poz. 34./OJ 2016, item. 34.

14 Konstytucja Rzeczypospolitej Polskiej z dnia 2 kwietnia 1997 r. (Dz. U. poz. 483, z późn. zm.)/Constitution of the Republic of Poland of 2nd April 1997 (Journal of Laws, item 483, as amended).

15 If the possibility of making such exceptions were allowed at the statutory level, it would be possible to justify, for example, the legislator's action, which would involve abandoning the requirement of political neutrality of the civil service or introducing solutions enabling non-compliance with this principle in the case of employees of certain government administration agencies.

In the absence of clearly established constitutional exceptions, it may therefore be concluded that the legislator's intention was to establish the civil service as a body covering the entire administrative state apparatus. If the legislator's intention was to set apart the status of civil servants working for the government, such a suggestion would be included in the Constitution as an exception to the principle of "universality" of the civil service within the government administration.

Pursuant to Art. 153 section 1 of the Constitution of the Republic of Poland, the civil service corps operates in the "government administration". The literature on the subject therefore states that "The term 'government administration' refers to an organizational structure with specific connections with the Council of Ministers, the Prime Minister or ministers. This structure includes government administration bodies and offices, understood as organizational units that form the auxiliary apparatus through which the bodies perform their tasks and exercise their competences. To recognize an office as a government administration office, two conditions must be met simultaneously: the performance of public administration tasks and location in the segment of state apparatus headed by the government, i.e. the Council of Ministers (...). The fulfilment of the latter condition is determined by submission to the 'management' as well as 'coordination and control' of the Council of Ministers, however these functions may also be exercised by the Prime Minister and ministers"[16].

In other words, it should be considered that according to the provisions of a fundamental and systemic nature – the civil service corps should be present in all those institutions that constitute government administration, referred to in Art. 153 of the Constitution of the Republic of Poland. Confirmation of this view may be found in the literature: "Article 153 allows for the thesis that the entire body of civil servants performing tasks for the public administration in its part subject to the Council of Ministers should be covered by the Civil Service Act and, as such, form part of it."[17].

The scope of the civil service also follows from statutory regulations. Article 2 of the Act of 21st November 2008 on the Civil Service[18] lists the offices where the Civil Service Corps operates. However, other statutory regulations show that this catalogue does not cover all those employed by the government administration. In this respect, reference may be made in particular to the Act of 16th September

---

16 P. Czarny [in:] *Konstytucja Rzeczypospolitej Polskiej. Komentarz*, 2nd edition, ed. P. Tuleja, Warszawa 2023, art. 153.

17 *Ibid.*

18 Dz. U. z 2022 r. poz. 1691, z późn. zm./OJ of 2022 item 1691, as amended.

1982 on employees of state offices[19], which in Art. 1 section 2 indicates that there are employees of government administration offices who are not subject to the regulations in the Civil Service Act[20].

In this context, it is rightly pointed out that "many acts lead to decomposition introduced by the commented taxonomy provision. A good example of this are regulations regarding the Customs and Tax Service. Although this institution falls within the scope of Art. 2 section 1 of the Civil Code, an analysis of the provisions of the Act on the National Tax Administration leads to a different conclusion. The employees of this entity constitute a separate category from the civil service. The above process, an example of which is the Customs and Tax Service, motivated by many things, often beyond the scope of reasons which are of legal nature (for instance a frequent motive for excluding particular groups from the civil service corps is the desire to give a given institution a special position), should be critically assessed. It leads to a distortion of the systematics and unnecessary inflation of regulations regarding the status of employees of individual institutions"[21].

The legislative practice which assumes this type of "weakening" the civil service is not justified by the constitutional norms, which clearly determine the need to maintain the comprehensiveness of the regulations defining the scope of the civil service. Any departures from the principle of universal corps in government administration are questionable from the point of view of the constitutional structure of the civil service.

3. The Second Paradox –Heterogeneity of the Civil Service

The second paradox refers to the internal structure of the civil service corps. Contrary to the framework structure of the system, the civil service is not

19 Dz. U. z 2023 r. poz. 917./OJ of 2023 item 917.

20 For instance, the Forest Seed Office is part of the government administration, because it is a budgetary unit whose purpose is to perform the tasks referred to in Art. 10 of the Act of 7th June 2001 on forest reproductive material (Journal of Laws of 2019, item 1097). This includes for issuing permits for the import of forest reproductive material from countries that are not members of the European Union, as well as for carrying out inspections of forest reproductive material in terms of meeting the requirements specified in the Act. Meanwhile, Art. 1 section 2 point 8 of the Act on employees of state offices indicates the Office as an office employing staff who do not form part of the civil service corps.

21 M. Wujczyk [in:] *Ustawa o służbie cywilnej. Komentarz*, ed. K. W. Baran, Warszawa 2021, art. 2.

uniform. In fact, it consists of two "subsystems", one of which covers only senior positions in the civil service while the other includes the remaining civil servant positions.

The basis for this division is the applicable legal status, in which the service includes:

1. employees and civil servants of the civil service;
2. persons employed in a higher position in the civil service[22].

It would be important to indicate the origins of this division into categories in the civil service. The distinction between employees and civil servants in the civil service was one of the principles specific to the civil service system and allowed for the identification of a promotion (development) mechanism for the corps members. This mechanism consisted, broadly speaking, of provided an opportunity to obtain a different legal basis for employment, additional remuneration rights, as well as other employee rights. Civil servants have been normatively defined as those members of the administrative apparatus whose status is more difficult to achieve and to whom increased qualification requirements apply. In other words, there was a differentiation of the civil service in terms of "quality", which was intended to define a promotion path – from an employee to a civil servant[23].

This traditional distinction was further added to by another one, interfering with the logic of the civil service system outlined above. Act of 30th December 2015 amending the Civil Service Act and certain other acts[24] significantly modified the civil service system by defining a new group of corps members, i.e. people holding senior positions in the civil service[25]. Characteristically,

---

22 See art. 3 of the Civil Service Act.

23 However, as it is pointed out in the literature, "It seems justified (…) to introduce a mechanism to uniform the status of a civil servant regardless of the basis for establishing an employment relationship, which in fact serves as a factor of differentiation in the subjective aspect in the group of employees in the civil service structure". See: M. Lekston [in:] *Ustawa o służbie cywilnej. Komentarz*, ed. K. W. Baran, Warszawa 2021, art. 3.

24 Dz. U. z 2016 r. poz. 34./OJ of 2016 item 34.

25 Pursuant to Art. 52 of the Act, these include the positions of the director general of the office; the head of a department or an equivalent unit in the Chancellery of the Prime Minister, a minister's office, an office supporting the chairman of a committee of the Council of Ministers, an office of a central government administration body, and the head of a department or equivalent unit in a voivodeship office, as well as their deputies; the provincial veterinarian and their deputy; district veterinarian and their deputy; the provincial inspector of commercial quality of agri-food products

the above-mentioned amendment resulted in an amendment to Art. 6 of the Act, which so far stipulated that recruitment for the civil service is open and competitive (without general exclusion of any category of positions). Since the entry into force of the amendment, an exception has been made in this important systemic rule: it has been indicated that it does not apply to matters regulated in Chapter 4 of the Act, i.e. the systematization unit that applies to senior positions in the civil service. The provisions contained in this chapter stated that "unlike the previous legal situation – persons holding higher positions in the civil service (referred to in Article 52(1)) will be selected by way of appointment, rather than by open and competitive recruitment"[26]. This exclusion means that in the case of filling these positions, there is no requirement to conduct recruitment for a vacant position in the civil service.

A number of objections were raised against this legislative solution such as for instance "Measures should be used that are sufficient to achieve an intended aim and which do not significantly exceed necessity. Therefore, if there is any doubt whether competition procedures are resolved according to substantive criteria leading to the selection of the best candidates, mechanisms (such as control mechanisms) should be introduced to ensure proper conduct of these procedures resulting in appropriate outcomes, rather than abolishing them altogether"[27]. Moreover, it was pointed out that the amendment in question "may be perceived as an action motivated by political conditions, standing in clear opposition to a directive for the politically neutral performance of state tasks provided in Art. 153 of the Constitution of the Republic of Poland. This view seems even more justified, taking into account the nature of positions defined as higher in the organizational structures of the civil service, where key decisions are made as part of the exercise of public authority"[28].

It should be recognized that the mentioned regulation, which excludes the principle of recruitment by way of competition for the highest positions

---

and their deputy; the head of the organizational unit in the Forest Seed Office, as well as the deputy of this person; the director of the National Tax Information Office, the director of the tax administration chamber, the head of the tax office, the head of the customs and tax office, as well as their deputies.

26 A. Banaszkiewicz, *Nowelizacja ustawy o służbie cywilnej z dnia 30 grudnia 2015 r. w kontekście wymogu neutralności politycznej członków korpusu służby cywilnej*, Studia Iuridica Lublinensia XXV, No. 4 (2016), p. 10.

27 Ibidem, p. 23.

28 M. Lekston [in:] *Ustawa o służbie cywilnej. Komentarz*, red. K. W. Baran, Warszawa 2021, art. 6.

in the civil service, constitutes a denial of the constitutional principle of professionalism of the service. As it is assumed that the service is to be moulded also by the political element basically without any normative limitations, it is difficult to maintain assurances of professionalism of the service. It seems that these assurances (updated initially at the stage of recruitment to the civil service) prove unnecessary in relation to senior officers in government administration offices. The legislator assumed that lower positions in the service should be filled with stricter requirements than in the case of recruitment for higher positions. This is a reversal of the order associated with the fundamental principles of the civil service. Before the discussed amendment to the law, the essence of office management included recruiting individuals for higher positions who had to demonstrate qualifications that exceeded those of the staff employed in lower positions. Currently, it is different: to become a general director or a department director there is no need to undergo any verification procedures, and the only necessary condition for taking up such a position is the support of the political factor[29].

4. The Third Paradox – Remuneration in the State Apparatus

The third paradox refers to remuneration of members of the civil service corps, and more precisely – to the subject of the relation of such remuneration to the remuneration of other groups operating in the public sector[30]. The paradox is that despite the important systemic role assigned to the civil service by the Constitution of the Republic of Poland, remuneration in this part of the public sector is lower than remuneration in some public institutions outside the civil service.

---

29 This follows from Article 53a (1) of the Civil Service Act, according to which a person for the position of Director General is appointed and dismissed by the competent Minister, Head of a Central Office, Head of the Prime Minister's Office (without any vetting procedure). This solution results in the Director General becoming a person who, by virtue of the regulations, "transfers" this method of filling positions in government offices to lower levels of government (Art. 53a (2) in conjunction with Art. 52(2) of the Act).

30 The term "public sector" should be understood in the broadest sense as a set of institutions comprising "the totality of public organisations whose main purpose is to fulfil the tasks arising from the functions assumed by the state". See: R. Przygodzka, *Efektywność sektora publicznego*, Optimum – Studia Ekonomiczne 4, Nr. 40 (2008), p. 159.

It should be pointed out that the Constitution distinguishes only several professional groups in the public sector. In particular, one must mention judges who were the only ones to receive direct constitutional authorization regarding the amount and method of remuneration[31]. These groups undoubtedly also include members of the civil service corps. It is true that in Art. 153 of the Constitution of the Republic of Poland, regulating the subject of this service, there is no equivalent regulation regarding the remuneration of judges, but it contains quite important conclusions of a systemic nature. First of all, the provision of Art. 153 section 1 of the Constitution of the Republic of Poland clearly requires members of the civil service corps to possess special features in terms of professional and ethical attitude, as well as qualifications. This service is to be "professional", which is not just a general meaningless guideline, but a normative determinant for the legislator who must form the system and principles of operation of the service in such a way that the corps includes only those who can meet numerous, sometimes strict, requirements meeting the concept of "professionalism". Doubtlessly, ensuring a high level of competence and ethics must involve recruiting appropriate staff and guaranteeing remuneration corresponding to competences and qualifications. In other words, the systemic requirement for professionalism in the civil service should be correlated with remuneration which sets this service apart.

However, the practice of Polish government administration is completely different. A situation has arisen in which institution employees performing

31 See: art. 178 ust. 2 Konstytucji RP, który stanowi, że sędziom zapewnia się warunki pracy i wynagrodzenie odpowiadające godności urzędu oraz zakresowi ich obowiązków. Jak się w tym zakresie wskazuje, „Norma ustrojowa wyrażona w art. 178 ust. 2 Konstytucji jest nakierowana na umocnienie pozycji władzy sądowniczej w systemie organów państwowych i zagwarantowanie sędziom takich warunków pracy i *wynagrodzenia*, które mają służyć prawidłowemu sprawowaniu wymiaru sprawiedliwości. W demokratycznym państwie prawnym dobrze działający wymiar sprawiedliwości jest gwarancją i warunkiem funkcjonowania rządów prawa. Ustrojodawca zakłada, że wymiar sprawiedliwości będzie funkcjonować prawidłowo, gdy warunki pracy sędziów oraz ich *wynagrodzenia* będą adekwatne do godności urzędu sędziego i zakresu jego obowiązków. Trzeba podkreślić, że sędziowie sądów powszechnych i szczególnych są jedyną kategorią zawodową, której *wynagrodzenia* stanowią przedmiot wyraźnej regulacji konstytucyjnej. Wypływa stąd obowiązek właściwych organów państwa szczególnej troski o kształtowanie należytego poziomu tych *wynagrodzeń*, także w relacji do *wynagrodzeń* innych funkcjonariuszy publicznych" See: R. Hauser, *Konstytucyjna zasada niezawisłości sędziowskiej*, Zeszyty Naukowe Sądownictwa Administracyjnego Nr 1 (2015), p. 11.

supervision tasks over entities lower in the administrative hierarchy are sometimes paid less, despite the tasks assigned to them in the field of "superiority" over these entities. Moreover, these "lower-level" institutions (subordinated to or supervised by the minister) are excluded from the civil service and therefore not covered by the indicated assurances sourced from the Constitution of the Republic of Poland. This does not mean, of course, that they are not subject to the requirements of professionalism of staff. However, this requirement was primarily assigned to the civil service and this circumstance cannot be ignored in administrative practice.

An example is the Ministry of Science and Higher Education. This structure is headed by a government administration body (minister) whose operation is ensured by a government administration office (ministry). The minister, in turn, supervises a number of public institutions which are not part of the civil service and which perform various tasks in the field of scientific research development, implementation, academic exchange, etc. It could be assumed that the responsibility for supervising efficient operation of these institutions, as well as working in an office providing services to a constitutional body (minister), are sufficient titles to bring high remuneration for people performing these tasks. In any case, it would be rational to expect the amount of remuneration of civil service corps members to be set at a higher level than that of employees who are at lower "levels" of the ministry. However, the opposite is true: employees of institutions supervised by the minister are, as a rule, better paid. The average salary of a ministry employee is up to several thousand zlotys lower than the salaries in entities supervised by the minister[32]. The reasons for such a situation may be found both in the fact that some of these entities usually employ staff with sought-after market skills (e.g. IT specialists), but also in the fact that they use resources to perform a number of tasks which significantly exceed the resources available to ministries.

The above paradox is only a part of a broader context relating to the competitiveness and attractiveness of remuneration in the civil service. This

---

32 According to the answer to interpellation No. 29299 of April 27, 2019. (8th Parliament) at the Ministry of Science and Higher Education, the average basic salary of women in civil service positions excluding senior positions was PLN 5,007, and that of men was PLN 5,397. At the National Information Processing Institute, the average salary for women was PLN 8,151.92 and for men PLN 11,041.87; at the Polish Technology Development Center, the average salary for women was: PLN 6,458.00, and for men it was: PLN 8,335.38; at The National Centre for Research and Development (NCBR), the average salary for women was: PLN 6,401.42, and for men: PLN 7,159.55.

segment of the administration, set apart in the constitution and with attributes defined at the systemic level as the only public service should be appreciated in a special way by the legislator and the "actual" employer, which is the state. This also applies to the subject of remuneration. Meanwhile, "practice shows that in many offices remuneration is lower than the national average, and increases in remuneration (…) were lower than in the national economy. Therefore, it may be concluded that salaries are not competitive and do not provide the opportunity to recruit good staff. Additionally, in practice, there are large discrepancies in remuneration in the civil service for the same positions within and between specific offices"[33].

5. Conclusion

Between 2005 and 2016, there was a significant increase in the number of bills that, under the guise of reorganisation, enabled far-reaching staffing changes in government administration. By the end of 2016, the Polish Parliament passed 37 such "staffing laws"[34].

Since political circles suspect that the Civil Service corps, as an elite group, is neither loyal nor motivated to identify with the ideology of the ruling camp and pursue its goals, they contest the significance of the Civil Service's political neutrality. Therefore, the legal changes of the Civil Service were a necessary step for its subordination to the execution of the policies of the ruling coalitions. This justification demonstrates the politician's scepticism toward the value of formal institutions as well as its unshakeable faith in the revolutionary idea of having devoted and politically loyal officials ready to carry out any political project of the ruling camp[35]. That is why from many years politicians effectively reverses the effects of constitutive concept of the Civil Service. This was influenced by, among others:

1. In recent years, the concepts of statism have gained traction in the Polish public sphere. They have become implanted into institutions that shape the way in which the state and public administration function.

---

33 D. Moroń, *Wynagradzanie członków korpusu służby cywilnej*, Studia Iuridica Nr 92 (2022), p. 162.

34 J. Paczocha, *Raport Partia w Państwie. Bezprecedensowa wymiana kadr w administracji rządowej i jej legislacyjne podstawy*, FOR, Warsaw2018.

35 A. Budzanowska, M. Radziewski, *The constitutional principle of common welfare at a time of a pandemic in Poland*, Horyzonty Polityki, 13 nr 45 (2022), pp. 203–217. DOI: 10.35765/HP.2389.

2. Public administration is subjected to strong pressures:
   (a) centralise power by expanding the government's remit and introducing centralised governance mechanisms;
   (b) politicise public administration and engage experts from outside the public sector who share the government's political visions and plans;
   (c) marginalise the role of expert advice in public governance;
   (d) the predominant type of organisational culture is bureaucratic oriented towards maintaining the *status quo*.

The Government Support Centre's dominant audit and control mechanisms are those inherent in the bureaucratic model of governance. It should be noted, however, that economic criteria, which characterise the market model of public administration, are also widely used. The problem is the Centre's relatively low capacity to use their findings to improve management processes.

The governments enacted a number of institutional reforms (2006–2016), their primary objective was not to improve institutions and governance mechanisms, but to centralise the system governance in order to coordinate key public policies, particularly economic and foreign ones by political Government Support Centre.

This resulted in the implementation in the area of Civil Service the populist drift more than professional neutrality of the public institutions.

Jarosław Czerw

Legal Standing of Local Government Staff in Poland: The Current Status and Proposed Changes in Selected Areas

The Constitution of the Republic of Poland of 2 April 1997[1] (hereinafter: the Polish Constitution), and more specifically Article 15(1), stipulates that the territorial system of the Republic of Poland shall ensure the decentralisation of public power. Decentralisation, as referred to by the legislator, is a way of organising the state apparatus, whereby lower-level bodies are not hierarchically subordinate to higher-level bodies[2]. As W. Skrzydło was right to note, the legislator did not specify in the Polish Constitution the degree or scope of this decentralisation[3]. Regarding this issue, the Constitutional Tribunal adopted a standpoint, in its judgement of 26 September 2013, noting that *"Article 15 of the Constitution imposes the obligation to decentralize public power by creating territorial units that will be able to perform public tasks"*[4]. Hence, the principle of decentralisation of public power, as set out in Article 15(1) of the Polish Constitution, is further specified in the first sentence of Article 16(2) of the Polish Constitution which stipulates that the local government shall participate in the exercise of public power. The participation in the exercise of public power regulated by this provision reflects the decentralisation of public power through local government. However, it should be stressed that decisions regarding the scope of tasks delegated to the local government under the decentralisation of public power are always taken by the state and not by the local government itself[5]. This was confirmed, *inter alia*, in the judgement of the Provincial Administrative

1 The Constitution of the Republic of Poland of 2 April 1997 (Journal of Laws of 1997 No. 78, item 483, as amended).

2 P. Tuleja, *Komentarz do art. 15 Konstytucji RP,* in: ed. P. Tuleja, *Konstytucja Rzeczypospolitej Polskiej. Komentarz*, WKP 2019, LEX.

3 W. Skrzydło, *Komentarz do art. 15 Konstytucji RP,* in: *Konstytucja Rzeczypospolitej Polskiej. Komentarz*, issue VII, Warsaw 2013, LEX.

4 The judgement of the Constitutional Tribunal of 26 September 2013, K 22/12, OTK-A 2013, No. 7, item 95.

5 D. Kurzyna-Chmiel, *Samorząd terytorialny – teraźniejszość i wnioski na przyszłość*, Samorząd Terytorialny *[Local Government]* No. 9, 2020, pp. 7–15.

Court in Kraków of 24 October 2017. The Court stated that *"In accordance with the fundamental principle of decentralisation arising from Article 15(1) of the Polish Constitution, the local government shall only perform the tasks delegated to it on statutory grounds and has no right to create public tasks for itself"*[6].

The modern local government in Poland began to take shape in 1990 due to the following three acts being adopted: the Act of 8 March 1990 amending the Constitution of the Republic of Poland[7], the Act of 8 March 1990 on Local Government[8] (hereinafter: the Local Government Act), and the Act of 8 March 1990 on Direct Elections to Commune Councils[9].

These Acts, together with restoring local government bodies in Poland after 40 years of their non-existence[10], gave rise to bringing the commune (Polish: *gmina*) back to life, which became the first-level and - as further underlined in Article 164(1) of the Polish Constitution - basic unit of the local government.

The concept of a Polish commune, as arising from the Acts adopted in 1990, and in particular from the Local Government Act, was consistent with the legal solutions stipulated in the European Charter of Local Self-Government drawn up by Members States of the Council of Europe in Strasbourg on 15 October 1985[11] (hereinafter: the ECLS)[12]. The ECLS defines local self-government as denoting

---

6 The judgement of the Provincial Administrative Court in Kraków of 24 October 2017, III SA/Kr 397/17, LEX No. 2381414.

7 The Act of 8 March 1990 amending the Constitution of the Republic of Poland (Journal of Laws of 1990 No. 16, item 94).

8 The Act of 8 March 1990 on Local Government (Journal of Laws of 1990 No. 16, item 95). Currently: the Act of 8 March 1990 on Commune Government. The heading of the Act was amended by way of Article 10(1) of the Act of 29 December 1998 amending certain acts in connection with the implementation of the constitutional reform (Journal of Laws of 1998 No. 162, item 1126) which took effect on 1 January 1999. Whenever the Act on Commune Government is mentioned in further deliberations, this shall be interpreted as the Act of 8 March 1990 on Commune Government in the wording as set out in the uniform text of the Act published in the Journal of Laws of 2022, item 559.

9 The Act of 8 March 1990 on Direct Elections to Commune Councils (Journal of Laws of 1990 No. 16, item 96).

10 W. Wytrążek, *Samorząd terytorialny w XX wieku w Polsce*, Lublin 2009, pp. 116–118.

11 The European Charter of Local Self-Government drawn up by Members States of the Council of Europe in Strasbourg on 15 October 1985, ratified by Poland on 26 April 1993 (Journal of Laws of 1994 No. 124, item 607, as amended).

12 P. Dobosz, *Dylematy konstrukcyjne samorządności terytorialnej w Polsce w kontekście przestrzegania w przez państwo wymogów Europejskiej Karty Samorządu Lokalnego,*

"the right and the ability of local authorities, within the limits of the law, to regulate and manage a substantial share of public affairs under their own responsibility and in the interests of the local population" (Article 3(1) of the ECLS). Furthermore, *"[t]his right shall be exercised by councils or assemblies composed of members freely elected by secret ballot on the basis of direct, equal, universal suffrage, and which may possess executive organs responsible to them"* (the first sentence of Article 3(2) of the ECLS)[13].

By way of the Local Government Act, communes were granted legal personality (Article 2(2) of the Local Government Act), municipal property (Articles 43 and 44 of the Local Government Act), and autonomy to conduct their financial management based on their budget (Article 51 of the Local Government Act).

The legislator divided the tasks performed by the commune into its own tasks and commissioned tasks. The former are meant to satisfy the collective needs of the local community (Article 7 of the Local Government Act) and the latter represent tasks assigned to government administration (Article 8 of the Local Government Act)[14].

The commune bodies include the commune council and the commune head (mayor). The commune council is the commune's decision-making and inspection body (Article 15(1) of the Commune Government Act). Its term of office lasts 5 years starting from the election date (Article 16 of the Commune Government Act). The commune council is composed of councillors elected by secret ballot on the basis of universal, equal and direct suffrage (Article 369 of the Act of 5 January 2011 - the Election Code[15], hereinafter: the Election Code). The commune head (mayor) is the commune's executive body (whenever further deliberations mention the commune head, this shall be interpreted as also including the mayor). The commune head's term of office begins on the date of commencement of the commune council's term of office, or on the date of his/her election by the commune council and ends upon expiry of the commune

---

in: ed. M. Ofiarska, *Europejska Karta Samorządu Lokalnego a prawo samorządu terytorialnego*, Szczecin 2015, p. 63.

13 E. Olejniczak-Szałowska, *Problematyka determinantów wyboru monokratycznego lub kolegialnego modelu organu wykonawczego na poszczególnych szczeblach jednostek samorządu terytorialnego*, in: ed. K. Małysa-Sulińska, M. Stec, *Pozycja ustrojowa organów wykonawczych jednostek samorządu terytorialnego*, LEX 2014.

14 A. Agopszowicz, Z. Gilowska, *Ustawa o gminnym samorządzie terytorialnym. Komentarz*, Warszawa 1999, p. 77.

15 The Act of 5 January 2011 - the Election Code (uniform text, Journal of Laws of 2020, item 1319).

council's term of office (Article 26 of the Commune Government Act). Pursuant to Article 471 of the Election Code, the election of the commune head shall be held by secret ballot on the basis of universal, equal, and direct suffrage[16].

The commune head implements resolutions of the commune council and the tasks assigned to the commune under legal regulations (Article 30(1) of the Commune Government Act). In performing his/her functions, the commune head is bound by the guidelines of the commune council as long as they have been issued (Article 30(3) of the Commune Government Act). The commune head is responsible for ensuring the proper financial management of the commune (Article 60(1) of the Commune Government Act). The commune head manages the local affairs of the commune (Article 31 of the Commune Government Act). The commune head is also the entity statutorily authorised to represent the commune before external bodies (Article 31 of the Commune Government Act). Finally, the commune head performs his/her tasks with the assistance of the commune office (Article 33(1) of the Commune Government Act) and organisational units of the commune[17].

Following the restoration of the local government at the commune level in 1990, the restitution process of the Polish local government was continued in the subsequent years, culminating in the creation of the district government by way of the Act of 5 June 1998 on District Government[18] (hereinafter: the District Government Act) and province government by way of the Act of 5 June 1998 on Province Government[19] (hereinafter: the Province Government Act) under the 1998 local government reform. The Polish district and province government system, resembling that at the commune level, is in line with the standards set out in the ECLS.

Following the entry into force of the District Government Act and the Province Government Act on 1 January 1999, the Polish local government system has been composed of three levels: the commune (*gmina*), the district (*powiat*) and the province (*województwo*).

The district performs its statutory public tasks in its own name and on its own responsibility (Article 2(1) of the District Government Act), has legal personality, which means that it may be a participant in economic transactions, as well as

16 See ed. M. Chmaj, *Prawo samorządu terytorialnego*, Warsaw 2013, pp. 64–70.

17 W. Kisiel, *Ustrój samorządu terytorialnego w Polsce*, Warsaw 2002, pp. 198–200.

18 The Act of 5 June 1998 on District Government (uniform text, Journal of Laws of 2020, item 920, as amended).

19 The Act of 5 June 1998 on Province Government (uniform text, Journal of Laws of 2020, item 1668, as amended).

is entitled acquire rights and contract obligations (Article 2 (2) of the District Government Act). The district's autonomy is subject to judicial protection, which implies that it can participate in court proceedings acting as a petitioner or a respondent (Article 2(3) of the District Government Act).

The district performs its statutory public tasks of a supra-commune character (constituting its own tasks). The tasks performed by the district have a compensatory and supplementary character in relation to those assigned to the commune, as it was not created to compete with the commune, but rather to complement it in performing its tasks[20]. In addition to fulfilling its own tasks, the district also performs certain commissioned tasks which are not originally assigned to the district government. These are government administration tasks which the district performs for and on behalf of that administration[21].

The district bodies include the district council and the district board (Article 8(2) of the District Government Act), with the former acting as the district's decision-making and inspection body (Article 9(1) of the District Government Act). Pursuant to Article 9(2) of the District Government Act, its term of office lasts 5 years, starting from the election date. The district council is composed of councillors elected by secret ballot on the basis of universal, equal and direct suffrage (Article 369 of the Election Code). The district board is the district's executive body. It is composed of 3–5 persons: the district governor (*starosta*) acting as the president of the district board, the deputy district governor, and other members (Article 26(2) of the District Government Act). The district board is elected by the district council (Article 27 of the District Government Act).

The district board implements resolutions of the district council and the tasks assigned to the district under legal regulations (Article 32(1) of the District Government Act). The district board is in charge of the proper performance of the district budget (Article 60(1) of the District Government Act). Finally, the district board performs its tasks with the assistance of the district office and organisational units of the district, including the district labour office (Article 33 of the District Government Act)[22].

The province government performs its statutory public tasks in its own name and on its own responsibility, is entitled to use provincial property, and

---

20 Z. Bukowski, T. Jędrzejewski, P. Rączka, *Ustrój samorządu terytorialnego*, Toruń 2003, p. 78.

21 M. W. Sienkiewicz, *Samorząd powiatowy w Polsce. Założenia i realizacja*, Lublin 2011, p. 19.

22 See more: J. Czerw, *Ustrój i funkcjonowanie rad i zarządów powiatów. Stan aktualny i postulaty zmian (w wybranych obszarach)*, Lublin 2014.

conducts its financial management based on its budget (Article 6(1) of the Province Government Act). The province government has legal personality, and its autonomy is subject to judicial protection (Article 6(2) and (3) of the Province Government Act)[23]. The province government defines the province development strategy and implements the province development policy (Article 11(1) and (2) of the Province Government Act). As noted by A. Szewc, the province government tasks indicate *"a fundamental difference between local (commune and district) and regional governments. While the former performs mainly service tasks, connected with meeting the ongoing needs of members of local government communities (the so-called service-provider administration), the province government mainly fulfils programming, planning and co-ordination functions"*[24]

The province government also performs statutory tasks of a provincial character (Article 14(1) of the Province Government Act). These are considered its own tasks[25]. In addition to these, certain acts may define matters falling within the scope of the province activities as tasks assigned to government administration, which are to be performed by the province board (Article 14(2) of the Province Government Act). Certain acts may also put the province under the obligation to perform tasks related to the organisation of preparatory work and conduction of universal elections and referenda (Article 14(3) of the Province Government Act). These are considered commissioned tasks.

The province bodies include the province assembly and the province board (Article 15 of the Province Government Act). The province assembly is the province's decision-making and inspection body (Article 16(1) of the Province Government Act). Its term of office lasts 5 years, starting from the election date (Article 16(2) of the Province Government Act). The province assembly is composed of councillors elected by secret ballot on the basis of universal, equal and direct suffrage (Article 369 of the Election Code). The province board is the province's executive body (Article 31(1) of the Province Government Act). It is composed of 5 persons: the marshal of the province acting as the president of the board, the deputy marshal (or 2 deputy marshals), and other members (Article

---

23 T. Lewandowski, *Samodzielność jednostek samorządu terytorialnego*, LEX/el. 2011, LEX.

24 A. Szewc, *Komentarz do art. 11 ustawy o samorządzie województwa,* in: ed. A. Szewc, *Ustawa o samorządzie województwa. Komentarz,* ABC 2008, LEX.

25 Z. Bukowski, T. Jędrzejewski, P. Rączka, op. cit., p. 83.

31(2) of the Province Government Act). The province board is appointed by the province assembly (Article 32(2) and (3) of the Province Government Act).[26]

The province board performs the tasks assigned to the province government, which are not reserved for the province assembly or organisational units of the province government (Article 41(1) of the Province Government Act). The province board is in charge of the proper implementation of the province budget (Article 70(1) of the Province Government Act). The province board performs its tasks with the assistance of the marshal's office and organisational units of the province government or its legal persons (Article 45(1) of the Province Government Act)[27].

The extensive scope of tasks performed by local government bodies has triggered the need to provide them with professional and specialised staff, including in particular clerical staff. To this end, the legislator has defined the legal standing of local government employees by separate legislation. The legal standing of local government employees results, first of all, from the provisions of the Act of 21 November 2008 on Local Government Employees[28] (hereinafter: the Act on Local Government Employees), as well as from the provisions of the Act of 26 June 1974 - the Labour Code[29].

Local government employees are employees hired in organisational units of the local government, including but not limited to marshal's offices and organisational units of the province government, district offices and organisational units of the district government, commune offices, town halls, commune budgetary units and local government budgetary establishments (Article 2 of the Act on Local Government Employees). However, employees hired in organisational units of the local government whose legal status is defined by separate regulations are not considered local government employees (Article 3 of the Act on Local Government Employees)[30].

---

26 J. Czerw, *Wybór organów wykonawczych jednostek samorządu terytorialnego – analiza aktualnego stanu prawnego i propozycje zmian w wybranych obszarach*, Przegląd Prawa Publicznego No. 7–8 (2014), pp. 178–187.

27 K. Sikora, *Samorząd województwa,* in: ed. B. Szmulik, K. Miaskowska – Daszkiewicz, *Administracja publiczna, Tom III, Ustrój administracji samorządowej. Komentarz*, Warsaw 2012, pp. 415–512.

28 The Act of 21 November 2008 on Local Government Employees (uniform text, Journal of Laws of 2019, item 1282).

29 The Act of 26 June 1974 - the Labour Code (uniform text, Journal of Laws of 2020, item 1320, as amended).

30 J. Szmit, *Pojęcie pracownika samorządowego (uwagi de lege lata)*, Samorząd Terytorialny No. 3 (2011), pp. 5–14.

The acquisition of the local government employee status results from the mere fact of being employed in the organisational units indicated by the legislator. As M. Wujczyk was right to note, *"Whether a person is considered a local government employee is, therefore, not determined by the nature of work, the manner of establishing the employment relationship or the fulfilment of a particular function, but by the place of employment"*[31]. Local government employees are hired in clerical positions, including managerial positions, as well as in support and service positions (Article 4(2) of the Act on Local Government Employees). However, the Act on Local Government Employees does not specify in detail local government employee positions, including clerical positions. This specification can be found in the Regulation of 25 October 2021 on Remuneration of Local Government Employees[32] (hereinafter: the Regulation on Remuneration of Local Government Employees). This Regulation contains, *inter alia*, a list of positions, including a division into managerial positions, clerical positions, support positions and service positions (§ 1(1) of the Regulation on Remuneration of Local Government Employees).

Local government employees in clerical positions, including managerial positions, as well as support and service positions, are hired under employment agreements (Article 4(1)(3) of the Act on Local Government Employees)[33].

Employment in a clerical position is usually based on recruitment, the rules of which are determined by the provisions of the Act on Local Government Employees. The recruitment of candidates for vacant clerical positions is conducted in both an open and competitive manner (Article 11(1) of the Act on Local Government Employees). As stated by the Provincial Administrative Court in Gliwice, in its judgement of 15 May 2018, *"[t]he recruitment of candidates for a vacant clerical position shall be open, which means that it shall take the form of a formalised recruitment procedure, and any person meeting the conditions stipulated in the recruitment announcement may put forward their candidacy. The open nature of recruitment is deemed preserved if the requirement for openness and transparency of the procedure is fulfilled. Free access to recruitment is guaranteed by the obligation to disseminate information about the vacant clerical position in*

---

31 M. Wujczyk, *Komentarz do art. 2 ustawy o pracownikach samorządowych,* in: ed. K. W. Baran, *Komentarz do ustawy o pracownikach samorządowych*, [in] *Prawo urzędnicze. Komentarz*, LEX 2014.

32 The Regulation of 25 October 2021 on Remuneration of Local Government Employees (Journal of Laws of 2021, item 1960).

33 J. Stelina, *Komentarz do art. 4 ustawy o pracownikach samorządowych*, in: ed. A. Rycak et al., *Ustawa o pracownikach samorządowych. Komentarz*, No. II, WK 2016, LEX.

the Public Information Bulletin and on the information board of the office where the recruitment procedure is conducted"[34]. As stipulated in Article 12(1) of the Act on Local Government Employees, a vacant clerical position is a position to which no local government employee hired in a clerical position, who has the qualifications required for the given position, has been transferred in accordance with the provisions of the Act or an agreement, or for which no recruitment procedure has been conducted, or in which no employee has been hired despite such a procedure having been conducted[35].

The recruitment announcement concerning a vacant clerical position contains, *inter alia*, the requirements (Article 13(2) of the Act on Local Government Employees) to be met by a candidate applying for a given position (essential requirements and additional requirements). The essential requirements are the requirements necessary to take up employment in a given position (Article 13(2a)(1) of the Act on Local Government Employees). Pursuant to Article 6(3), in conjunction with Article 6(1) of the Act on Local Government Employees, a local government employee hired under an employment agreement in a clerical position can be a person who:

1. is a Polish citizen (a person who does not have Polish citizenship may be employed in the position in which the work performed does not involve direct or indirect participation in the exercise of public power or functions aimed at protecting the general interests of the state, if he/she has the command of the Polish language confirmed by a document specified in the civil service regulations),
2. has full legal capacity and enjoys full public rights,
3. has the professional qualifications required to perform work in a given position,
4. has at least secondary education,
5. has not been sentenced by a final court judgement for an intentional offence prosecuted under indictment or for an intentional fiscal offence (Płażek 2010: 131–153),
6. has an impeccable reputation.

34 The judgement of the Provincial Administrative Court in Gliwice of 15 May 2018, IV SA/Gl 1133/17, LEX No. 2505669.

35 B. Przywora, Problematyka zgodności z Konstytucją RP alternatywnego trybu obsadzania stanowisk urzędniczych w administracji samorządowej (tzw. awansu wewnętrznego), No. 7–8, 2014, pp. 104–113.

The qualification requirements for particular clerical positions, apart from the Act on Local Government Employees itself, are specified in the Regulation on Remuneration of Local Government Employees. The qualification requirements for individual clerical positions are also stipulated in the rules and regulations concerning remuneration of local government employees established by the head of a given organisational unit of local government (Article 39(1)(1) of the Act on Local Government Employees). These requirements may be more stringent than the qualification requirements set out in the provisions of the Act on Local Government Employees and in the Regulation on Remuneration of Local Government Employees. If the candidate for a clerical position fails to meet the essential requirements, he/she is disqualified from participating in the recruitment procedure.

The additional requirements specified in the recruitment announcement (Article 13(2)(3) of the Act on Local Government Employees) are other requirements allowing the employee to perform tasks in a given position in the best possible way (Article 13(2a)(1) of the Act on Local Government Employees). Additional requirements in the case of recruitment for a clerical position include, *inter alia*, impeccable manners, exemplary work record, an ability to interpret legal provisions or computer literacy. If the candidate for a clerical position fails to meet the additional requirements specified in the recruitment announcement, this does not disqualify him/her from participating in the recruitment procedure; however, he/she stands lower chances compared to the candidates who meet those requirements[36].

Recruitment for a clerical position is conducted by a committee appointed by the head of an organisational unit of the local government (the Recruitment Committee) (Article 14(2)(5) of the Act on Local Government Employees). The task of the Recruitment Committee is to select, from among all candidates, no more than five best candidates who meet the essential requirements and preferably also the additional requirements (Article 13a(1) of the Act on Local Government Employees). The committee presents these candidates to the head of the organisational unit of the local government with the aim of ultimately hiring the selected candidate. The head of the organisational unit of the local government selects the ultimate candidate from among the candidates presented, but is not obliged to select the candidate who best meets the requirements set out in the recruitment procedure (as stated by the Provincial Administrative Court

---

36 The judgement of the Provincial Administrative Court in Warsaw of 20 May 2016, I OSK 1996/14, LEX No. 2064205.

in Wrocław in its judgement of 3 March 2020, "*[t]he commune head is not obliged to employ the candidate who scored the highest number of points. The body in charge of recruitment has the possibility of reviewing the candidates presented and to selecting from among them the one who, in its opinion, will provide a guarantee of proper performance of the entrusted tasks*"[37]). This can result in recruiting a candidate who, for various non-substantive reasons, appears the most suitable to the head of the organisational unit although he/she is not the best candidate. This method of selecting candidates for clerical positions does not ensure that local government units have the best employees. In order to ensure that the best candidate is selected for a clerical position, the candidate to be employed should be selected by the recruitment committee and the head of the organisation unit should be obliged to employ that candidate[38].

A local government employee hired in a clerical position, including a managerial position, can be transferred to work in another unit, in the same or another town/city, at any time, at the request or upon consent of that employee, if this does not infringe on the vital interest of the unit which previously employed that local government employee, and if it is dictated by vital needs of the unit to which that employee is to be transferred (Article 22(1) of the Act on Local Government Employees). As stressed by P. Zuzankiewicz, the transfer under Article 22(1) of the Act on Local Government Employees constitutes "*a special legal instrument which, with regard to local government employees hired in clerical positions, including managerial positions, under an employment agreement enables a prompt change of the employer*"[39]. The transfer of an employee can be performed at the initiative of that employee (at the employee's request) or at the initiative of the employer. However, in the latter case, the employee's consent is required – in other words, the employee cannot be transferred against his/her will (without obtaining his/her consent). The transfer is only permissible if, on the one hand, it does not infringe on the vital interest of the unit which previously employed the local government employee and, on the other hand, it is justified by important needs of the unit to which that employee is to be transferred. In order for the transfer to be effected, both of these conditions must be fulfilled

---

37 The judgement of the Provincial Administrative Court in Wrocław of 3 March 2020, IV SA/Wr 412/19, LEX No. 2973907.

38 J. Czerw, *Recruitment as a way of employing self-government employees in clerical positions in Poland*, International Journal of Legal Studies 3, No. 1 (2018), pp. 47–60.

39 P. Zuzankiewicz, *Komentarz do art. 22 ustawy o pracownikach samorządowych*, in: W. Drobny, M. Mazuryk, P. Zuzankiewicz, *Ustawa o pracownikach samorządowych. Komentarz*, Oficyna 2010, LEX.

simultaneously[40]. The transfer is made by way of an agreement between the employers (Article 22(2) of the Act on Local Government Employees)[41]. The transfer of an employee under Article 22(1) of the Act on Local Government Employees does not result in termination of the employment relationship with the previous employer and establishment of a new employment relationship with the employer that is to hire the employee. As stated by the Supreme Court in its judgement of 12 June 2013, *"[t]he change of the employer in the mode stipulated in Article 22 of the Act on Local Government Employees of 2008 takes place within the same employment relationship, which is only subject to modification, inter alia, as regards the employing unit"*[42]. Agnieszka Rzetecka-Gil also argued that *"as a result of the transfer, a new employment agreement is not drawn up, but the content of the existing agreement is merely modified with regard to the definition of the employer and the place where the employment relationship is provided, as well as other terms and conditions of employment, including the name of the position to be held by the employee, the amount of remuneration or the scope of responsibilities"*[43].

Despite the positive assessment of the transfer under Article 22(1) of the Act on Local Government Employees, it seems justified to extend that instrument by enabling transfer of employees who are not employed by local government units. This change will enable a greater supply of professional staff to the local government administration.

A local government employee (including an employee working in a clerical position) is entitled to remuneration composed of the basic pay, a multi-annual service bonus, a jubilee award, a one-off severance pay due to going on retirement or disability pension, and an additional annual pay (the so-called "13th-month salary") (Article 36(2) of the Act on Local Government Employees). The above-mentioned remuneration components for a local government employee constitute obligatory components and must be awarded and paid to the employee as long as the conditions set out by the legislator are satisfied. A local government

40 See also: The judgement of the Provincial Administrative Court in Warsaw of 7 March 2012, VIII SA/Wa 110/12, LEX No. 1139883.

41 J. Stelina, *Komentarz do art. 22 ustawy o pracownikach samorządowych,* in: A. Rycak et al., *Ustawa o pracownikach samorządowych. Komentarz,* No. II, WK 2016, LEX.

42 The judgement of the Supreme Court of 12 June 2013, I PK 2/13, Judicature of the Supreme Court, Labour Chamber of 2014, No. 3, item 38. See also: H. Szewczyk, *Glosa do wyroku SN z dnia 12 czerwca 2013 r,* I PK 2/13, Judicature of Polish Courts 2015, No. 1, item 6.

43 A. Rzetecka-Gil, *Glosa do wyroku SN z dnia 28 czerwca 2013 r.,* I PK 27/13, LEX/el. 2014.

employee may additionally be granted a function allowance (Article 36(4) of the Act on Local Government Employees) and a special allowance in respect of temporarily increasing their professional duties or for delegating additional tasks (Article 36(5) of the Act on Local Government Employees). In addition, a local government employee may receive an award for special achievements in his/her professional work (Article 36(5) of the Act on Local Government Employees). The above-mentioned remuneration components for a local government employee are of an optional nature; if the conditions set out by the legislator are fulfilled, they may be granted to a local government employee, but this is done at the discretion of the head of the organisational unit[44].

Apart from the Act on Local Government Employees, issues concerning remuneration of local government employees are also set out in the Regulation on Remuneration of Local Government Employees. The Regulation defines, *inter alia*, the conditions and manner of remunerating local government employees hired under employment agreements, including the minimum basic pay in particular positions (§ 1 of the Regulation on Remuneration of Local Government Employees). The detailed conditions regarding remuneration, including the maximum basic pay for local government employees hired under employment agreements, are determined in the rules and regulations concerning remuneration by the head of a given organisational unit of local government (Article 39(1)(2) of the Act on Local Government Employees). Granting leeway to the manager of an organisational unit of the local government to determine the maximum basic pay for local government employees should be assessed in a very positive way.

As noted by L. Florek, *"the employer may, in the rules and regulations concerning remuneration (which cover only local government employees hired under employment agreements), specify the conditions and manner of granting allowances other than those provided for in the Act"*[45]. In addition, the rules and regulations concerning remuneration may also specify the conditions and manner of granting awards other than the jubilee award and the award for special achievements in professional work, referred to in Article 36(6) of the Act on Local Government Employees. The rules of remunerating local government employees determined in this way enable managers of organisational units of the

44 J. Czerw *Wynagrodzenie pracowników samorządowych zatrudnionych na kierowniczych stanowiskach pracowniczych – wnioski de lege ferenda*, Samorząd Terytorialny, No. 5 (2020), pp. 25–35.

45 Ed. L. Florek, *Powszechne a szczególne prawo pracy*, WK 2016, LEX.

local government to adjust the remuneration of local government employees in an appropriate manner. In consequence, the actual amount of remuneration of local government employees can be adjusted to the situation on the local labour market and to the needs of a given organisational unit of the local government as regards recruiting highly qualified staff. In practice, managers of organisational units of local government very rarely introduce some remuneration components for local government employees other than those specified by the legislator (e.g. it is uncommon for these organisational units to use allowances connected with employees' additional qualifications or command of foreign languages). The manner in which heads of organisational units of the local government apply optional remuneration components, including special allowances and awards, very often has a demotivating effect on local government employees. The amount of the special bonus is often unrelated to the actual increase in professional duties or additional tasks entrusted to an employee, while awards are almost always treated as an obligatory remuneration component to which all employees are entitled. All this not only makes it difficult to recruit and retain highly qualified staff but also results in local government employees not being properly motivated to perform their professional duties. Nor are they prompted to improve their qualifications, as such efforts are not usually associated with an increase in their remuneration. In order to change this situation, managers of organisational units of the local government should fully use their powers related to determining the amount of remuneration of local government employees, placing greater emphasis on reviewing and rewarding both individual commitments and additional qualifications of their employees[46].

A vast part of the tasks of local government units is performed by local government employees working in commune offices (city halls), district offices, and marshal's offices. The commune (municipal) office is an auxiliary vehicle of the commune head who also acts as the head of that office (Article 33(3) of the Commune Government Act); the district governor's office is an auxiliary vehicle of the district board and the district governor who also acts as the president of the district board and the head of the district governor's office (Article 35(2) of the District Government Act); and the marshal's office is an auxiliary vehicle of the province board and the marshal who also acts as the president of the province board and the head of the marshal's office. Activities related to the labour law of local government employees are performed on behalf of

46 See also: J. Czerw, B. Liżewski, *Influence of Hybrid Legal Institutions on the Management in Local Government on the Example of the Institution of Public-Private Partnership*, LEX Localis – Journal of Local Self-Government 19, No. 3 (2021), pp. 805–835.

the commune (municipal) office, the district governor's office and the marshal's office by the commune head, the district governor and the marshal, respectively (Article 7(3) of the Act on Local Government Employees)[47]. The head of the office also determines the organisational rules and regulations for the office, and its organisational structure (in the case of the commune head) or has a significant impact on the content of the organisational regulations, and the organisational structure of the office (in the case of the district governor and the marshal). The combination of the political function of the executive body (the commune head) or the president of the executive body (the district board - the district governor, the province board - the marshal) with the function of the head of the office managing the staff employed in the office should be assessed in a negative manner. This solution does not foster the professionalisation of clerical staff, nor does it facilitate determining an optimal organisational structure of the office. The head of the office – a politician managing the office and its employees – may prefer to select local government employees not for substantive reasons, but for some other reasons, including political ones when it comes to employment, working conditions, the scope of responsibilities, promotions or the level of remuneration. With a view to mitigating this situation, the legislator should distinguish between political functions (commune head, district governor, marshal) and administrative functions (head of the office) in the commune, district and province government. The performance of activities related to the labour law of local government employees and the function of the head of the office should be entrusted by the legislator to the secretary (secretary of the commune, secretary of the town/city, secretary of the district, secretary of the province)[48]

As can be concluded from the conducted analysis, the legislator entrusted the Polish local government with a number of tasks as part of decentralisation. By introducing separate statutory regulations specifying the legal position of local government employees, it gave the possibility to provide the government with appropriate staff. However, the dynamically changing environment, including the entrusting of additional tasks to local government, necessitate further professionalisation of local government staff. Nonetheless, this will not be possible without introducing changes to the legal standing of local government

47 E. Ura, *Pozycja prawna pracowników terenowej administracji rządowej i samorządu terytorialnego*, Lublin 1995, pp. 89–95.

48 K. Mroczka, Samorządowa służba cywilna - szansa dla obywateli czy zagrożenie dla samorządności? Wnioski z badania jakościowego, in: ed. M. Ćwiklicki, Sprawne państwo. Systemowe zmiany w funkcjonowaniu polskiego samorządu terytorialnego *[An efficient state. System changes in the functioning of the Polish local government]*, Kraków 2015. See also: J. Czerw, B. Liżewski, op. cit., pp. 805–835.

employees, including the changes proposed in this study. These changes will enable local governmental employers to retain the current highly qualified staff and, at the same time, to recruit new employees.

Anna Deryng-Dziuk

Judicial Review of the Refusal to Consent to an Additional Employment of a Member of the Civil Service Corps

He who serves his country serves himself[1].

I.

In the light of the labour law in force, as a rule, employees[2] may take up additional employment[3] outside their basic employment relationship[4]. Nowadays, this phenomenon has become an important and permanent element of the labour market in Poland[5], as well as in other countries, regardless of the socio-economic system in force[6]. It can be observed that more and more people, including civil servants, in the light of galloping inflation and changing economic situation, are looking for new sources of income[7].

---

1 P.Skarga, quoted from the introduction after H. Szewczyk, *Stosunki pracy w służbie cywilnej*, Warsaw 2010, p. 11.

2 Article 2 of the Labour Code. "An employee is a person employed on the basis of a contract of employment, appointment, election or cooperative employment contract".

3 "The term 'additional employment' is used in both legal and juridical language. However, the scope of the term has not been clearly defined anywhere so far. This is mainly due to the fact that additional employment is regulated in a great number of legal acts with different subject and object scope", B.Cudowski, Dodatkowe zatrudnienie pracowników samorządowych i radnych (zarys problematyki), in: ed. B. M. Ćwiertniak, *Prawo pracy, zabezpieczenie społeczne (z aktualnych zagadnień)*, Opole 2001, p. 131.

4 A.Dubowik, *Dodatkowe zatrudnienie i inne zajęcia pracowników służby publicznej*, Praca i Zabezpieczenie Społeczne, No. 10 (2005), p. 15.

5 B.Cudowski, *Ograniczenia swobody zatrudnienia pracowników samorządowych i członków korpusu służby cywilnej*, in: ed. W.Sanetra, *Stosunki pracy w służbie cywilnej i samorządzie terytorialnym*, Białystok 2001, p. 56.

6 From the abstract of B.Cudowski, *Zmiany regulacji prawnej dodatkowego zatrudnienia*, Studia Iuridica Lublinensia, XXIV, No. 3 (2015), p. 131.

7 B.Cudowski, *Ograniczenia swobody zatrudnienia pracowników samorządowych i członków korpusu służby cywilnej*, *op.cit.*, p. 56.

The normative basis for the above should be sought, for example, in Article 65(1) of the Act of 2 April 1997, the Constitution of the Republic of Poland (hereinafter: "the Constitution of the Republic of Poland")[8]. Indeed, this provision states that: "everyone shall be guaranteed the freedom to choose and exercise his profession and to choose his place of work. Exceptions shall be determined by law". At the same time, these exceptions must fall within the limits indicated in Article 31(3) of the Constitution of the Republic of Poland[9]. As Boguslaw Banaszak aptly pointed out at the same time, "freedom of work thus means the focus of the legislator on granting work-related freedoms to the individual"[10]. The principle of freedom of work finds its normative expression also in Article 10 § 1 of the Act of 26 June 1974 of the Labour Code (hereinafter: "the Labour Code")[11] in the light of which, everyone is guaranteed the freedom to choose freely selected work. No one, except in cases specified by law, may be prohibited from exercising a profession[12]. This principle is also complemented by Article 11 of the Code of Labour constituting the principle

8 Journal of Laws 1997, No. 78, item 483.

9 K. Jaśkowski, E. Maniewska, *komentarz do art. 10 k.p.*, in: ed. K. Jaśkowski, E. Maniewska, *Komentarz aktualizowany do Kodeksu pracy*, published: LEX/el.2022, www.sip.lex.pl (accessed 21.10.2022). Article 31(3) of the Polish Constitution: "Limitations on the exercise of constitutional freedoms and rights may be established only by statute and only if they are necessary in a democratic state for its security or public order, or for the protection of the environment, public health and morals, or the freedoms and rights of others. Such limitations may not impair the essence of the freedoms and rights".

10 B.Banaszak, *Konstytucja Rzeczypospolitej Polskiej. Komentarz*, Warsaw 2009, p. 337. See also W. Skrzydło, *Konstytucja Rzeczypospolitej Polskiej. Komentarz*, 4th edition, Cracow 2005, p. 79; B. Banaszak, M. Jabłoński, *komentarz do art. 65 Konstytucji RP*, in: ed. J.Boć, *Konstytucje Rzeczypospolitej Polskiej oraz komentarz do Konstytucji RP z 1997 r.*, Wrocław 1998, p. 122. These authors pointed out that "the provision constructs the principle of freedom of undertaking and performing work, according to which no one may be forced to perform work. Everyone is free to choose the place of work and the type of work provided. However, this principle is not universal; exceptions are possible. However, it is necessary to define them explicitly by law", p. 122.

11 T.U. 2022, item 1510, as amended.

12 I.Wieleba, *Umowne ograniczenie podejmowania dodatkowego zatrudnienia jako przejaw lojalności pracowniczej. Wybrane zagadnienia*, Annales Universitatis Mariae Curie-Skłodowska. Lublin-Polonia LXV, No. 2, (2018), p. 31. The author pointed out that "In the doctrine it is emphasised that despite some differences in the content of the provision of Article 65(1) of the Constitution and Article 10 of the Labour Code, it is necessary to recognise that both cases are about the guarantee of the free choice of the performed profession and work in the sense of the place of work, and thus the principle has the character of civil liberty and thus employee freedom. This position is justified in particular by the placement of this principle among the constitutional freedoms,

of freedom of establishment of the employment relationship[13]. According to this provision, the establishment of the employment relationship and the determination of the terms and conditions of work and pay requires a consensual declaration of will by the employer and the employee. This therefore means that each party is free to decide on the conclusion of the employment contract[14] .

It already follows from the above that freedom of work cannot therefore be considered in absolute terms. Jacek Borowicz rightly pointed out that "it does, in fact, experience a number of statutory limitations (absolute, relative or related to the adoption of an act by a competent authority permitting employment)"[15]. It is also possible that the legislator provides the parties to the employment relationship themselves with the right to narrow the limits of the principle of freedom of work[16]. It can therefore be concluded that the legal regulation of restrictions on additional employment is quite diverse and problematic[17] .

In view of the subject matter of this study, attention will be focused on members of the civil service, in relation to whom the prohibition to undertake additional employment (or other gainful activities) without the written consent of the Director General of the office is formulated, as well as the prohibition to perform actions or activities contrary to the duties under the Act or undermining confidence in the civil service[18] – Article 80(1) of the Act of 21 November 2008 on the civil service (hereinafter: "CSA")[19]. Unfortunately, this regulation, as well as the Civil Service Act as a whole, does not contain provisions on the possibility of challenging in court the employer's lack of consent for additional employment. This raises the rather obvious question whether, in such a situation, the employee (member of the civil service) is deprived of the right to judicial review of the employer's refusal of such consent?[20]. Next, could such an

---

rights and duties of human and citizen in the section on economic, social and cultural freedoms and rights", p. 317 and the literature cited therein.

13 *Ibid*, p. 317.

14 L.Florek, *Chapter 3. Swoboda umów w stosunku pracy*, in: K.W. Baran (ed. nauk.), G.Goździewicz (ed.nauk.), *System prawa pracy. Tom II. Indywidualne prawo pracy. Część ogólna*, Warsaw 2017, p. 74.

15 J.Borowicz, *Wolność pracy*, [w:] B. Banaszak, A. Preisner, *Prawa i wolności obywatelskie w Konstytucji RP*, Warsaw 2002, p. 519.

16 *Ibid*, p. 519.

17 B. Cudowski, *Zmiany regulacji prawnej dodatkowego zatrudnienia, op.cit.*, p. 132.

18 J. Borowicz, *Wolność pracy*, [w:] B. Banaszak, A. Preisner, *Prawa i wolności obywatelskie w Konstytucji RP, op.cit.*, p. 531.

19 Uniform text, Journal of Laws of 2022, item 1691.

20 B. Cudowski, *Dodatkowe zatrudnienie*, Warsaw 2007, p. 183.

action by the employer constitute a manifestation of discriminatory behaviour and perhaps even mobbing? If so, what then are the employee's legal remedies against discrimination[21] (Article 11 of the Code of Civil Procedure 3[22]) or mobbing (Article 94 of the Code of Civil Procedure 3[23]) on the part of the employer?

II.

The right to a court[24] also referred to as the right to justice, the right to a trial, the right to a fair (honest) trial, the right to an action or to a defence before a court[25] is one of

21 Anna Deryng-Dziuk, *Dyskryminacja pracownika jako naruszenie konstytucyjnych praw i wolności człowieka*, in: ed. M. Malczyńska-Biały, *Bezpieczeństwo. Prawa człowieka. Stosunki międzynarodowe*, Rzeszów 2021, p. 32 in.

22 Article 11^3 of the Labour Code [Prohibition of discrimination] "Any discrimination in employment, direct or indirect, in particular on the grounds of sex, age, disability, race, religion, nationality, political opinion, trade union membership, ethnic origin, religion, sexual orientation, employment for a definite or indefinite period of time, full-time or part-time employment – is unacceptable".

23 Art. 94^3 of the Labour Code [Mobbing] "§ 1. The employer is obliged to prevent mobbing.

§ 2. Mobbing means actions or behaviours concerning an employee or directed against an employee, consisting of persistent and prolonged harassment or intimidation of an employee, causing an employee's appraisal of his/her professional usefulness to be lowered, causing or aimed at humiliating or ridiculing an employee, isolating him/her or eliminating him/her from his/her team of co-workers.

§ 3. An employee who has been subjected to harassment which has resulted in disorder of health may claim from the employer an appropriate sum as monetary compensation for the harm suffered.

§ 4. An employee who has been subjected to harassment or who has had his/her employment contract terminated as a result of harassment shall have the right to claim compensation from the employer in an amount not lower than the minimum remuneration for work, as determined on the basis of separate regulations.

§ 5. The employee's declaration of termination of the employment contract shall be made in writing, stating the reason referred to in § 2 justifying the termination of the contract".

24 J. Gołaczyński, A. Krzywonos, *Prawo do sądu*, in: ed. B. Banaszak, A. Preisner, *Prawa i wolności obywatelskie w Konstytucji RP*, Warsaw 2002, p. 725.

25 H. Mądrzak, *Prawo do sądu jako gwarancja ochrony praw człowieka (studium na tle polskiego prawa konstytucyjnego, prawa cywilnego materialnego i procesowego)*, [w]: ed. L. Wiśniewski, *Podstawowe prawa jednostki i ich sądowa ochrona*, Warsaw 1997, p. 187 and literature cited therein; A. Deryng, *Rzecznik Praw Obywatelskich*

the fundamental assumptions of a democratic legal state[26], whose duty it is to provide institutional and procedural guarantees for its implementation[27]. The Constitution of the Republic of Poland defines the right to a court in general terms[28] – as the right of everyone to a fair and public hearing of a case without undue delay by a competent, independent, impartial and independent court (Article 45(1) of the Constitution of the Republic of Poland)[29]. Therefore, it can be concluded that this refers to all cases, both, criminal, civil, administrative, criminal fiscal, etc.[30], as well as cases concerning labour law[31]. On the other hand, the trial may be excluded from public view on the grounds of morality, state security and public order as well as on the grounds of protection of private life of the parties or other important private interest. The verdict is announced publicly (Article 45(2) of the Constitution of the Republic of Poland)[32].

---

jako wnioskodawca w postępowaniu przed Trybunałem Konstytucyjnym, Warsaw 2014, p. 207 and literature cited therein.

26 Z. Kwiatkowski, *Prawo do sądu w demokratycznym państwie prawnym*, Ius Novum, No. 2 (2019), p. 33.

27 S. Lisowska-Krakowiak, *Instytucje kuratorów a realizacja prawa do sądu w cywilnym postępowaniu rozpoznawczym*, Warsaw 2018, p. 15.

28 A. Kubiak, *Konstytucyjna zasada prawa do sądu w świetle orzecznictwa Trybunału Konstytucyjnego*, Łódź 2006, p. 60.

29 W. Skrzydło, *Konstytucja Rzeczypospolitej Polskiej. Komentarz, op.cit.*, p. 56.

30 P. Winczorek, *Komentarz do Konstytucji Rzeczypospolitej Polskiej z dnia 2 kwietnia 1997 r.*, Warsaw 2000, p. 65; J. Boć, Commentary *to Article 45 of the Constitution of the Republic of Poland*, in: ed. J. Boć, *Konstytucje Rzeczypospolitej Polskiej oraz komentarz do Konstytucji RP z 1997 r.*, Wrocław 1998, p. 90; see also, A. Deryng, *Sąd polubowny a realizacja konstytucyjnej zasady prawa do sądu*, in: ADR. Arbitraż i Mediacja, No. 1 (2009). *"Perspektywy rozwoju sądownictwa arbitrażowego", Katowice, 20–21.11.2008 r. – materiały pokonferencyjne (part 1)*, p. 50 and the literature cited therein.

31 According to Zbigniew Kwiatkowski, "The broader treatment of the right to a court in the Polish Constitution results not only from the fact that it is not limited to certain categories of cases, but also from the linking of this right to the principle of two-instance court proceedings, included in Article 176(1) of the Constitution of the Republic of Poland, and the right to appeal decisions at least to the second instance, granted not only to persons accused of a crime to which guilt has been attributed, but to all litigants. This follows expressis verbis from Article 78 of the Polish Constitution, which states that: "Each party has the right to appeal against judgments and decisions rendered at first instance. Exceptions to this principle and the mode of appeal shall be determined by law", p. 36, Z. Kwiatkowski, *Prawo do sądu w demokratycznym państwie prawnym*, Ius Novum, No. 2 (2019), p. 36.

32 "This general formula is supplemented by Article 77(2) containing the prohibition of closing the judicial path to the assertion of infringed freedoms or rights, and Article

The doctrine of constitutional law emphasises that the right to a court appears in two senses. Firstly, as a constitutional principle, i.e. a legal norm addressed to the organs of the state obliging them to shape an independent, impartial, independent judiciary to resolve all types of legal disputes[33]. Secondly, as a constitutional subjective right[34]. In this second sense, the content of the subjective right to a court includes: the right of access to a court, the right to a proper procedure, and the right to a binding settlement of the case[35]. According to Bogusław Banaszak, court proceedings may be initiated in this situation by any entity that seeks to resolve a dispute. Thus, a violation of the constitutional right to a court will be any closure of the court path to him or her and deprivation of the possibility to present to the court one's own arguments for the defence and interests of a given entity[36].

The principle of the right to a court thus implies the entitlement of every subject of the law to obtain protection of his subjective rights by means of legal proceedings in an appropriate form and in compliance with the requirements of the procedure in question, and without undue delay[37].

III.

As indicated above, Article 80 of the CSA does not provide for the possibility to challenge in court the lack of consent of the employer for additional employment by a member of the civil service[38]. Interestingly, this is in contrast, for example, to the possibility of challenging negative periodic evaluations[39] provided for directly in

---

78 guaranteeing the right of the parties to challenge judgments and decisions issued at first instance. In turn, the individual constitutional institutions referred to in Article 45(1) are concretised by: Article 173 emphasising the independence of courts and tribunals, Article 177 assuming the monopoly of courts in the exercise of justice and Article 178(1) containing the principle of judicial independence", in: J. Gołaczyński, A. Krzywonos, *Prawo do sądu*, *op.cit.*, p. 730.

33 D. Lis-Staranowicz, *Chapter VIII Konstytucyjne środki ochrony wolności i praw*, in: ed. M. Chmaj, *Wolności i prawa człowieka w Konstytucji Rzeczypospolitej Polskiej*, Cracow 2006, p. 244.

34 Z. Kwiatkowski, *Prawo do sądu w demokratycznym państwie prawnym*, *op.cit.*, p. 34.

35 D. Lis-Staranowicz, *Chapter VIII Konstytucyjne środki ochrony wolności i praw*, *op.cit.*, p. 244 and the literature cited therein.

36 B. Banaszak, *Konstytucja Rzeczypospolitej Polskiej. Komentarz*, *op.cit.*, p. 240.

37 J. Gołaczyński, A. Krzywonos, *Prawo do sądu*, *op.cit.*, p. 730; P. Wiliński, *Proces karny w świetle Konstytucji*, Warsaw 2011, p. 117.

38 S. Płażek, *Commentary to Article 80 of the Civil Service Act*, in: ed. K. Baran, *Ustawa o służbie cywilnej. Komentarz*, published: JPC 2021, www.sip.lex.pl (accessed 22.10.2022).

39 S. Płażek, *Commentary to Article 80 of the Civil Service Act*, *op.cit.*, www.sip.lex.pl (accessed 22.10.2022). Article 83 u.s.c. "[Objection to periodic evaluation].

Article 83 of the CSA[40] .

The remainder of this article will consider whether such refusal by the employer can be challenged in court? Including whether such action by the employer can be qualified in terms of discrimination[41] or mobbing[42]? And if so, what remedies are then available to the employee?

---

1. The periodic evaluation is subject to an objection to the Director General of the Office within 7 days from the date of knowledge of the evaluation.

2. (repealed).

3. The objection shall be dealt with within 14 from the date of filing.

4. If an objection is upheld, the periodic evaluation shall be revised or made a second time. A second interim evaluation may be challenged under the conditions set out in paragraphs 1 and 3.

5. If an objection is not dealt with in time or if an objection to a periodic evaluation is not upheld, the appraisee may, within 14 days of the date of notification of the decision or of the expiry of the time limit referred to in paragraph 3, appeal to an employment tribunal".

40 Article 83 u.s.c. "[Objection to periodic evaluation].

1. The periodic evaluation is subject to an objection to the Director General of the Office within 7 days from the date of knowledge of the evaluation.

2. (repealed).

3. An objection shall be considered within 14 days of being lodged.

4. If the objection is upheld, the periodic evaluation shall be revised or made a second time. A second interim appraisal may be protested under the conditions set out in paragraphs 1 and 3.

5. In the event that an objection is not dealt with in time or an objection to a periodic evaluation is not upheld, the appraised person may, within 14 days from the date of delivery of the decision or from the expiry of the time limit referred to in paragraph 3, appeal to an employment court."

41 "In common parlance, the word '*discrimination*' means distinction (*discrimination*). Dictionaries and encyclopaedias consider discrimination to be 'the disadvantage or persecution of individuals or groups in society because of their origin, race, ethnicity, religion, nationality or class.' Discrimination in this general sense consists in treating individuals or groups worse in relation to the general population because of their 'otherness', J. Marciniak, *Mobbing, dyskryminacja, molestowanie przeciwdziałanie w praktyce*, Warsaw 2020, p. 46.

42 "Mobbing is a process of harassment of an employee lasting not less than six months, applied systematically at least once a week, harming the dignity, personality or mental or physical integrity of a person, endangering his or her employment and impairing the atmosphere and productivity at work"; "H. Leymann defines mobbing as a phenomenon from the sphere of communication – as hostile (angry, negative) and unethical communication between one employee or group of employees and another who is pushed into a defensive position and deprived of help. This type of

There are two opposing positions in the doctrine[43]. According to Bogusław Cudowski[44] "(...) the refusal to give consent does not fall into the category of the employer's discretion. For if this were to be assumed, the employee would have no subjective right to pursue his claim before the labour court. In the labour law literature, such views were propounded. It has been argued that the consent to additional work by civil servants is purely discretionary and not subject to any control, and that there are no provisions that would allow a possible refusal of such consent to be challenged. These views stem from the erroneous assumption of the total discretionary nature of the decision to consent to additional employment"[45]. Moreover, Bogusław Cudowski referring to the judgment of the Supreme Court of 06 January 1999, ref. no. III RN 180/98 in the thesis of which it was stated that "a retired judge may pursue claims resulting from the employment relationship before the labour court"[46], i.e. the Supreme Court accepted the admissibility of the court route in this case[47].

---

action occurs frequently (according to Leymann – statistically at least once a week) and persists over a long period of time (according to Leymann – statistically at least six months). Due to the high frequency and long duration of the hostile behaviour, the result of this maltreatment is psychological, psychosomatic and social damage to the victim. It is worth emphasising at this point that this communication can take both verbal and non-verbal forms (it can be gestures – humiliating or insulting, for example). Obviously, frequency and duration are very important for the phenomenon of mobbing, but it should also be remembered that the term 'statistically' means a large approximation – referring to the duration of phenomena over time", J. Marciniak, *Mobbing, dyskryminacja, molestowanie przeciwdziałanie w praktyce*, *op.cit.*, pp. 20–21.

43 P. Zuzankiewicz, *Commentary to Article 80 u.s.c.*, in: ed. W. Drobny, M. Mazuryk, P. Zuzankiewicz, *Ustawa o służbie cywilnej. Komentarz*, published: LEX 2012, www.sip.lex.pl (accessed 19.11.2022) – "There is a dispute in the doctrine as to whether the consent of the Director General (Head of the Civil Service) in the above-mentioned respect falls into the category of the employer's discretion, and thus whether the employee (member of the civil service) has a subjective right to pursue his claim before the labour court."

44 P. Zuzankiewicz, *Commentary to Article 80 u.s.c.*, *op.cit.*, www.sip.lex.pl (accessed 09.11.2022); B. Cudowski, *Dodatkowe zatrud*nienie, *op.cit.*, p. 183.

45 B. Cudowski, *Dodatkowe zatrud*nienie, *op.cit.*, p. 183.

46 B. Cudowski, *Dodatkowe zatrud*nienie, *op.cit.*, p. 183; Supreme Court judgment of 6 January 1999, ref: III RN 180/98, http://www.sn.pl/sites/orzecznictwo/orzeczenia1/iii%20rn%20180-98.pdf (accessed 09.11.2022); P. Zuzankiewicz, *Commentary to Article 80 u.s.c.*, *op.cit.*,www.sip.lex.pl (accessed 09.11.2022).

47 P. Zuzankiewicz, *Commentary to Article 80 u.s.c.*,*op.cit*, www.sip.lex.pl (accessed 09.11.2022).

Indeed, in that judgment, the Supreme Court stated that "(…)the First President of the Supreme Court may (should) consent to a judge of this Court taking up (continuing) his or her work, unless its performance could offend the dignity of the judge's profession (Article 68 § 1 and 2 of the Law on Retired Judges). On the other hand, there is no concern as to the possibility of a restriction of a judge's independence related to taking up another job, as a retired judge does not perform the judicial function"[48] .

The position presented by Anna Dubowik in her article "Additional employment and other activities of employees in the public sphere"[49] corresponds with the above view. Anna Dubowik pointed out that "a decision allowing or prohibiting an employee to perform additional employment or other gainful activity is not, therefore, of a strictly discretionary nature. The refusal to give consent to additional employment/remunerated activities may in no way constitute a manifestation of discrimination against the employee. An employee who believes that a decision of his/her superior depriving him/her of the possibility to perform additional employment/other activities has been made on the basis of criteria that the Labour Code lists as prohibited reasons for discrimination (Article 11^3, Article 18^{3a} contain exemplary catalogues of such criteria), may appeal to the labour court on general principles"[50] .

An opposing view on this issue has been expressed by, among others, Beata Klink[51]. According to the author: "The granting of permission for additional work by officials is purely discretionary and is not subject to any control. Officials have no right to appeal against a refusal. However, this situation does not imply complete arbitrariness, as the entity granting the consent cannot be guided by personal dislike or particular interests when taking the decision. As long as the taking up of additional employment does not contradict the objectives of the

---

48 B. Cudowski, *Dodatkowe zatrudn*ienie, *op.cit.*, p. 183; Supreme Court judgment of 6 January 1999, ref. III RN 180/98, http://www.sn.pl/sites/orzecznictwo/orzeczenia1/iii%20rn%20180-98.pdf (accessed 09.11.2022); P. Zuzankiewicz, *Commentary to Article 80 u.s.c., op.cit*, www.sip.lex.pl (accessed 09.11.2022).

49 P. Zuzankiewicz, *Commentary to Article 80 u.s.c.,op.cit.*, www.sip.lex.pl (accessed 09.11.2022); A. Dubowik, *Dodatkowe zatrudnienie i inne zajęcia pracowników sfery publicznej*, Praca i zabezpieczenie społeczne, No. 10 (2005), p. 18.

50 A. Dubowik, *Dodatkowe zatrudnienie i inne zajęcia pracowników sfery publicznej*, *op. cit.*, pp. 18–19.

51 P. Zuzankiewicz, *commentary to art. 80 CSA„op.cit.*, www.sip.lex.pl (accessed 09.11.2022)]; B. Klink, *Podejmowanie dodatkowego zatrudnienia przez pracowników administracji publicznej – problematyka prawna*, Radca Prawny, No. 6 (1999), p. 106.

prohibition, there are no obstacles to granting permission. Such a regulation, however, encourages abuse on the part of the subject on whose consent the possibility of additional work depends"[52]. A similar position on this issue was expressed by Maria Teresa Romer[53]. Indeed, she stated that "there are no legal provisions that would allow a possible refusal of such consent to be challenged"[54].

In my view, the refusal of the employer to take on additional employment, as indicated in Article 80 CSA, cannot be arbitrary. It is not sufficient merely to communicate to the employee the refusal to grant such consent. Indeed, it is important to indicate also the reasons for the refusal, so that the employee is in no doubt as to what obstacles, in the opinion of the employer, prevent the employee from taking up additional employment. In this context, I am sympathetic to those positions that allow the refusal of consent to be subject to judicial review. What remains problematic, however, is the question of what specific claim can be made by a civil servant who has been refused consent. The demand to order the employer to give consent or to issue a judgment in lieu of such consent (Article 64 of the Civil Code Act of 23 April 1964[55]) should be considered here. The assessment of the effectiveness of such actions will depend on the specifics of each case. Conducting a detailed analysis in this respect taking into account the most characteristic situations would exceed the framework of this study. Particularly as the CSA does not specify detailed criteria to be followed by the employer when consenting to additional employment, nor does it specifically indicate the conditions and principles for undertaking additional employment.

As part of further analysis of the problem presented, he therefore wishes to focus on situations in which the refusal to grant consent for additional employment may be a manifestation of discrimination[56] or mobbing[57] on the

---

52 B. Klink, *Podejmowanie dodatkowego zatrudnienia przez pracowników administracji publicznej – problematyka prawna*, *op.cit.*, p. 106.

53 P. Zuzankiewicz, *commentary to article 80 CSA*, *op.cit.*, www.sip.lex.pl (accessed 09.11.2022); M. T. Romer, *Dodatkowe zatrudnienie a uprawnienia pracownicze*, Warsaw 1995, p. 14.

54 M. T. Romer, *Dodatkowe zatrudnienie a uprawnienia pracownicze*, Warsaw 1995, p. 14.

55 T.U. 2022, item 1360, as amended.

56 B. Mróz, A. Chudzicka-Czupała, M. Kuśpit, *Kompetencje osobowościowe i twórcze. Psychologiczne uwarunkowania kreatywności pracowników*, Warsaw 2017, p. 95.

57 More on mobbing, e.g. H. Szewczyk, *Mobbing w stosunkach pracy. Zagadnienia prawne*, Warsaw 2012, p. 15; M. Gamian-Wilk, *Mobbing w miejscu pracy. Uwarunkowania i konsekwencje bycia poddawanym mobbingowi*, Warsaw 2018, p. 15; J. Wachowiak, *Dysfunkcjonalne zachowania pracowników*, Warsaw 2011, p. 70; W. Warecki, M. Warecki, *Słowo o mobbingu, czyli jak sobie radzić z dręczycielem*, Warsaw 2005, p. 13.

part of the employer. However, the possibility of challenging the refusal to consent to additional employment is not self-explanatory here. Instead, the protection against unjustified refusal to consent to additional employment is indirect and limited. The indirectness of this protection stems from the fact that, when recognising the validity of a discrimination or mobbing claim manifested by a refusal to consent to additional employment, the court in its judgment cannot order the employer to give such consent, nor can it issue a judgment that would supersede the employer's statement of additional consent. Indeed, in upholding such an action, the court may award damages from the employer to the employee. However, the issuance of such an otherwise favourable judgment does not mean that the employee can take up additional employment. Indeed, the employer may still refuse to consent to such employment and the employee will only be left with the possibility of suing the employer again, this time in respect of a further period. Of course, assuming the reasonableness of the employer's action, it is impossible to assume that, once the discrimination or mobbing action has been upheld, the employer will continue to refuse consent and thus continue the discriminatory or mobbing actions. However, this cannot be ruled out and, should such a situation arise, the employee will be left with the option of bringing a further claim.

Furthermore, the review of the reasonableness of the refusal of consent discussed here is limited in nature. Not every refusal of consent, even if obviously groundless, will constitute a manifestation of discrimination or mobbing. If only one employee requests such consent from a particular superior, it will be difficult for him to show that he is treated worse than the others, if none of the employees sought such consent. The use of the possibility to make the protection against discrimination an instrument to protect against unjustified refusal of consent for additional employment will only apply to situations where such consent has been sought and obtained by a number of employees and not by others. Those employees who have not received such consent will then be able to claim that they are being treated less favourably than those who have received consent. In such a situation, it will be up to the employer to show what considerations it had in refusing consent to some employees and giving consent to others. It should be noted that if the adopted differentiating criteria do not have an objective justification, the court may consider individual refusals to be a manifestation of discrimination. As a consequence, this will open up the possibility to take up additional employment, although, as indicated above, only in an indirect manner. It is worth noting at this point that the anti-discrimination measures will, however, not be able to succeed if the employer consistently refuses consent to all employees requesting it, even if in all cases the lack of such consent has no justification. Thus, the limited nature of the review of the refusal to consent to additional employment in the exercise of the option to bring a discrimination claim is also expressed in this respect.

Even more indirect and limited in nature is the protection against unjustified refusal to consent to additional employment under legal measures against mobbing. In doing so, it appears that a mere one-off refusal of consent will not exhaust the prerequisites necessary to be considered a mobbing action[58]. This is a consequence of how the concept of mobbing is understood[59]. Therefore, it is only when the refusal to consent to additional employment is accompanied by other actions of a mobbing nature that the employee will be able to effectively avail

---

58 According to the judgment of the Supreme Court of 29 January 2019, ref. III PK 6/ 18: "the definition of mobbing contained in Article 94^3 § 2 of the Labour Code does not set rigid time limits or frequency of behaviour qualifying as mobbing for a period of at least six months. However, it unquestionably shows that it is not sufficient to use mobbing once or several times in a short period of time, as the relevant characteristic of mobbing is persistent and prolonged harassment or intimidation of an employee"- Judgment of the Supreme Court of 29 January 2019, act III PK 6/18, LEX no. 2619173, www.sip.lex.pl (accessed 05.12.2022).

59 The Supreme Court, in its judgment of 29 January 2019, ref: III PK 6/18, indicated that: "mobbing is actions or behaviour: (1) concerning an employee or directed against an employee; (2) involving persistent and prolonged harassment or intimidation of an employee; (3) causing an employee's appraisal of his/her professional usefulness to be lowered; (4) causing or intended to humiliate or ridicule an employee; (5) isolating him/her or eliminating him/her from the team of employees.

The Supreme Court in its jurisprudence accepts that the above-mentioned statutory prerequisites of mobbing must be fulfilled jointly and demonstrated by the employee (cf. judgment of 11 February 2014, I PK 165/13, LEX No 1444594 with gloss by K. Stępnicka, LEX/el 2014; of 5 October 2007, II PK 31/07, OSNP 2008 No 21–22, item 312; of 5 December 2006, II PK 112/06, OSNP 2008 No 1–2, item 2). It is stressed that the prerequisites of mobbing listed in Article 94^3 § 2 of the Labour Code are undefined phrases, the abstract definition of which is basically impossible, and their clarification is performed by referring to the entirety of the specific factual circumstances occurring in the case (cf. the decision of the Supreme Court of 6 June 2012,, LEX No. 1216839) – judgment of the Supreme Court of 29 January 2019, ref. III PK 6/18, LEX no. 2619173, www.sip.lex.pl (accessed 05.12.2022).

According to one of the theses of the Supreme Court expressed in the judgment of 18 December 2018, ref: II PK 243/17: "Mobbing is committed by a supervisor who repeatedly annoys, harasses or hinders a subordinate in the exercise of his/her entitlements for raising minor children, as a result of which the employee has developed an adaptive depressive-anxiety disorder (Article 94^3 § 2 of the Labour Code)." – Supreme Court judgment of 18 December 2018, ref: II PK 243/17, published: OSNP 2019/8/97, www.sip.lex.pl (accessed 05.12.2022).

himself of protection through the courts against an unjustified refusal to consent to additional employment. This is because, in the case of a mobbing lawsuit, the burden of proof is on the employee. Thus, it is not the employer who has to prove (as in a discrimination lawsuit) that he or she is treating the employee properly, but the employee has to show that the refusal of consent and other actions (which must accompany the refusal of consent) are a manifestation of mobbing. In practice, this means that in the case of a discrimination lawsuit, it will be the employer who will have to show whether other employees also applied for consent for additional employment, how many were refused and how many were granted consent and, above all, for what reasons, and that any differentiation here was based on objective criteria. The employee will be able to trigger such a judicial review of the refusal of consent (albeit indirect and limited) without knowing whether he or she is the only one to whom consent was refused. In the case of bullying, the situation is quite different. Indeed, this means that the protection against unjustified refusal of consent in the case of a bullying lawsuit is even more limited.

IV.

It follows from the considerations carried out that the issue of the admissibility of a judicial challenge to a refusal to consent to additional employment of a member of the civil service, as referred to in Article 80 of the Civil Service Act, has not been directly regulated in the Act. On the other hand, in the doctrine this issue is quite debatable. Nevertheless, it can be concluded that the refusal to grant consent for additional employment of a member of the civil service is not of a discretionary nature and may be subject to court review. Thus, an employee who has been refused such consent may bring a claim before the court in defence of his or her rights. However, the question of the basis of the employee's claim remains problematic. In other words, with which claim would the employee have to go to court if he or she was refused permission for additional employment.

On the other hand, it must be recognised that a civil servant may challenge through the courts the employer's refusal to consent to additional employment by availing himself of his legal remedies against mobbing and discrimination. In such a situation, however, the triggering factor for the possibility of judicial protection is, in fact, the concurrence of the refusal to consent to the additional employment with the mobbing or discriminatory action on the part of the employer. In the situation of the coincidence indicated here, the protection against unjustified refusal to consent to additional employment will be indirect and limited. The mere refusal to consent to additional employment is therefore not sufficient to trigger judicial review.

Wojciech Drobny

About the Polish Civil Service on Its 100th Anniversary

1. Introduction

In the debate about the civil service, the authors of the statements refer to the ethos of this service, ethics, attitudes and behaviours required of members of the civil service corps[1]. They indicate the elements of the employment status of this group of people, such as the appointment act, periodic appraisals or disciplinary liability. At the same time, they usually ignore the proper quantifier of these concepts and elements, i.e. their public-law dimension. All of the above instruments, ordered and logically applied by the legislator, together constitute clerical law, the essence of which is its separation from labour law and its original affiliation with administrative law. The subject of further considerations will be the presentation of changes in the public-law nature of the Polish civil service law, an attempt to indicate the reasons for these changes and their assessment.

2. The Public-Law Status of the Civil Service Law in an Abstract Approach

The use of the term "public law" is synonymous with the use of the concept strictly defined in the dogma of administrative law, belonging to the family, the so-called "Administrative law institutions"[2]. In the well-established systematics of administrative law, this category includes the most important intellectual models for this branch of law, e.g. public subjective law, the administrative-legal relationship, or administrative recognition[3]. The fact of this affiliation has far-reaching consequences. Administrative law institutions are characterized by the *a priori* features of administrative law as part of the public law. These features are specific axiology, sources, principles, and features in the *strict sense*[4].

---

1 G. Rydlewski, *Służba cywilna w Polsce,* Warszawa 2001, s. 13–15.

2 R. Hauser [w:] Z. Duniewska, R. Hauser, M. Jaśkowska, M. Matczak, Z. Niewiadomski, Z. Wróbel, *Instytucje prawa administracyjnego* [w:] R. Hauser, Z. Niewiadomski, A. Wróbel, *System prawa administracyjnego. Tom 1,* s. 199 i n.

3 Ibidem.

4 J. Zimmermann, *Prawo administracyjne,* Warszawa 2018, s. 59 i n.

The catalogue of these mentioned attributes determines the special position of an individual in relation to the state. It is in the axiology of this law that there are universal values, internal values (including human welfare, morality, justice, rationality, clarity, transparency, speed and economy) and values protected by administrative law (including public interest, public law subjective). In the principles of administrative law, the doctrine places the principles derived from the concept of a democratic state of law (e.g. protection of acquired rights, subsidiarity, proportionality), principles relating to public administration bodies (e.g. good administration, competence, efficiency) and general principles of the Code of Administrative Procedure (including the rule of law, objective truth or increasing trust in the website). The sources of this law are the sources *sensu stricto* (indicated by the Constitution), *sensu largo* (constitutionally defined acts of internal law) and other (various law-making facts not mentioned by the Constitution). *Sensu stricto* features of administrative law directly determine whether this branch of law belongs to public law, which, according to Ulpian, is defined as "serving the public interest", while "private law serves private interests"[5]. Therefore, administrative law as part of public law is a branch of law that regulates the state as the subject of power and serves to justify and define state competences. As J. Zimmermann aptly notices: "the state has a superior character over other entities. Administrative law is the result of the will of not every entity, but special public entities. Its norms express the competences of these special entities implementing public administration. Within the limits of this law, goals, interests, public good and tasks are realized, and the organization and operation of public administration are regulated."[6] Such a widely repeated statement in fact touches on a key issue in the discussion about the nature of the Polish civil service. The question of whether this legal institution belongs to public or private law.

I have no doubts, just like the interwar legislature[7], that the civil service is a public-law category belonging to administrative law. The practical effects of this qualification, against the background of the above-mentioned attributes of administrative law, are fundamental. The unique axiological assumptions, specific only to this branch of law, as well as its sources, principles and features

5 A. Dębiński, J. Misztal-Konecka, M. Wójcik, *Prawo rzymskie publiczne,* Warszawa 2010, s. X.

6 J. Zimmermann, *Prawo administracyjne..*, s. 59–60.

7 J. Kopczyński, *Przepisy normujące stosunek państwowej służby cywilnej,* Warszawa 1925, s. 9; M. Jaroszyński, M. Zimmermann, *Polskie prawo administracyjne, część ogólna.* Warszawa 1956, s. 293 in.

in the strict sense, should directly and without intermediaries translate into the regulations of statutes that belong to this branch of law. Therefore, if the clerical law, which includes the pragmatics of the civil service, belongs identically to administrative law, then the logical consequence of such classification is the inclusion in the provisions of pragmatics of the provisions implementing the listed attributes of administrative law.

3. The Public-Law Status of the Civil Service Law in Practical Approach

Moving the above considerations from an abstract level to practical legal solutions in the status of the civil service, a good illustration may be the diametrically different legal situation of a member of the civil service corps in the regime of administrative law or labour law. In the first case, the legal relationship between the official and the state will be an administrative one of the service type. Due to the belonging to administrative law, and thus having the attributes of this law, in this specific legal relationship there will be an inequality of parties[8].

The interest of the state will take precedence over the interest of the official (i.e. individual interest)[9]. This will translate into a catalogue of the rights and obligations of an official, including legitimate, constitutionally permissible restrictions on political, union and labour rights[10]. Based on this basic assumption, the pragmatics in the part concerning the system of civil service bodies, the jurisdiction of administrative courts or the application of administrative procedure should be shaped by the legislator in such a way as to enable the control of an official's actions under the Code of Administrative Procedure, and then under the Act on Procedure before administrative courts[11]. It is worth noting that this is the direction that was followed by the legislator in the first pragmatics of members of the civil service corps after the political transformation[12].

---

8 R. Hauser [w:] Z. Duniewska, R. Hauser, M. Jaśkowska, M. Matczak, Z. Niewiadomski, Z. Wróbel, *Instytucje prawa..*, s. 201.

9 T. Kuczyński [w:] T. Kuczyński, E. Mazurczak-Jasińska, J. Stelina, *Stosunek służbowy* [w:] R. Hauser, Z. Niewiadomski, A. Wróbel, System prawa administracyjnego, Tom 11, Warszawa 2011. s. 3.

10 Art. 31 ust. 3 Konstytucji Rzeczypospolitej Polskiej z dnia 2 kwietnia 1997 r., Dz.U.1997, Nr 78, poz. 483.

11 T. Kuczyński [w:] T. Kuczyński, E. Mazurczak-Jasińska, J. Stelina, *Stosunek służbowy..*, s. 112.

12 The point is: ustawa z dnia 5 lipca 1996 o służbie cywilnej, Dz.U. Nr 89, poz. 402.

The legal situation of a Civil Service Corps member will be completely different when his pragmatics is adopted by the legislator as part of the labour law. This branch of law, as part of private law, is characterized by the equality of the parties to the legal relationship (employment relationship)[13].

This attribute will determine the legal position of this official, thus making it equal to the status of code employees[14]. This means the application of the Labour Code regime and – as a subsidiary – possible clerical pragmatics, within which the legislator will have very limited possibilities to create restrictions, including trade union, political and employee rights.

The private-law identity of this clerical law makes no sense to create a special system of civil service organs and the mode of their operation, because disputes concerning an official – in this model – may be resolved on general terms by institutions of common judiciary. The solutions from the post-war period illustrate this type of approach to the Polish civil service (state administration staff)[15]. Undoubtedly, the decision to qualify clerical pragmatics to the appropriate branch of law is of paramount importance. The direction of further legislative and legislative work should depend on this preliminary decision. Both the logical and historical look at the role of the civil service undoubtedly locates it – in my opinion – in the area of public law.

The type of civil service tasks, i.e. the performance of state tasks and the location of this corps in government administration offices[16], imply the necessity to place these members of the civil service corps in the legal regime applicable to public administration. The public-law type of tasks translates into the manner of their implementation, and the required manner of carrying out the tasks translates into the status of their contractors. At each stage of this process, the aforementioned attributes of administrative law (axiology, sources of law, *sensu stricto* features and principles) are applied.

The above-mentioned qualification is also confirmed by the historical perspective and the genesis of the civil service law. In the interwar period, in the face of the post-partition problems of harmonizing the apparatus of the national

13 M. T. Romer [w:] *Prawo pracy. Komentarz*, wyd. V, Warszawa 2012, art. 11, Lex.

14 The point is: ustawa z dnia 26 czerwca 1974 r. – Kodeks Pracy, Dz.U.2020, poz. 1320 t.j.

15 The point is term from 1974 r. (established Kodeks pracy) to 1982 r. (established ustawa z dnia 16 września 1982 r. o pracownikach urzędów państwowych, Dz.U.2020.537 t.j.).

16 Pursuant to Art. 153 paragraph. 1 of the Constitution of the Republic of Poland which reads as follows: "In order to ensure professional, reliable, impartial and politically neutral performance of the state's tasks, the civil service corps operates in government administration offices."

administration[17], the legislator consistently established the public-legal status of the staff of the state civil service. Taking a form adequate to these unprecedented challenges, he subjected civil servants to administrative law regulations, effectively ensuring the reconstruction of the state apparatus[18].

The pragmatics of 1922 was the starting point for the history of the Polish civil service, a model for creating the civil service in the public-law model, from which the legislator abandoned the following years for legal and non-legal reasons.

4. The Impact of International Law on Polish Clerical Law

Among the legal, objective, existing reasons for the Polish legislator to depart from public-law solutions in the civil service, there is a paradigm shift in Western European legislation of applying the institution of official relations in public administration and the extensive appropriation of the issues of clerical law in the legal discourse by the administrative law. Until recently, administrative law, in particular official law, was an area of national law that was subject to the influence of international law to a limited extent[19]. At the international level, there are no legal regulations that would directly refer to the principles of organization and functioning of public administration bodies in specific countries.

It can be recalled from the literature that such a state is the result of the assumption that the competence to create the apparatus of public administration is a traditional domain of a sovereign state[20], which is independently responsible for the choice of the concept, system and procedures of the state's operation[21]. For this reason, until recently the view was that there were no European standards that would shape the status of public administration employees[22].

17 P. Górski, *Profesjonalizacja administracji państwowej w Polsce 1918–1939. Uwarunkowania społeczne i kulturowe,* Kraków 2011, s. 41 i n.

18 Ustawa z dnia 17 lutego 1922 r. o państwowej służbie cywilnej, Dz.U. 1949, Nr 11, poz. 72.

19 T. Górzyńska, *Standardy europejskie dotyczące pracowników administracji publicznej*, Studia Prawnicze, Warszawa 2001, s. 119.

20 J. Czaputowicz, *Implikacje integracji z Unią Europejską dla polskiej służby cywilnej*, Służba Cywilna, Nr 1 (2000) s. 22.

21 I. Corte-Real, *Administracja publiczna a Unia Europejska*, Służba cywilna, Nr 1 (2000), s. 11.

22 T. Jasudowicz, Kilka uwag o europejskich standardach administracyjnych – ze szczególnym uwzględnieniem służby cywilnej – w świetle europejskich standardów praw człowieka [w:] Księga pamiątkowa profesora Eugeniusza Ochendowskiego, Toruń 1999, s. 97–136.

However, a progressive real Europeanization of national public administrations is noticeable, manifested by the unification of rules, behaviour and procedures regulating its operation. It results to some extent from the expanding cooperation of national administrations with international institutions and bilateral cooperation between the states[23]. This led to the creation of an area known in the literature as the European Administrative Space[24]. Its legal environment is constituted by public international law which regulates the mutual relations between the subjects of this law, i.e. between states and international organizations[25].

Undoubtedly, international law as well as legal solutions within international institutions or comparative legislation of other states and communities directly, indirectly, or at least inspire the national legislator to act towards approximation to these solutions. The most important legal acts affecting the perception of clerical law as part of labour law include the International Covenant on Civil (Personal) and Political Rights[26], the European Social Charter[27] or Convention No. 151 of the International Labour Organization on the protection of the right to organize and the procedure for determining employment conditions in the public service[28]. In the scope of regulations concerning, for example, trade union and employee rights, the rights of association or the pursuit of claims, the cited legal acts do not take into account the specificity of the public service, often equating the public status of an official with the ordinary status of an employee.

The impact of European Union law on the status of the Polish civil service is similar. As it is noted in the literature, the European Union does not have the possibility of direct legal interference in the shape of public service in the Member States, but it cannot be stated that this area is completely excluded from the influence of this law[29]. The strength of this influence comes primarily

---

23 J. Itrich-Drabarek, *Uwarunkowania, standardy i kierunki zmian funkcjonowania służby cywilnej w Polsce na tle europejskim*, Warszawa 2011, s. 332–333.

24 J. Czaputowicz, *Implikacje integracji z Unią..*, s. 23.

25 W. Czapliński, A. Wyrozumska, *Prawo międzynarodowe publiczne. Zagadnienie systemowe,* Warszawa 1999, s. 5.

26 Międzynarodowy Pakt Praw Obywatelskich (Osobistych) i Politycznych z 19.12.1966, Dz. U. 1977, nr 38, poz. 16.

27 Europejska Karta Społeczna, Dz. U. 1999, Nr 8, poz. 67.

28 Konwencja nr 151 Międzynarodowej Organizacji Pracy dotycząca ochrony prawa organizowania się i procedury określania warunków zatrudniania w służbie publicznej, Dz.U. 1994, Nr 22, poz. 78.

29 D. Bossaert, Ch. Demmke, *Służba cywilna w państwach akcesyjnych. Tendencje i wpływ procesów integracyjnych*, Łódź 2003, s. 83.

from the fact that it has the nature of a community of values that gives great importance to the law, which formulates these values and secures their actual functioning[30]. The shape of the national regulations in the field of civil service, in this respect will be guaranteed under Art. 45 of the Treaty on the Functioning of the European Union[31] (and, above all, the established jurisprudence in this respect), the right of access to the national public service and the Charter of Fundamental Rights of the European Union[32]. It is also worth noting that outside the EU legal system, public law regulations, such as the Recommendations of the Committee of Ministers of the Council of Europe on the status of public employees in Europe[33] and Recommendations on codes of conduct for public employees, remain in some unjustified oblivion[34].

5. Final Remarks

The above reasons resulted in a situation in which the present actual legal status of the Polish Civil Service Act, objectively to a large extent, shows law-labour elements. However, it is a logical error to draw conclusions from the current shape of these provisions as to the correct model of the civil service. The current legal act is – in my opinion – an example of instrumentalization of the law, and its shape is the result of the legislator's reactive action due to the need of the moment.

The legislator's approach to the issue of the civil service was instrumental from the very beginning. With the exception of the interwar period, most legal interference in this area was marked by a misunderstanding of the essence of this institution and was dictated by the current, short-sighted interests of the political elite.

Therefore, the idea of guaranteeing the elementary framework of the civil service in the constitution was fully reasonable. Potentially, it was the only effective counteracting the instrumentalization of clerical law and ensuring its status understood as a public service, i.e. as the superior value of the rule of law. Unfortunately, in the light of the current solutions in Polish civil service law, it is reasonable to assess that this potential has been wasted.

30 J. Itrich-Drabarek, *Uwarunkowania, standardy i kierunki..*, s. 333.
31 Traktatu o funkcjonowaniu Unii Europejskiej, Dz.U.2004, Nr 90, poz. 864/2.
32 Karta Praw Podstawowych Unii Europejskiej, Dz.U.UE.C.2007, Nr 303, poz. 1.
33 Zalecenia Nr R (00) 6 Komitetu Ministrów Rady Europy dotyczące statusu pracowników publicznych w Europie z 24 lutego 2000 r.
34 Zalecenia Nr R (00) 10 w sprawie kodeksów postępowania pracowników publicznych z 11 maja 2000 r.

Jadwiga Glumińska-Pawlic, Lidia Zacharko

Model of Employment in Public Administration in the Interwar Period: Some Reflections

1. Introduction

According to Maurice Hauriou, "public service is a work to be carried out by public administration and public authority as a means of implementation[1]*."* The article aims to present the employment model in public administration after regaining independence in Poland in the interwar period, pointing to the public law nature of the employment relationship of state officials. As emphasized by H. Izdebski, in the first years of independence, the executive power developed spontaneously. Its structure and organizational principles were ad hoc, according to emerging needs. However, it also needed more financial possibilities and staff qualifications[2].

The functionality of public administration is based on a professional, well-prepared staff made up of officials. People employed in public administration and dealing with public affairs are called officials[3].

There is no defined concept of public service in the Polish legal system. The word "public" comes from Latin and means something related to the state – for example, public property[4].

As emphasized by J. Łętowski, public service is the collective name of all professions in Poland that are established to perform specific tasks for the state[5]. As J. Jagielski adds, the Polish state should have a staff whose duty is to serve the needs of a state apparatus, especially its administration. Staff should be professional, disciplined, and loyal, meeting the competencies of their authorities to ensure the efficient and effective operation of the entire mechanism of power in the state[6].

---

1 M. Hauriou, *Precis de droit administratif*, Paris 1927, p.VII.
2 H. Izdebski, *Historia administracji*, Warsaw 2001, p. 112.
3 G. Rydlewski, *Służba cywilna w Polsce*, Warsaw 2001, p. 17.
4 M. Kulesza, M. Niziołek, *Etyka służby publicznej*, Warsaw 2010, p. 76.
5 J. Łętowski, *Pracownicy administracji w PRL*, Wrocław 1994, p. 30.
6 J. Jagielski, *Przepisy ogólne*, in: ed. Z. Cieślak, J. Jagielski, K. Rączka, *Komentarz do ustawy o służbie cywilnej*, Warsaw 1998, p. 5

On the other hand, M. Kulesza and M. Niziołek point out that the standard definition of civil service law comes from the concept of a tool called a legal relationship. This means that two people can be in a legal relationship when one law is essential to them. Public service is working for a state salary to provide services directly related to state functions. Public service is a legal relationship between a specific person and the state, consisting of the performance by that person continuous and ongoing services related to these functions for remuneration[7].

F. Longchamps stated that legal provisions define relations between public officials and the state[8].

Public service should be created for the common good. It is a special kind of service that only bureaucracy can perform[9].

The state has the authority to determine the duties and rights of a government official by law. Voluntary access to the service is supported by the public law nature of the service relationship, which is expressed in an administrative and legal act based on the admission to service. Moreover, this relationship has a unilateral character. The relationship between the state and its workers must be stable and committed to service to society. This can only be achieved through a legally imposed hierarchical structure. Society must also have access to its officials, who should put aside their interests when undertaking activities for the benefit of the state[10].

2. Model of Employment in Administration in the Interwar Period

In 2022, we celebrated the 100th anniversary of the civil service in Poland. An essential act in the interwar period was the Act of February 17, 1922, on the State Service[11], which was preceded by the previously issued interim regulations, i.e., the Council Rescript Regency and Temporary Service Regulations for Government Officials and Pay Table of government officials[12]. This was mainly due to regaining

---

7 M. Kulesza, M. Niziołek, *Etyka służby publicznej…*, p. 79.

8 F. Logchamps, *O pojęciu stosunku prawnego w prawie administracyjnym*, AUWr 1964, Prawo XII, No. 19, p. 45.

9 M. Kulesza, M. Niziołek, *Etyka służby publicznej*, Warsaw 2010, p. 76.

10 Z. Kubot, T. Kuczyński, Z. Masternak, H. Szurgacz, *Prawo pracy. Zarys wykładu*, Warsaw 2008, p. 333 and next.

11 Journal AT. No. 21, item 164.

12 Journal of Laws, 1918, No. 6, item 13.

independence after the period of partitions and the need to introduce uniform rules and solutions around the country. The interim provisions indicated the public law nature of the relationship business. As stated in Art. 1 of the interim provisions, the legal relationship of the official to a State falls within the scope of public law. It may not be established, changed, suspended, or terminated by agreement or at the request of an official but only on the law's principle and the authorities' legal orders.

J. Stelina emphasizes that the following was of fundamental importance for the newly reborn state: normalization of the political system, the appointment of authorities, and the creation of professional body of officials[13].

E. Ura points out that the Act of 1922 introduced the basic principles of law official, which were:

1. the public law nature of the service relationship;
2. establishing a service relationship in the administrative and legal mode through appointment;
3. full subordination to superior authority;
4. disciplinary responsibility to corporate bodies in the form of a disciplinary commission[14].

According to Art. 4 of the Act mentioned above, the service relationship of an official was concluded by appointment upon delivery of the nomination letter. In the nomination letter, the office in which the appointed official was to serve, his title as official was mentioned and his rank. The appointment was announced in the manner established for government announcements.

The candidate applying for the appointment had to meet the rigors indicated in Art. 6 of the Act, namely, an official could be appointed when he was:

- a Polish citizen with an impeccable past,
- with legal capacity,
- physically and mentally fit to perform the relevant official duties, and fluent in spoken and written Polish.

These rigors were adapted to a given category of officials, divided into three categories. Candidates in the first category had to have higher education and complete a year's preparatory service, ending with an exam. Candidates for the second category had to have general secondary or vocational education, and for

13 J. Stelina, *Prawo urzędnicze*, Warsaw 2013, p. 36 and next.
14 E. Ura, *Prawo administracyjne*, Warsaw 2009, pp. 233–234.

the third category – education at the level of a primary school or completed lower secondary school.

It is worth emphasizing that the Act regulated public officials' legal status in the state administrative apparatus. However, outside the scope of regulation, state functionaries served in state education, state-owned enterprises (e.g., in PKP *[Polish State Railways]* or the post office), persons employed in the army, and provisions for judges, prosecutors, and court trainees[15].

The state civil service included government administration officials employed in various departments of the state administration, divided into two categories: civil servants and lower functionaries[16]. Whereas officials were divided into three categories, which covered individual positions from Prime Minister and field marshal to messenger and usher. Positions classified into individual categories corresponded to specific grade ranges[17]. Despite the indicated distinction between the groups mentioned above, the basis for establishing a service relationship for both was the appointment.

The Act introduced inequality of the subjects of the service relationship because, on the one hand, the subject of the service relationship was the state (endowed with state authority)[18], and on the other hand, the official (deprived of this authority). Thus, civil servants became public officials bounded by a service relationship with the state characterized by durability. On the other hand, they were firmly subordinate to their superiors and this state[19].

The model of personnel selection in the interwar period referred to the traditional continental model, where efforts were made to create a permanent and professional clerical corps that could function independently of political changes. As noted by H. Izdebski and M. Kulesza, the symbol of this approach was the highly accurate statement that governments and parliaments are leaving, and the administration is staying[20]. In turn, D. Gręzicki emphasizes – referring

15 J. Stelina, *Prawo urzędnicze…*, p. 39.

16 A. Dubownik, Ł. Pisarczyk, *Prawo urzędnicze*, Warsaw 2011, p. 53.

17 L. Hass, *Pracownicze organizacje zawodowe w Polsce 1918–1939, Roczniki Dziejów Społecznych I Gospodarczych,* T.XXV, 1963, p. 154.

18 E. Ura, *Prawo administracyjne, Warsaw* 2009, p. 234.

19 H. Izdebski, *Fundamenty współczesnych państw,* Warsaw 2007, p. 215; J. Stelina, *Prawo urzędnicze*, Warsaw 2009, p. 14; Ł. Pisarczyk, *Model zatrudnienia w administracji publicznej*, in: *Prawo administracyjne wobec współczesnych wyzwań. Księga jubileuszowa dedykowana Profesorowi Markowi Wierzbowskiemu*, Warsaw 2018, p. 536.

20 H. Izdebski, M. Kulesza, *Administracja publiczna. Zagadnienia ogólne*, Warsaw 2004, p. 265.

to current solutions – that in the interwar period, a state official was a carrier of values and ideas on an unprecedented scale[21] whose employment relationship (based on appointment) was subject to special protection.

The regulations of the interwar period can be compared to a model of personnel selection similar to the career model. The service career model means that stability and the possibility of gradual promotion were guaranteed for candidates for service, i.e. successive moving to higher positions in connection with improving qualifications and gaining experience in professional work. A political change of government remains indifferent to staffing in public administration, which means that in the event of a change of political power, people employed in the administrative apparatus are not at risk of dismissal[22].

As J. Sługocki adds, the career system is closed because entering the service guarantees to stay in it until retirement because the state takes care of qualified people and provides them with a career[23]. The career system is closely related to – what particular attention is paid in the literature – to the bureaucratic way of organizing the state's activity. This is essentially about the concept of bureaucracy in a neutral sense, i.e. the one given to it by Max Weber[24].

---

21 D. Gręzicki, *Służba cywilna w Polsce- rys historyczny*, in: red. R. Bruski, J. Joachimowski, T. Koczur, *Współczesna administracja publiczna w Polsce. Wybrane zagadnienia prawne, polityczne i ekonomiczne*, Toruń 2010, p. 250.

22 Z. Cieślak (red.), *Nauka administracji*, LexisNexis, Warsaw 2012, p. 53.

23 J. Sługocki, *Prawo administracyjne. Zagadnienia ustrojowe*, Wolters Kluwer, Warsaw 2012, p. 432.

24 A. Dubownik, Ł. Pisarczyk, *Prawo urzędnicze*, Wolters Kluwer, Warsaw 2011, p. 71 and next., and also about the model of organization according to Max Weber, L. Zacharko, M. Janik, *Nauka administracji. Paradygmaty współczesnego zarządzania w administracji publicznej*, red. L. Zacharko, ed. PWSZ Raciborz, Racibórz 2016, p. 11 and next., and literature cited there. The second basic model is the station model, which is called the position model. Recruitment takes place here for a specific position (usually through open competitions), but there is no guarantee of employment in this model. Recruitment of civil servants in the system of positions differs from the solutions adopted in the career system, but the differences do not concern the procedures, because in both models one can talk about free, competitive recruitment, but they concern more the criteria for assessing the suitability of the candidate. Unlike the career model, the position system does not require formal education from the candidate but pays attention to his experience and specific qualifications. This system is an open system (A. Dubownik, Ł. Pisarczyk, *Prawo urzędnicze…*, p. 75).

The analysis of the regulations regarding personnel selection in the interwar period confirmed that the central administration bodies were free to recruit and hire employees for official positions.

However, the problem faced by the governments during the wars was the low level of education of officials. In the first half of the 20s of the last century, the education of state officials was a concern not only for the government but also for community professionals and law professors. As it was emphasized in the literature on the subject, until the mid-1920s, the regulations governing the duties of state officials were concise, required them to know the rules, effectively perform their duties, and ordered officials to be trained so that "they were fully familiar with the regulations of the relevant state authorities." Although no training activities were planned at that time, thanks to the involvement of the management of offices, it was possible to train officials so that they could understand their goals and tasks[25].

3. Conclusions

The changes introduced in the legal status of the civil service in the 1990s referred to the classic continental concepts and based employment on official employment. However, the legislator did not decide to transfer earlier solutions and the use of employment of a public law nature while maintaining the employment relationship. Consequently, it was assumed that an official is not employed by the state (a local government unit) but by an office[26].

Particularly noteworthy was the dissemination of the competition procedure, which gave rise to qualitative changes in public administration. The competition became a presentation of knowledge and skills; this applies to staffing positions requiring high and specialist qualifications. Efficiency depends on the strength of the organization, i.e. a combination of qualified staff, financial resources, and other factors that imply specific results.

The role performed by an official is crucial from the point of view of civil rights and shaping the relationship between the office and the citizen. They must have appropriate knowledge and skills, as well as have appropriate social

25 K. Baranowski, *Inteligencja łódzka w latach II RP*. Ed. Lodz University of Technology, Łódź 1996.

26 Ł. Pisarczyk, *Model zatrudnienia w administracji publicznej*, in: *Prawo administracyjne wobec współczesnych wyzwań. Księga jubileuszowa dedykowana Profesorowi Markowi Wierzbowskiemu*, Warsaw 2018, p. 537.

qualifications, which were supported by personal qualities, to determine their prestige[27].

At this point, it is worth paying attention to the regulation contained in the Constitution of the Republic of Poland of April 2, 1997. The civil service is directly devoted to two provisions: Art. 153 and Art. 60, in which it is possible to find both provisions regarding establishing the service and the right to access the civil service.

The provision of Art. 153 of the Constitution of the Republic of Poland indicates that a civil service corps operates in government administration offices to ensure professional, reliable, impartial, and politically neutral performance of state tasks.

As emphasized by W. Sokolewicz, the legislator draws attention to professionalism, which means the requirement to establish appropriate qualification requirements for recruitment to the civil service corps, and then to introduce appropriate requirements and skills against members of the civil service corps, checked during periodic qualification assessments. Hence the obligation for a member of the civil service corps to develop professional knowledge[28]. The Constitution indicates the general purpose of establishing the civil service in the form of professional performance of state tasks, specified in detail in the currently binding Civil Service Act.

Secondly, the legislator draws attention to the reliability of the performance of state tasks, which should be understood in the sense of simple honesty, but also due diligence in the performance of employee duties. As J. Jagielski adds, the requirement of reliability includes (…) the obligation imposed on the official to act efficiently, timely, and economically in the performance of the functions entrusted to him[29].

In turn, impartiality is a certain standard of performing tasks by the civil service. As emphasized by T. Górzyńska, it requires maintaining objectivity in action and not succumbing to any external influences or one's sympathies or preferences. This is important because the civil service works for the common good of all citizens, and therefore there is no room for individual interests[30].

---

27 A. Potoczek, *Model współczesnego urzędnika administracji publicznej*, in: red. B. Sprengel, A. Strzelecki, *Urzędnik w administracji publicznej*, Ed. WSH-E in Włocławek, Włocławek 2005, p. 27 and next.

28 W. Sokolewicz, *Komentarz do art. 153*, in: red. L. Garlicki, Wyd. Sejmowe *Konstytucja Rzeczypospolitej Polskiej, Komentarz*, t. II, Warsaw 2001, p. 1.6.

29 J. Jagielski, K. Rączka, *Ustawa o służbie cywilnej, Komentarz*, LexisNexis, Warsaw 2010, p. 27.

30 T. Górzyńska, *Konstytucyjne podstawy służby cywilnej*.., p. 430.

On the other hand, political neutrality means that an official is to perform his duties in an apolitical manner. According to the judgment of the Constitutional Tribunal of December 12, 2002, K 9/02, political neutrality means "the lack of influence of the world of politics on the activities of the civil service corps." It is about the order of political neutrality in the performance of state tasks – above all, neutrality towards the interests of political groups and fought by these groups or individual politicians addressed to the civil service corps[31].

Article 60 of the Constitution provides the right of access to the civil service, which means that "Polish citizens enjoying full public rights have the right to access service public on equal terms." The cited provision of Art. 60 is guaranteed to apply for admission to service but does not guarantee admission and employment. It gives the basis for stating that the Constitution provides equal opportunities to apply for the civil service after meeting the qualifying conditions specified in the Act (e.g. in terms of education, the requirement to have a specific diploma, age limit, language skills, skills team management, seniority, etc.), as well as equality in access to information about vacancies in the civil service. This right is not absolute because regulations' special provisions give the possibility of applying for admission to the service to the Union European citizens. There should also be transparency in the career system (public announcement of vacancies) and a fixed promotion system.

However, the changes introduced to the Civil Service Act, the so-called December amendment[32], fundamentally modified the recruitment rules by limiting the application of the principle of openness and competitiveness of recruitment concerning filling senior positions in the civilian service. The December 2015 amendment introduced a new category to the corps, i.e. persons employed in senior positions in the civil service[33].

According to the justification of the draft amendment to this Act, the MPs alleged that the existing practice of applying the provisions of the Civil Service Act in the current legal situation often indicates lengthy and ineffective procedures – which implied the statement that this is an undesirable phenomenon. Especially

31 Journal AT, 2002, no. 228, item 2025.

32 Act of December 15, 2015. on amending the Civil Service Act (Journal AT 2016, item 34).

33 More about this J. Glumińska-Pawlic, L. Zacharko, *Wybrane aspekty funkcjonowania służby cywilnej we Francji i w Polsce*, in: *Państwo, Administracja i prawo administracyjne w europejskiej kulturze prawnej. Księga jubileuszowa dedykowana Janowi Andrzejowi Jeżewskiemu z okazji osiemdziesiątej rocznicy urodzin*, Warsaw 2018, p. 89 and next.

"in the case of senior positions in civil service," which are "particularly related to the implementation of government policy and ensuring the efficient administration and human resources management"[34]. Therefore, employment in these positions should be flexible and less formalized. However, the above changes differ from the standards adopted in the interwar period.

34 Print no 119 of December 15, 2015, http://www.sejm.gov.pl/Sejm8.nsf/PrzebiegProc.xsp?nr=119.

Marcin Grzybowski

Principles of Staffing Managerial Positions in National Regulatory Authorities of Infrastructural Sectors in Comparison with the Principles of Promotion in the Civil Service

1. Introductory Notes

The article compares the rules for staffing managerial positions in the national regulatory authorities operating in the energy sector, in rail and air transport, with the current rules for staff promotion in the Polish civil service. Both the establishment of independent national regulatory authorities and the creation of the civil service were based on a similar premise. Regulatory authority's activities ought to be conducted on a non-discriminatory and equally accessible market with its equally accessible infrastructural devices (for both the professional as well as end users)[1]. In the case of the civil service – actions of their officers should be conducted impartially and professionally by the appropriately appointed individuals[2].

It is worth noting that there out of the two concepts of the Polish regulation of the civil service – in which its regulation either: (a) covers all employees employed in the state administration or; (b) extends only to those holding "official" positions; in the course of expert discourse design, the second concept was given priority. The dispute over the subjective scope of statutory civil service regulations has historically become the reason for the hesitation of J.K. Bielecki's cabinet in promoting the draft of a civil service act on the parliamentary forum. After the government of J. Olszewski came to power, the draft act on the state

---

1 More on this topic: M. Grzybowski, *Krajowe organy regulacyjne w sektorach infrastrukturalnych w świetle polskich ustaw sektorowych*, Białystok 2021, pp. 12–17. Also: M. Szydło wrote convincingly about the importance of regulating infrastructural sectors convincingly in: *Regulacja sektorów infrastrukturalnych jako rodzaj funkcji państwa wobec gospodarki*, Warsaw 2005, pp. 52–57.

2 K. Szczerski, *Demokracja, nowoczesne państwo i korpus urzędniczy*, "Służba Cywilna" 2006, No. 15, pp. 23–24; B. Przywora„ *Transformacje ustrojowe polskiej służby cywilnej*, Kraków 2012, pp. 74–75.

public service was withdrawn from the Sejm and sent for further expert work and revisions[3].

After refining the drafted regulations, its new version – authorized by the team of the government plenipotentiary for the civil service's reform headed by prof. M. Kulesza – was sent to the Sejm by the government of H. Suchocka[4]. The act was finally adopted, although after the resignation of H. Suchocka's cabinet and after the new parliamentary elections of 1993 – as the Act of 5 July 1996 on the Civil Service[5].

The limited scope of the statutory regulation of July 5, 1996 resulted in its coverage of officials employed in the chief and central government administration bodies and in local government administration bodies on the basis of appointment[6]. The limited scope of regulation revealed an unregulated circle of administrative positions, especially in central bodies. Characterised by novel tasks and functions, differing from typical forms of administration or management of state assets (property), the positions were taken by national independent regulatory authorities, established in the process of systemic transformation of the state and economy, initiated in Poland in the beginning of the 1990s.

2. Origin, Systemic Location, Function, and Forms of Operation of Independent Regulatory Authorities in the Energy, Rail and Air Transport Sectors

Before the economic reforms of the 1990s – an attempt to remedy the economic crisis manifested at the turn of the 1960s and 1970s, at the end of the 1970s and in the 1980 – the infrastructural sectors: energy and collective transport – rail and air, were monopolized by state-owned enterprises. Polish State Railways (PKP) and LOT Polish Airlines were the instances of such type of economic oligopolies.

Large state-owned enterprises allowed access of business entities and citizens (residents or local communities) to infrastructural services: supply of electricity or natural gas, telecommunication services, radio and television communications, based on the conditions set by legal regulations along with preferences, politics

3 K. Zonn-Pastemak (ed.), *State Civil Service*, Warsaw 1993, pp. 71–73.

4 B. Przywora, *op. cit.*, p. 76.

5 Act of 5 July 1996 on the civil service (Journal of Laws 1996, No. 89, item 402). The act was subsequently amended many times.

6 J. Jagielski, *Komentarz do ustawy o służbie cywilnej*, Warsaw 2001, p. 119.

and dispositions of state authorities. Moreover, central state regulations affected the conditions of use and prices of such services.

Staffing of managerial positions in national or regional enterprises of the infrastructural sectors – as a rule – fell within the competencies of ministers of economic ministries or, during periods of operation of intermediate management links, to those appointed by ministers – association directors or presidents of central (industry) management boards. An important role in the selection of management staff was played by central, provincial (less often: local) recommendations of the management links of the hegemonic PZPR party, in connection with the functioning of the party nomenclature system[7]. The proclamation – primarily in the statutory form (in 1988)[8] and subsequently in the constitutional form (with the amendment to the Constitution of December 29, 1989) – of the freedom of economic activity opened a new chapter for the undertakings in the infrastructure sector. The transforming sector relatively rapidly departed from the monopoly or strong dominance of state-owned mega-enterprises. Central planning of activities of business entities in the infrastructural services sector was severely limited, in favor of market mechanisms, under which the supply of infrastructural services and resources (electricity, gas, transport capacity of railways and civil aviation), began to be established.

At this stage of economic and political transformation, the regulatory activities of the state required the formation of specialized bodies whose activities – mainly of a regulatory nature – were to be aimed at guaranteeing equality and fair competition in the access to infrastructural resources and devices (transmission facilities, tracks, airports and ground facilities) – for both the private (end-) and professional users. Therefore, an equal and socially fair use of such infrastructure sector's equipment, services was set as an objective to be obtained.

The economic and social importance of a professional and impartial staffing of state authorities – tasked with monitoring, regulating and enforcing of established rules for the functioning of segments of the infrastructure sector – is unquestionable. The economic importance concerns – above all – guaranteeing continuous and uninterrupted supply of electricity and natural gas and ensuring efficient rail and air transport. Every disruption in the supply of electricity or gas for state or industrial purposes results in a chain of distortions on the market – in industry, transport and trade of goods that use such resources. It also generates

---

7 M. Tymiński, *PZPR i przedsiębiorstwo. Nadzór partyjny nad zakładami przemysłowymi*, Warszawa 2001, p. 17 et seq.

8 Act of 23 December 1988 on economic activity, Journal of Laws 1988 No. 41 item 324.

irremovable disturbances in railway transport (on electrified lines), as well as in the operation of ground control and air traffic control devices.

The component of professionalism is linked with the requirement of exceptional responsibility due to the scale of threats that stem from lack of professionalism and the costs of disruptions in the functioning of the infrastructure. Furthermore, such requirement applies due to the common nature of infrastructural services' usage, which satisfies more than basic life needs (lighting and heating of apartments and workplaces) but also fulfils the needs of educational, healthcare and cultural institutions as well as the needs to ensure the operation of electronic communication and transport devices in the state.

The potentially limiting element of public interest, which often restricts the exercise of freedom of economic activity, is exceptionally strong when it comes to regulation of activities of entities that operate in the infrastructure sector. Therefore, it is a constituting factor which reinforces the expectations addressed to the staff of state regulatory authorities. In particular, it does so in relation to their managerial staff and persons who serve substantive and decision-making functions (who determine the content of regulatory acts).

The nature of regulatory activities in infrastructural sectors comes down to restraining freedom of economic activities in these sectors and subjecting it to rules established by the relevant regulatory authority. Those rules are formulated in normative acts based on statutory regulations or in administrative acts, or in both, and define roles of entities in the infrastructural resources and services market.

When it pertains to individual segments (sub-sectors) of infrastructure, regulatory authorities are obliged to balance regulatory objectives oriented towards achieving pro-efficiency effects (stability and reliability of infrastructure networks, energy supply, gas transmission or uninterrupted operation of railway and air transport), with the obligation to satisfy the needs of end recipients and users of infrastructural supplies and services, whilst ensuring their availability, quality, reliability and reasonable costs (affordable prices)[9].

In the infrastructural sub-sector of energy, the President of the Energy Regulatory Office, who heads the Energy Regulatory Office (URE) acts as the national regulatory authority. Their existence was established on the basis of a sub-sectoral "substantive act" (regulating the functioning of the energy sector),

9 M. Grzybowski, *Op. cit.*, pp. 15–16.

established (in its original version) by an act – the Act of 10 April 1997 – Energy Law (in its articles 21–31)[10].

In the infrastructural sub-sector of rail transport, the national regulatory authority is the President of the Office of Rail Transport, who heads the Office of Rail Transport (UTK). The office of the President of UTK and the Office of Rail Transport were established by virtue of the Act of 28 March 2003 on rail transport[11]. The systemic position, powers and procedure for filling the position of the President of UTK and members of the management of his Office (deputies of the President) were regulated in Chapter 3 of the aforementioned act (entitled: "President of the Office of Rail Transport"). Its text has been amended numerous times; the last significant amendment, made on 23 July 2021[12], did not, however, alter the guidelines for staffing positions in the management of the UTK Office.

In the infrastructural sub-sector of air transport, the increase in number of air operators and the diversification of their statuses made it necessary to shift from the notion of state-administering of this sub-sector towards the model of its regulation (regulation of the aviation market). These tasks were assumed by the Civil Aviation Authority (ULC), established by the Act of 3 July 2002[13], headed by the President of the Civil Aviation Authority. His political position, scope of activity, competences and the structure of the Office, together with the principles of staffing were regulated by the provisions of Section II, Chapter 2 of the Aviation Law and the provisions of the Civil Aviation Authority's statute.

To confront the principles of filling the positions of the presidents of the three national regulatory authorities: URE, UTK, ULC, the positions of further members of their management and persons employed in these bodies in official positions with the principles of appointments adopted for the civil service, both the provisions of the current Act of 21 November 2008 on the civil service[14], as well as – retrospectively – the civil service regulations that are no longer in force must be considered. The latter need stems from the fact that all 3 NRAs in the infrastructure sector were established and were operating in the period prior to the entry into force of the 2008 Civil Service Act. At the same time, it

10 Act of April 10, 1997 – Energy Law, Journal of Laws 1997 No. 54 item 348 as amended.
11 Act of 28 March 2003 on railway transport, Journal of Laws 2003 No. 86 item 789 (as amended).
12 Act of 23 July 2021 amending the act on rail transport, Journal of Laws 2021 item 1556.
13 Act of 3 July 2002 Aviation Law, Journal of Laws 2002 No. 130 item 1112 (as amended).
14 Act of 21 November 2008 on the civil service, Journal of Laws 2008 No. 227 item 1505 (as amended).

must be noted that the principles for the creation of the civil service and the principle for the creation of national regulatory authorities remained common and unchanged, i.e. ensuring professional, impartial and politically neutral performance of the state's tasks. With regard to the presidents of: URE, UTK and ULC and the offices they manage, the main goal was for them to remain "professional, impartial and politically neutral" in performing their tasks in the field of the energy, rail transport and air transport infrastructural sub-sectors.

The analysis of the statutory regulations concerning the staffing of the positions of the aforementioned presidents of regulatory authorities indicates common elements in the procedure of their appointment. Their aim is to guarantee the professionalism and impartiality of the group of candidates for appointment to the position of the president of a given regulatory authority.

On the eve of the end of the term of office or other (regulated by law) situations of vacancy of the position of the President of the Energy Regulatory Office, the Head of the Chancellery of the Prime Minister appoints a team (a panel consisting of at least 3 people) to select a group of candidates for the position of the President of URE. Pursuant to Art. 21 sec. 2e of the amended text of the Energy Law, the recruitment team evaluates the professional experience of individual candidates, whether they possess knowledge necessary to perform their future tasks and whether they have managerial competences. Art. 21 sec. 2 f the Energy Law permits – with a view to objectifying the evaluation – that the assessment of the candidates' knowledge and managerial skills be conducted by competent persons from outside the team. The statutory requirement for candidates is to have at least 6 years of work experience, including: at least 3 years of work experience in a managerial position[15]. Both the information on the recruitment for the position of the President of the Energy Regulatory Office, and the result of the recruitment process, are announced in the Public Information Bulletin of the Chancellery of the Prime Minister, as it ensures the transparency of the recruitment process[16]. The information includes, but is not limited to, job requirements, data on recruitment methods and techniques, and data on both the successful candidate and, alternatively, information on the fact that no candidate was selected.

Both the recruitment procedure, the term of office (5-year long with the possibility of one repetition) and the closed catalogue of grounds for dismissal before the end of the term of office (contained in Article 21 sec. 2m of the Energy

---

15 See: art. 21 sec. 2b of the Energy Law.

16 See: art. 21 sec. 2c, 2j of the Energy Law.

Law Act) serve to guarantee the impartiality and political neutrality of the person who will be appointed from among 3 candidates, ranked by the recruitment team according to "the level of their compliance with the requirements specified in the recruitment announcement"[17].

A similar procedure has been established with regard to the recruitment for the position of the Vice-President of the Energy Regulatory Office. Pursuant to Article 21 sec. 5 of the Energy Law, the Vice-President of the URE is appointed by the President of the URE after an open and competitive recruitment process; furthermore, the President has the power to dismiss the vice-president of the Energy Regulatory Office. To carry out vice-presidents' recruitment process, a recruitment team – panel – (again: consisting of at least 3 people), composed of persons who guarantee the selection of the best candidates, is appointed. In the course of recruitment, the candidate's professional experience, knowledge – necessary to perform tasks in the position – and his managerial competences are assessed[18]. The President of URE appoints the Vice-President from among no more than 3 candidates selected by the recruitment team. The Vice-President of the Energy Regulatory Office is appointed for a 5-year term. He may be reappointed only once, and shall perform his function until the appointment of his successor[19].

The recruitment and staffing of the positions of the President and Vice-President of the Office of Rail Transport (UTK) and the President and Vice-President of the Civil Aviation Authority (ULC) were based on principles similar to the abovementioned ones.

A candidate for the position of the President of UTK must meet seven statutory requirements[20] for appointment to this position. Several of these

17 See: art. 21 sec. 2i of the Energy Law. This provision requires the provision of data relevant to the recruitment process, including: information on the recruitment methods and techniques used and justification for the selection of the best candidate (alternatively: providing reasons for not selecting a candidate).

18 See: art. 21 sec. 5a of the Energy Law Act.

19 See: art. 21 sec. 5d of the Energy Law.

20 These requirements are listed in Art. 11 sec. 2 of the Railway Transport Act. These include: having managerial competences, at least 6 years of work experience (including: at least 3 years in a managerial position and the requirement of education and knowledge in the field of matters falling within the competence of the President of UTK.

An important statutory provision is that the President of UTK may not belong to a political party, trade union or conduct activities with explicit features of politics. This immunizes the office of the President of UTK from party or trade union discipline and meets the requirement of political neutrality.

requirements: possession of managerial qualifications, education and knowledge in the field of matters falling within the competence of the President of UTK, are subject to a – mostly – discretionary assessment. The level of discretion increases the importance of the recruitment, which is appointed by the Head of the Chancellery of the Prime Minister. Prime Minister appoints the President of UTK from among 3 candidates selected by the team, which leaves him a possibility of choice from within the group of selected candidates.

Recruitment for the positions of two vice-presidents of UTK was also based on the principles of openness and competitiveness. Both the requirements relating to the candidates and the rules of recruitment conducted by the team appointed by the President of UTK are communicated in advance (in the Public Information Bulletin of the Office), and the provisions governing the recruitment procedure for the position of the President of UTK apply accordingly to the appointment of UTK's Vice-Presidents.

The appointment process of the President of the Civil Aviation Authority remains coherent with the guideliness for the appointment of the Presidents of URE and UTK. Regarding vice-presidents, the quantitative difference is the admission of up to 3 vice-presidents (this is also due to the fact that, apart from regulatory tasks, the ULC President and – on his behalf – ULC vice-presidents perform supervisory tasks). Recruitment takes place in an open and competitive procedure conducted by a recruitment team appointed by the minister responsible for transport. The requirement for the team to present no more than three candidates, ranked according to the level of fulfilment of the competition requirements – initially to the minister responsible for transport, who then submits candidatures (with a request for the appointment of a specific person) to the Prime Minister, constitutes a procedural difference between the presented recruitment processes. The Prime Minister has the power to dismiss the President of the Civil Aviation Authority before the end of the term of his office in instances prescribed by law. Recruitment for the positions of vice-presidents of the Civil Aviation Authority takes place in a similar manner, with the recruitment team being appointed by the President of the Civil Aviation Authority.

The comparison of the rules for filling managerial positions in national regulatory authorities, leads to the conclusion that they are convergent with the procedure for filling "senior positions in the civil service" as defined in the provisions of Chapter 4 of the Act of 21 November 2008 on the Civil Service[21]. The basic difference concerns not so much the mode of selection of persons for

21 The amended and consolidated text announced as an attachment to the announcement of the Marshal of the Sejm of the Republic of Poland of 7 April 2022 (Journal of Laws 2022, item 1691).

the positions, but the range of positions themselves. In the Civil Service Act of 2008, "higher positions in the civil service" are defined as "important and decisive, substantive positions in central or regional offices of government administration bodies". Nevertheless, they still are positions subordinated to the heads of these offices (bodies), which are monocratic government administration entities ("maintainers" of the governing functions of a given body). In the matter of hereby characterised national regulatory authorities, the discussed procedure of recruitment and appointment applies to positions (offices) synonymous to the authorities themselves. Pursuant to the regulations of the Energy Law, Railway Transport Law and Aviation Law, considered as the authorities of the regulatory nature – in the strict sense (and *de iure*) – are the presidents themselves: the President of the Energy Regulatory Office, the President of the Rail Transport Office, the President of the Civil Aviation Authority, rather than the Offices (Authorities) which they manage (URE, UTK, ULC).

Looking retrospectively at the issue of recruitment for certain (senior) official positions within the civil service – for legal and comparative purposes[22]- it is worth noting that the model of recruitment for such senior official positions, in its basic principles, remains constant. That recruitment model was subjected to a particular extrapolation (extension with displacement) to the procedure of recruitment and appointment of the managerial staff of national regulatory authorities.

The principles of the aforementioned model of recruitment were for it to be open for participation to all interested parties, provided, that they met the requirements specified by law in the form of a multi-point enumerative list (catalogue). The candidates were obliged to meet each of these requirements, without omissions or possibility of compensation for failure to meet one of the requirements by extraordinary fulfilment of other requirement contained in the statutory catalogue[23].

---

22 For example, in the Act of 5 July 1996 on the Civil Service, this concerned "certain groups of officials supervised by the supreme government administration body and certain groups of officials of this body" (Article 20 of the cited act). For the categories of civil servants indicated here, the Prime Minister could create special sections within the Qualification Committee to conduct the qualification procedure.

23 It should be considered as highly rational to assume that meeting all the requirements to a high degree, with particular intensity, concerned the civil servants with category A, distinguished in the Act of 1996, in which category the legislator included "persons capable of holding senior managerial positions, characterized by – in particular – the ability to lead complex human teams, by creativity, by the ability to manage financial, material and information resources". The features indicated here seem to be highly

In the years 2006–2009 in the Republic of Poland, in addition to the Civil Service Act of 24 August 2006 (which replaced the previous Civil Service Act of 1996), another regulation of similar matters – the Act of 24 August 2006 on the State Personnel Resources and high state positions[24] – was in force. That Act, later repealed on 24 March 2009, was characterised by its focus on the issues of manning "high state posts". Indirectly, such scope of regulation – in the light of the coexistence of both acts – resulted in duality of statutory regulations of the procedures of recruitment for posts in state authorities. While the provisions of a special act, i.e. the Act on State Personnel Resources, were applied to positions considered as "high state posts", the Act on Civil Service, enacted on the same date, was applicable to the act of filling of other official (state) positions.

Given that the positions of presidents and vice presidents of the previously mentioned national regulatory authorities corresponded with the parameters of "high state posts (positions)", the attempt to confront the provisions of the Act on State Personnel Resources with the specific regulations of the Energy Act, the Railway Transport Act and the Aviation Act – relating to recruitment for the positions of: President and Vice-President of the Energy Regulatory Office, President and Vice-Presidents of UTK and President and Vice-Presidents of the Civil Aviation Authority – seems to be worthwhile. It should be noted that the comparison concerns the legal standing, which ceased to exist on the date of repeal of the Act on State Personnel Resources, i.e. on 24 March 2009.

According to the Art. 2 point 1 of the Act of 2006 on the State Personnel Resources, the resource created under the Act was to be understood as "a set of candidates for high state positions". In turn, in the Art. 4 of the Act, in a multi-part enumeration, formulated was a statutory catalog of such "high state positions". Within this enumeration, the national regulatory authorities: Presidents of the URE, UTK and ULC – have not been listed literally (listed *expressis verbis*). A problem has arisen, whether the category of posts referred to as "heads of central government administration offices and their deputies" – covered by the Act on State Personnel Resources – included these national regulatory authorities.

---

compatible with the expectations addressed to the heads of national regulatory authorities and their deputies. A civil servant classified in category A could not, pursuant to Art. 49 sec. 3 of the 1996 Act belong to a political party or trade union; once he was included in this official category, his membership in a party or trade union ceased by operation of law.

24 Act of 24 August 2006 on the State Personnel Resources and High State Positions, Journal of Laws 2006 No. 170 item 1217 (as amended).

An affirmative answer to such question would result in an obligation to recruit for managerial positions in the URE, UTK and the ULC only from among persons belonging to (included in) the state personnel resources. It seems, however, that despite the fact that the adoption of the such interpretation would coincide with the intentions of the creators of the institution of the "state personnel resources" and the creators and supporters of the Act on the State Personnel Resources of 2006, there were at least two circumstances that prompt the interpretation hereby outlined to be subjected to a more thorough consideration in the context of Art. 4 of the Act.

The first circumstance is the specificity of national regulatory authorities, whose basic functions rely not on the administration (management) of separate substrates of state assets, institutional entities and human resources – in a sectoral or branch arrangement – but on the act of determining the rules for the coexistence (cooperation) of entities having infrastructural resources, performing infrastructural services and buyers, users and recipients of these services. In this sense, national regulatory authorities are distinctive state authorities (different than the "typical" managers of central government administration offices, referred to in Article 4(1) of the 2006 Act on State Personnel Resources). The authors of the said Act noticed such specificity of certain bodies and entities operating on the borderline between the management of state assets (e.g. agencies) and government administration in the "classic" understanding, and activities of specialized inspection or supervision bodies. Some of these bodies and institutions were covered by the Act on State Personnel Resources, enumerating them in Article 4(2), Items 3–7 and Items 8–11. The enumeration, however, did not cover national regulatory authorities operating in sub-sectors of the infrastructure sector.

The Act on State Personnel Resources regulated the scope of its application to filling (manning) managerial positions in:

1. the Head Office of State Archives (in relation to the director and his deputies);
2. Chief Sanitary Inspectorate (Referring to the Chief Inspector and his deputies);
3. General Directorate for National Roads and Motorways (in relation to the General Director and his deputies);
4. office of the Chief National Surveyor;
5. State Agricultural Insurance Fund (in relation to the President of the Fund and his deputy);
6. Agricultural Property Agency of the State Treasury (in relation to the President and Vice-President of the Agency);

7. Agency for Restructuring and Modernization of Agriculture (in relation to the President and Vice-President of the Agency);
8. the State Mining Authority (in relation to the President and Vice-Presidents of the State Mining Authority);
9. the Main Inspectorate of Construction Supervision (in relation to the Chief Inspector and his deputies);
10. Central Statistical Office (in relation to the President and Vice Presidents of the Central Statistical Office);
11. State Reserves Agency (in relation to the President and Vice-President of the Agency);
12. Military Property Agency (in relation to the President and its vice-presidents).

In this particular part of the regulations the Act on State Personnel Resources determined the extension of its provisions to national regulatory authorities. Specifically, the Art. 48 point 1 of the Act stipulated that the President of the Energy Regulatory Office (URE) is appointed by the Prime Minister from among persons belonging to the state personnel resources. The appointment and dismissal took place at the request of the minister responsible for the economy.

Article 65 of the Human Personnel Act[25] applied to the position of the President of the Civil Aviation Authority (ULC) and the position of its vice-presidents. Moreover, Art. 68 of the Act[26] extended the use of the state personnel resource to the position of the President of UTK and his (two) vice-presidents.

Thus, during the period when the Act of 26 August 2006 on the State Personnel Resources was in force (2006 – 24.03.2009), managerial positions in three national regulatory authorities of the infrastructure sector were subject to the recruitment narrowed down to the candidates from within the scope of this "state personnel resource" and to appointments concluding such recruitment. The repeal of the Act in March 2009 was tantamount to extension of the personnel framework (scope) for the selection of candidates for offices of those regulatory authorities.

25 This provision changed Art. 20 sec. 2 of the Act of July 3, 2002 – Aviation Law.
26 Art. 68 of the Act of 2006 on State Personnel Resources amended the provisions of Art. 11 sec. 1 and sec. 3 of the Act of 23 March 2003 on railway transport.

Hubert Izdebski

On the 100th Anniversary of the First Polish Civil Service Law[1]

I. Introduction

On the 17 February 1922 the Legislative Sejm – the Constituent Assembly of the Polish State – elected in 1919 and working until November 1922, passed the Law on the State Civil Service[2]. 1922 was the first year when the Polish State reborn after the World War, I was not engaged in armed hostilities as well as the year following that of adoption of the Constitution of the Republic of Poland[3]. The Legislative Sejm, fulfilling its mission of setting out foundations of the legal system of the Republic, left an enormous legislative output, including rich legislation in the field of administrative law. Within it, the Civil Service Law belonged to the most important, and from this point of view it could be compared, it may seem, only with the other great 1922 law – the Law of the 3 August 1922 on the Supreme Administrative Tribunal[4]; they both were fundamental markers of the system based on the rule of law, however, to be subverted after 1926.

Another law adopted in 1922 relating to the state service has, nevertheless, also to be borne in mind. That was the Law of the 23 March 1922 on Basic Duties and Rights

---

1 In the present survey, fragments of the author's article *Wpływ rozwiązań prawnych i tradycji służby cywilnej RP na obecny model służby cywilnej* „Studia Iuridica", 93 (2023); are used. See B. Przywora, *Transformacje ustrojowe polskiej służby cywilnej*, Kraków 2012, and also A. Łukaszczuk, *Służba cywilna II Rzeczypospolitej,* Acta Universitatis Wratislaviensis. Przegląd Prawa i Administracji, 83 (2010), 233 et sqq.

2 Journal of Laws No. 21, item 164, with subsequent amendments. The qualifier "state" was used to underscore a limitation of the scope of application of the Law to officials of the state administration, and, therefore, not all public officials, i.e. those of territorial self-government. The status of employees of territorial self-government was not newly regulated under the Second Polish Republic, though in 1939 there was a respective draft law subject to advanced legislative procedures.

3 The Constitution of the 17 March, 1921 – Journal of Laws No. 44, item 267, with subsequent amendments.

4 Journal of Laws No. 67, item 600, with subsequent amendments – consolidated text in Journal of Laws of 1926 No. 68, item 400. The Law was replaced by the regulation of the President of the Republic of 27 October, 1932 – Journal of Laws No. 94,item 806, with subsequent amendments.

of the Polish Army Officers[5], and there was a certain concatenation of that Law and the 1922 Civil Service Law. In particular, they both concerned in a similar way the status of officials of top categories, and, in general, civil service and professional military service constituted jointly the state service. It should be noted that the adjective "civil" was added precisely to the title of the Law and the denomination of the institution only in the course of parliamentary works concerning the draft law in order to distinguish between civil and military service for the State – and not modelling after appellation of the British institutional and terminological contribution to global history of public administration and governance.

What is more, whereas the Supreme Administrative Tribunal was not restored (and a similar institution, i.e. the High Administrative Court was introduced only in 1980), in so called "People's Republic of Poland" after 1944, governed by the Communists and being a part of the Soviet camp, the 1922 Civil Service Law was maintained in force, though its provisions were essentially changed in their letter as well as in their practical application. The Law, in wording of the 1949 consolidated text[6], could last until 1974, but, it has to be noted, though it had been extended over employees of people's councils, having replaced in 1950 according to the Soviet model traditional territorial self-government, in 1968 its scope of application was sensitively reduced as a result of adoption of the Law on People's Councils Employees[7]. The 1968 Law, moreover, lost its legal force in 1974 together with the 1922 Civil Service Law – in consequence of entering into force of the Labour Code.

II. The 1922 Law as a *Lex Generalis*

The 1922 Civil Service Law contained general provisions, was a *lex generalis*, what meant that it had to coexist with particular service regulations and/or other particular regulations it referred to: on salaries (Articles 39 and 106)[8], on medical assistance (Articles 44 and 109), on retirement pay (Articles 46 and 111), on organization of disciplinary authorities and disciplinary procedures (Article 88). Thanks to its general character, the Law had a large scope, relating to persons employed by the state on the public law basis, even including, though to a certain

5 Journal of Laws No. 32, item 256, with subsequent amendments.

6 Journal of Laws No. 11, item 72.

7 Journal of Laws No.25, item 164.

8 See A. Karwowska-Sokołowska, A. Stawicka, P. Stawicki, J. Woźniczko, *Kształtowanie wynagrodzeń w państwowej sferze budżetowej. Cz. II. Wynagrodzenia urzędników w II RP*, Warszawa 2021.

extent, ministers. The formal exclusion from its provisions of judges, public prosecutors, legal interns, employees of state railways, post and telegraphy, and teachers of all state schools, including universities (Article 118) meant that to be excluded from the Law regulation a given group of public employees had to be expressly indicated in a respective piece of legislation (or in the 1922 Law itself).

III. Basic Solutions of the 1922 Law

The 1922 Law fixed a classical model of the service, modelled to a large extent after solutions having been introduced in Germany, in particular in Prussia, and in Austria – that is to say a career model, based on the assumption that an official ("functionary") remained in a service relationship during the whole period of his or her professional activity. Such assumption explained the sense of Article 8 of the Law, according to which nomination of an officer (*urzędnik*, to be distinguished from a „junior functionary")[9] – and (Article 89) of a junior functionary – needed an assent of the competent supreme authority not only when the candidate was less than 18 years old (what was not strange) but also when he or she was over 40 and had never been in the state service; therefore, experience resulting from a work for business entities or from self-employment was not held in high esteem, and expected.

The "service relationship" (Article 3 of the Law) of an official of the state civil service could be "changed, suspended or dissolved exclusively while applying provisions of public law, in particular provisions of this Law". Within that classical model, officials were totally outside the scope of labour law, as they were in the service relationship, and were not performing work in terms of labour law. The word "service" as an adjective (*służbowy*) related not only to the service relationship (set by appointment: permanent or provisional, until dismissal – Article 5), but also to responsibility (Article 66 et sqq.); within the service responsibility there was a distinction between disciplinary responsibility (for service misdemeanours) and responsibility for failure to obey work rules (*porządkowa*). Officials enjoyed particular rights, relating to leave, retirement, medical assistance, family allowances, and, except for those appointed provisionally, enjoyed a stabilisation of the service relationship (expulsion or exclusion from the service exclusively on the basis of the final decision of the authority taken in conformity to the Law or of the disciplinary commission decision – Articles 33 and 104). On the other hand, they were charged with special obligations, partially differentiated with respect to officers and junior functionaries.

---

9 There were no fundamental differences of the status of those two groups of officials, except, what should be obvious, mainly for education requirements.

The basic duty of officers as well as of junior functionaries was – the formula, it has to be noted, lacking in the post-war legislation, including that in force at present – "taking, according to the best will and knowledge, care of the good of the public cause, and doing everything what serves the good, fighting shy of everything that could do harm to it" (Articles 21 and 95).

IV. The 1922 Law After 1926

The 1922 Law was not fully applied after May 1926, marking a gradual passage to an authoritarian regime. Generally authoritarian regimes (and authoritarian like ones as well) are not interested in having an internal institutional check in the form of real civil service within the executive power. In particular, the post-1926 authorities infringed upon the principle of stabilisation of the service relationship of officials having been given permanent appointment.

After 1944 the Law, still formally in force, was essentially amended in short order. Instead of categories of civil service officers and junior functionaries, a uniform category of state employees was introduced, that itself suggested a tendency of assimilating to labour law – though wording of Article 1 relating to the public law character of the civil service relationship remained preserved. Preservation concerned, however, a technical side of the Law only, because its spirit had to be rejected in the so-called socialist state based upon a politicisation of everything within the state.

V. Formal End of the 1922 Law

The 1922 Civil Service Law lost its force definitively on the 1 January 1975 – the date of entering into force of the Labour Code. An important element of the technical side of the Law, that is to say the public law character of the service (with the notion of service as well) was, therefore, rejected. State employees were to be employed on the basis of regular labour law relationship – majority of them in the simplest form, that is to say the labour law appointment, subject to dissolve any time by the employer[10]. One of formal expressions of full politicisation of the state administrative apparatus were the following words of the regulations of the Council of Ministers of the 20 December 1974 on rights and duties of the state employees, opening the enumeration of duties[11]: "to follow the principles of

10 In the Polish legal terminology, there is a distinction of appointment (*powołanie*) fully belonging to the field of labour law, and appointment (*nominacja*) containing, at least partially, elements of public law.

11 Journal of Laws No. 49, item 300, para. 8.

people's legality, being guided by social interest and requirements of the socialism building, to uphold authority of the people's power, and to strive for intensification of citizens' confidence in the people's power and in its authorities".

VI. The 1982 Law on Employees of State Offices

The approach to employment in the state service represented by the Code of Labour was shaken, as many other elements of socialist orthodoxy, in 1980–1981, in the period of emergence and regular activity of the massive social movement "Solidarność". The movement was suppressed by force in December 1981, but the Communist rulers – influenced also by a phenomenon of "legal nostalgia", that is to say a (selective) search, having been present since the 1970s, in the pre-war legislation for solutions better adapted to reality than those of socialist orthodoxy – decided to adopt some reform ideas, limited, however, to their technical aspects. The Law of the 16 September 1982 on Employees of State Offices was one of such reform acts[12].

The 1982 Law restored a part of technical solutions of the 1922 Civil Service Law – without, however, coming back to the construction of the relationship of public law. In the first place, the comeback concerned institution of appointment (*mianowanie*) ensuring a relative employment stabilisation, but one should also note, for example, restoration of the division of forms of responsibility into disciplinary and for failure to obey work rules.

VII. The 1996 Law and Constitutionalization of Civil Service

The radical political change that took place in 1989 and inaugurated the process of "regime transformation" had to lead also to a comeback to the idea of state civil service. A comeback to all solutions of the 1922 Law was not, however, possible – in the first place because of changes having been effected since 1922 or even since 1974 in legal environment, but also because of the evolution of employment in Western public administrations leading to flexibilization of its forms. Nevertheless, a lack of stronger interest of subsequent ruling teams in limiting their appointment powers should also be noted.

At last, on 5 July 1996 the Parliament adopted the Law on Civil Service[13]. Though adopting many elements of the 1922 Law, the 1996 Civil Service Law differed from the 1922 Law, first of all, by limitation of its scope of application to employees of offices of government administration, that is to say administrative

12 Journal of Laws No. 31, item 214, with subsequent amendments.
13 Journal of Laws No. 89, item 402, with subsequent amendments.

apparatus, bureaus of authorities subject directly or indirectly to the President of the Council of Ministers and/or to the Council of Ministers. That effected exclusion not only of persons employed in public entities other than bureaus but even also of those employed in offices of state authorities situated outside the government administration, like chancelleries of the both chambers of Parliament or the Chancellery of the President of the Republic. Therefore, the 1982 Law (partially amended) had to be left to apply to.

What is more, that limited scope of application of the institution of civil service was transferred to the 1997 Constitution. According to Article 153, "a corps of civil servants shall operate in the bodies of government administration in order to ensure a professional, diligent, impartial and politically neutral discharge of the State's obligations"[14]. There has been a comeback to the traditional denomination (without "state") and to fundamental ideas of the 1922 Law (without, however, idea of a totally separate public law relationship), but the significant departure from the tradition has acquired constitutional status.

VIII. Closing Remarks

The 1996 Civil Service Law was followed by a series of subsequent laws relating to the same object, passed in 1998, 2006 (together with the Law on the State's Staff Resource and High State Positions, meaning the formal "decapitation" of the civil service, reduced to less important posts), and 2008 – the latter substantially amended in 2016 in the sense of an internal "decapitation", i.e. politicization, of higher posts. Changes in the civil service legislation effected since the adoption of the Constitution are not a subject of the present research – but it is necessary to note that it is not possible to say that Poland has been lucky in establishing any stable system of civil service that could be regarded as a decent continuation of the principles of the 1922 Law.

However, that should also mean that the 1922 Civil Service Law plays, and it still does, a more important role as a source of inspiration in thinking about a stable system of civil service Poland still needs. Such system, though adapted to the challenges of the third decade of the 21st century, should uphold the principles and values expressed in the 1922 Law – and should be based on them.

---

14 See H. Izdebski, *Komentarz do Konstytucji RP. Art. 149, 152, 153*, Warszawa 2023, 122 et sqq.

Aleksander Lipinski

On the Defectiveness of Certain Administrative Structures in Geology and Mining

1. Administrative Bodies and Mining Supervisory Authorities

Geological and Mining Act[1] distinguishes between the following authorities:

- geological administration, and
- mining supervision.

The geological administration bodies are:

- minister responsible for the environment,
- voivodship marshals,
- starosts (Art. 156 and 164).

Unless otherwise stipulated by law, the tasks of the geological administration "shall include the performance of certain tasks, and in particular:

- making decisions and performing other acts necessary to comply with and apply the Act, including the granting of licenses,
- control and supervision of activities regulated by the Act, including the design of geological activities and the preparation of geological reports" (Art. 158 of the PrGG).

The details of the division of competences between the various bodies of the geological administration, as well as some problems of the division of competences between them and other public administration bodies, can be omitted (see Art. 160–161 of the PrGG). Instead, it is worth mentioning that they have become the subject of numerous competence disputes, which (it seems) should be attributed to the lack of imagination of the lawmaker (although, in fact, the drafter)[2]. Indeed, the formulation of the said Art. 158 can hardly be assessed as unambiguous and sufficiently communicative. The source of doubts

1 Act of 9 June 2011, Law Gazette 2024, item 1290 with amendments, referred to as "PrGG".

2 Zob. A. Lipiński, Z problematyki właściwości rzeczowej organów administracji geologicznej. Przegląd Ustawodawstwa Gospodarczego 2013 No 6, pp. 2 et seq.

is the term "in particular", suggesting that the tasks of the said authorities go beyond the scope set out in this provision.

The tasks of the voivodship marshals and starosts defined by the Act under discussion are tasks of government administration (Art. 156 para 3 of the PrGG).

The mining supervisory authorities are the President of the Higher Mining Authority and the directors of the district mining offices (Art. 164 et seq. of the PrGG). Their tasks include supervising and controlling the operations of mining plants, in particular regarding:

1. occupational health and safety,
2. fire safety,
3. mine rescue,
4. the management of mineral deposits in the process of their extraction,
5. environmental protection and deposit management, including according to the criterion of performance by entrepreneurs specified in separate regulations or on the basis thereof,
6. damage prevention,
7. the construction and decommissioning of a mining site, including the reclamation of land after mining activities.

Regarding the design of construction works and their execution, as well as the maintenance of construction works in the area of the mining facility, the said authorities "perform tasks of architectural and construction administration and construction supervision"[3] (Art. 168 para 1–2 of the PrGG). However, the scope of the tasks of the mining supervisory authorities thus defined is far from clear. This applies in particular to supervision (and control) in matters concerning environmental protection defined on grounds other than the Geological and Mining Act. An example is the trivial problem of cutting down a tree in order to open up a mineral deposit below. Suffice it to mention that elements of the application for approval of a mining plant's operation plan are, *inter alia*, "copies of decisions required for the intended works issued by other authorities, in particular those concerning environmental protection" (Art. 108 para 9 item 2 of the PrGG). The framework of the study does not allow to elaborate on the details. The scope of the tasks of the mining supervisory authorities presented above is therefore not exhaustive. An analysis of the Geological and Mining Act leads to the conclusion that the tasks of the said authorities are broader (see Art. 4 para

3 Determined in Construction Act of 7 July 1994, Law Gazette 2024, item 725 with amendments.

2–4; Art. 27a; Art. 141 para 1 item 3 of the PrGG). In principle, however, the view should be defended that the competences of the mining supervisory authorities do not include matters belonging to other public administration bodies, unless the law expressly provides otherwise.

2. The License and Some Problems of Licensing Procedures

The basic instrument for the regulation of geological and mining activities is the license. Pursuant to Art. 21 para 1 of the PrGG, it is required to carry out activities in the field of:

- exploration or prospecting of mineral deposits referred to in Art. 10 para 1[4],
- extraction (mining) of minerals from deposits,
- underground tankless substance storage,
- underground waste storage,
- underground storage of carbon dioxide[5] .

The primary task of the geological administration authorities is the licensing of the activities described above[6]. The chief organ of geological administration is the minister responsible for the environment (currently the Minister of Climate and Environment). His tasks (as a licensing authority) include matters of most[7] licenses for activities regulated by the Geological and Mining Act (see Art. 21

.4 According to art. 10 para 2 and 4 of the PrGG they are the deposits of hydrocarbons, hard coal, methane existing as an associated mineral, lignite, metal ores excluding bog iron ores, native metals, radioactive ores, native sulphur, rock salt, sylvinite, potassium-magnesium salts, gypsum and anhydrite, precious stones, rare-earth elements, noble gases and hydrogen. They are covered by mining property wherever they occur. This enumeration does not include all deposits (spaces) that are the subject of mining property. The subject of mining property also includes deposits of therapeutic waters, thermal waters and brines. The subject of the aforementioned right is also covered by parts of the rock mass located outside the spatial boundaries of the land property, in particular those located within the boundaries of the maritime areas of the Republic of Poland.

5 Admittedly, the terminology of the Act is somewhat different, but it can be successfully reduced to the enumeration presented above.

6 The President of the Higher Mining Authority is to say, first and foremost, adjudicating on the granting of a license, its amendments, withdrawal, declaration of expiry.

7 The tasks of the starosts include granting concessions for the extraction of minerals not covered by mining property, if the area of the documented deposit does not exceed 2 hectares, and at the same time the extraction of minerals in a calendar year will not exceed 20,000 m^3, and the activity will be conducted using the open-pit method

para 1). A license, on the other hand, is never an independent decision of the licensing authority. Depending on the details (such as the type of activity, the type of mineral, the place where the activity is to be carried out), it must be preceded by an opinion or agreement with at least one administrative authority (a so called co-operating authority), and in practice most often with several such authorities. Most of the related details, especially relating to the procedural issues of such cooperation[8], can be omitted. What is relevant from the point of view of the subject matter, however, is the licence for:

- extraction of minerals referred to in Art. 10 para 1,
- underground tankless substance storage,
- underground storage of carbon dioxide

"shall require the agreement of the minister responsible for the management of mineral deposits" (Art. 23 para 1 and 3 of the PrGG).

3. The Minister Responsible for Mineral Resources Management

In the current legal state of affairs mineral deposit management are the responsibility of the Minister of Industry, who also supervises the President of the Higher Mining Authority.[9]

Affairs of state assets include matters relating to the management of state property, including the exercise of property and personal rights vested in the State Treasury, as well as the protection of the interests of the State Treasury – with the exception of matters which, by virtue of separate provisions, are included in other branches of government administration (Art. 9b of the Act of 4 September

---

and without the use of explosives. The voivodship marshal licenses the extraction of minerals not covered by the tasks of the minister and the starosts.

8 Zob. A. Lipiński, Z *problematyki współdziałania organów administracji publicznej*, in: ed. A. Matan, *Administracja w demokratycznym państwie prawa. Księga jubileuszowa Profesora Czesława Martysza*. Wolters Kluwer 2022, p. 332 et seq.; G. Łaszczyca, A. Matan, Współdziałanie decyzyjne w ogólnym postępowaniu administracyjnym, op.cit., p. 380 et seq.

9 Rozporządzenie Prezesa Rady Ministrów z 19 grudnia 2023 r. w sprawie szczegółowego zakresu działania Ministra Przemysłu, Dz. U. 2023, poz. 2727 (Regulation of the Prime Minister of 19 December 2023 on the detailed scope of activities of the Minister of Industry, Law Gazette 2023, item 2727)

1997 on Branches of Government Administration[10]). The minister in charge of state assets represents the State Treasury in the scope specified in paragraph 1; he may initiate state policy with respect to the use of state assets in order to ensure their rational and effective use, increase their value and implement state economic policy.

In the light of Art. 11a of the Act of 4 September 1997 on Branches of Government Administration[11], the section "mineral deposit management" covers matters concerning:

1) carrying out, in consultation with the minister responsible for the environment, the rational management of deposits of hydrocarbons, lignite, hard coal, indigenous sulphur, rock salt, potassium salt, potassium-magnesium salt, in the mining area,
2) agreeing on mining licenses granted by the minister responsible for the environment, with respect to minerals covered by the State Treasury's mining property,
3) cooperating in the supervision of the extraction of the minerals referred to in point 1,
4) mining (professional) qualifications.

4. Some Tasks of the Minister of Climate and Environment[12]

He oversees the following sections of government administration:

---

10 Czego przykładem może być chociażby wykonywanie uprawnień Skarbu Państwa wynikającym z własności górniczej. Wedle art. 12 ust. 1 PrGG w zasadzie wykonują je organy koncesyjne (z wyjątkiem starostów), a niekiedy zarządy województw (Which is exemplified, for example, by the exercise of the State Treasury's powers arising from mining property. Acording to art. 12 para 1 PrGG, in principle, these are exercised by concession authorities (with the exception of starosts) and sometimes by voivodship boards).

11 Dz. U. 2024, poz. 1370 ze zm., dalej powoływana jako "DzAR" (Law Gazette 2024, item 1370 with amendments, hereinafter referred to as "DzAR").

12 Nazwa tego organu sugeruje, że klimat nie jest elementem środowiska, co nie koresponduje z ustawową definicją tego ostatniego. Prawo ochrony środowiska (ustawa z 27 kwietnia 2001 r., Dz. U. 2024, poz. 54 ze zm., dalej cyt. jako "PrOŚr") definiującpojęcie "środowiska" (art. 3 pkt 39) bezspornie zalicza do niego "klimat" (The name of this authority suggests that climate is not an element of the environment, which does not correspond to the statutory definition of the latter. The Environmental Protection Law (Act of 27 April 2001, Law Gazette 2024, item 54 as amended, hereinafter cited as "PrOŚr"), defining the concept of "environment" (Art. 3 point 39) indisputably includes "climate").

1. energy,
2. climate,
3. environment.

Pursuant to Art. 7a of the DzAR, the energy section covers matters of energy, energy raw materials and fuels; the tasks of the minister responsible for these matters include, in particular:

1. the country's energy policy and participation in the shaping of the European Union's energy policy,
2. energy markets,
3. the country's energy security, including security of supply of energy,
4. energy infrastructure, including the operation of energy systems, taking into account the principles of rational economy and the needs of national energy security,
5. initiating, coordinating and supervising international cooperation in the field of energy and to participate in the work of European Union bodies.

The climate section covers climate and sustainable development issues, in particular with regard to:

1. participation in climate policy-making, including within the European Union, in particular in negotiations on international climate and sustainable development policies,
2. implementation of the European Union's climate policy, including the management of funds for ecological and climate transformation, in particular the management of auctions of greenhouse gas emission allowances and the management of the funds obtained as a result, taking into account the country's energy security, including security of energy supply, energy raw materials and fuels,
3. protection and shaping of the environment and the rational use of its resources, subject to Art. 28 (i.e. matters covered by the "environment" section),
4. ecological living conditions resulting from air protection, protection of the earth's surface, protection against noise and protection against electromagnetic fields,
5. monitoring compliance with environmental protection requirements and studying the state of the environment,
6. the system for managing and trading greenhouse gas emissions and other substances,
7. waste management, including as part of a circular economy,

8. support, including the promotion, of green innovations and technologies, taking into account climate and energy transition objectives,
9. managing and coordinating programmes for the dissemination, development, and promotion of the use of low and zero carbon technologies, including in particular renewable energy sources and transport,
10. the socio-economic aspects of environmental and climate transformation,
11. energy efficiency,
12. development and use of renewable energy sources,
13. environmental education and promotion of ecological living conditions – within the scope of the tasks belonging to the department.

The minister responsible for climate matters supervises the President of the State Atomic Energy Agency, the Chief Inspector of Environmental Protection, the Institute for Environmental Protection – State Research Institute, the Institute for Ecology of Industrial Areas, as well as the activities of the National Fund for Environmental Protection and Water Management and the provincial funds for environmental protection and water management (Art. 13 of the DzAR).

The environment section, in turn, covers matters of protecting and shaping the natural environment and the rational use of its resources, in particular with regard to:

1 the protection of nature, including in national and landscape parks, nature reserves, and biodiversity, the protection of plant and animal species, legally protected forests, wildlife and other natural creations,
2. geology,
3. management of natural resources,
4. forestry,
5. protection of forests and forest land,
6. hunting,
7. environmental education and promotion of ecological living conditions – within the scope of the tasks belonging to the department,
8. genetically modified micro-organisms and genetically modified organisms, including the supervision of GMO cultivation within the meaning of the legislation on genetically modified micro-organisms and genetically modified organisms, with the exception of matters related to the issuing of authorisations for the placing on the market of food and pharmaceuticals, matters of genetically modified organisms intended for use in feed and genetically modified feed within the scope of certain tasks or activities defined by the relevant legislation and the control of cultivation in the field of genetically modified organisms.

The Minister responsible for the environment controls, among others, the General Director of Environmental Protection. This Minister supervises the activities of the State Forest Holding "State Forests", the Forest Research Institute and the State Geological Institute – State Research Institute, as well as the activities of the Forest Seed Bureau in Warsaw (Art. 28 of the DzAR). Analysis of the requirements in question leads to critical conclusions. The distinction between the "climate", "environment" and "geology" or "management of natural resources sections[13] " does not find sufficient basis and becomes a source of unnecessary doubts.

5. Certain Tasks of the Minister Responsible for Mineral Deposits

In the light of Art. 23 para 1 and 3 of the PrGG, agreement with the minister responsible for the management of mineral deposits is required only for a license for the extraction of minerals listed in Art. 10 para 1 of the PrGG, and not (as the Prime Minister wishes to do in the aforementioned regulation of 18 November 2019) for all minerals constituting the subject of mining property. The order to co-operate (decision-making) in administrative proceedings can only arise from the law and not from the executive order entrusting the minister with tasks defined by the provisions on government administration sections. This leads to the conclusion that the regulation in question of 18 November 2019, partly goes beyond the solutions of the Geological and Mining Act and, to this extent, does not have the legal effects envisaged therein. This is because the jurisdiction (competence) of a public administration body can only be shaped by way of an Act of Parliament, or by way of an act implementing the Act of Parliament if the statutory basis for issuing such an implmentation would expressly allow for such a solution.

A license for underground tankless storage of substances and underground storage of carbon dioxide is also required to be agreed with the minister responsible for mineral deposit management, which is not mentioned in the requirements for government sections. There is also no answer to the question of what is to guide the said authority in making the said arrangements (or refusing to make them). The Act does not specify any rationale for its position. It is

13 Do których niewątpliwie zaliczają się geologiczne zasoby środowiska, a przede wszystkim złoża kopalin (What undoubtedly includes geological environmental resources and, above all, mineral deposits).

assumed that the purpose of such cooperation "is to obtain, by the administrative body conducting the main proceedings, the position of the administrative body dealing with this area of social life, which does not fall within the scope of activity of the administrative body conducting the main proceedings. The administrative body that conducts the interlocutory proceedings expresses its position on the subject matter of the main proceedings by assessing it through the prism of its own knowledge of that area of social life that falls within the scope of its activity"[14]. However, there is no denying that in practice it becomes extremely difficult, even discretionary, to establish these premises. It is true that one can defend the view that the prerequisite for the reconciliation is the compliance of the intended concession with the principle of rational management of mineral deposits, however, the mentioned Art. 11a item 1 of the DzAR applies only to certain deposits covered by mining property. The issue of underground, tankless storage of substances is included in the energy section, covered by the tasks of the minister in charge of the climate, although a license for such activity requires agreement with the minister in charge of mineral deposit management (Art. 23 para 1 and 3 of PrGG). Not surprisingly, there are known situations in which the position of the authority agreeing the concession is determined by entirely extra-legal premises, especially those related to the person of the applicant[15].

Another difficulty relates to the establishment of legal instruments to be used by the minister responsible for the management of mineral deposits regarding the rational management of deposits of hydrocarbons, lignite, hard coal, indigenous sulphur, rock salt, potassium salt, potassium-magnesium salt, in the area covered by mining, as well as the supervision of such activities. Above all, for unknown reasons, this solution applies only to certain deposits which are the subject of mining property rights. While it is possible to defend the view that one of the prerequisites for establishing a concession for the mining of the aforementioned minerals should be a determination that such activity will be in compliance with the principle of rational management of the deposit, the order of rational management of a mineral deposit applies to all mineral deposits, regardless of their type (Art. 125 and 126 of the PrOŚr in conjunction with Art. 29 para 1 et seq. of the PrGG). The essence of "rational management of mineral deposits" has not received a statutory definition. Linguistically, "rational" means as much

14 Judgment of the Supreme Administrative Court of 23 January 2015, II OSK 1390/13.

15 See the final judgments of the Voivodship Administrative Court in Warsaw issued in the same case: of 9 June 2006, VI SA/Wa 839/06 and of 24 April 2007, VI SA/Wa 178/07.

as: (1) "based on modern scientific methods; well thought out and justified (…)", (2) "based on reason, reasoned, rationalistic, guided by reason (…)".[16] It must be assumed that "management" is in fact synonymous with "using". According to Art. 3 of the PrOŚr, there is no doubt that "minerals" are (in principle non-renewable) components of the environment (para. 39), while the protection of the latter consists in particular in "the rational shaping of the environment and the management of environmental resources in accordance with the principle of sustainable development" (para. 13(a)). On the surface, it might seem that the essence of "rational management of mineral deposits" should be the fullest possible use (extraction) of their resources. Most of the time, however, this is not possible, primarily for technological reasons, and may not be justified for economic reasons. Sometimes a part of the resources in question must be left behind, if only because of the need to ensure safety in the broad sense[17]. Finally, it may not be economically viable to extract some parts of the deposit[18]. An additional source of difficulty is the legal definition of "mineral deposit"[19]. It is only known that the "rational" management of a mineral deposit "is to consist, among other things, in the comprehensive use of the main mineral and associated minerals"[20]. The injunction to manage the deposit rationally is addressed primarily to entrepreneurs carrying out mineral extraction activities. It is also indirectly incumbent on administrative bodies making decisions regulating such activities. However, it is unquestionable that invoking the premise of rational management of a mineral deposit requires establishing what the essence of the premise is in a given state of facts[21]. It is not uncommon to find situations in which the licensing authorities refuse a license for the exploration of a deposit on the grounds of a threat to the rational management of the mineral deposit, without any attempt to explain the meaning of this term and to demonstrate how

16 Mały słownik języka polskiego, ed. S. Skorupka, H. Auderska, Z. Łempicka 1969, p. 683.

17 Examples include so-called mining protection pillars defined in Article 104 para 5 of PrGG.

18 Examples include thin seams, in additions highly contaminated.

19 According to Article 6 para 1 item 19 of PrGG, such a deposit "is a natural accumulation of minerals, rocks and other substances, the extraction of which may bring an economic benefit". The said "possibility", on the other hand, is derived from a number of factors (technological, environmental, economic, legal), which, in addition, may be extremely variable over time.

20 See. § 1.1 of the Regulation of the Minister of the Environment of 24 April 2012 on Detailed Requirements for Deposit Development Projects, Law Gazette 2012, item 511.

21 See e.g. judgments of the Supreme Administrative Court of 13 January 2015, II GSK 1841/13; of 1 October 2021, II OSK 3282/18.

the intended activity may violate the said principle of "rationality"[22]. It is also not true that administrative bodies (including the minister responsible for mineral deposit management) carry out "rational management of mineral deposits". Indeed, this is not the task of the administrative body, but of the entrepreneur. It is also unclear what legal instruments are to comprise the "supervision" exercised by the minister responsible for the management of mineral deposits.

The list of organisational units subordinate to or supervised by the Minister of Industry includes only:

1. National Research Institute – Central Mining Institute in Katowice,
2. KOMAG Institute of Mining Technology in Gliwice,
3. Institute of Energy and Fuel Processing Technology in Zabrze,
4. "Poltegor- Institute" Institute of Opencast Mining in Wrocław[23].

6. Conclusions

The analysis made above shows that the lawmaker shaping the legal model of regulation of geological and mining activities and defining tasks within the scope of the department of government administration covering "management of mineral deposits", was not fully aware of the consequences of the solutions adopted. In part, they were modelled on the solutions of a centrally managed economy, which (as a relic of a socialist state) became obsolete more than 30 years ago. On the other hand, there is a lack of any information on initiatives aimed at rationalising the legal status in question. *De lege ferenda,* however, it should be proposed that the tasks of the minister responsible for deposits management be restructured and included in the "geology" section.

22 See non-final Judgment of the Voivodship Administrative Court in Warsaw of 4 June 2018, VI SA/Wa 570/18.

23 Notice of the Minister of Industry of 3 June 2024 on the List of Organisational Units Subordinated to or Supervised by the Minister of Industry, Official Journal Monitor Polski 2024, item 453.

Olgierd Kucharski

Working Time Systems and Schedules in the Civil Service

1. Introduction

The civil service was established to carry out the tasks of the state in a professional, reliable and politically neutral manner.[1] The fundamental idea behind the civil service is the desire to ensure the continued professional performance of the tasks of the state, despite the political changes of ruling teams. This is to be achieved by separating political positions from politically neutral and stable civil servant positions. Understood in this way, the idea of the civil service is a negation of the idea of spoils, i.e. the assumption of all official positions by representatives of the party that won the elections.[2] To realise these assumptions, the legislator decided to create a separate law exclusively concerning the functioning of the civil service, classified among the so-called employee pragmatics.[3] As an aside, it should be noted that such a solution is criticised by some representatives of the labour law doctrine because, in their opinion, it harms the coherence and functionality of labour law.[4]

Irrespective of the assessments concerning such, and not other, positioning of the provisions concerning the employment of civil servants and their rights and obligations, it should be pointed out that the legislator also foresaw from the outset in Article 9 of the Act that in matters concerning the employment relationship of members of the civil service corps and not regulated by the Act, the provisions of the Labour Code and other provisions of the labour law will

---

1 As evident from Article 1 of the Act of 21 November 2008 on the Civil Service (Journal of Laws 2022.1691, uniform text), hereinafter referred to as the Act.

2 Prawo urzędnicze pod red. T. Liszcz, Lublin 2005, s. 16 [Clerical Law, ed. by T. Liszcz, Lublin 2005, p. 16.]

3 W. Sanetra, *Pragmatyki zawodowe. Pojęcie i systematyka. Miejsce w systemie źródeł prawa* [w:] red. K. W. Barana, Z. Górala, *System prawa pracy Tom IX Pragmatyki pracownicze pod*, Warszawa 2021, s. 50 [W. Sanetra, *Professional pragmatics. Concept and systematics. Place in the system of sources of law*, in: ed. K. W. Baran, Z. Góral, Labour Law System Volume IX Employee pragmatics, Warsaw 2021, p. 50].

4 Ibid, p. 66.

apply, which will be particularly relevant to the issues described in this article.[5] On the other hand, an analogous regulation can be found in Article 5 of the Labour Code, from which it follows that if the relations of a specific category of employees are regulated by special provisions, the provisions of the Labour Code apply to the extent not regulated by these special provisions. In terms of scope, therefore, these independent provisions overlap.

Moving on to outline the subject matter of the article, it should be pointed out that the working time of members of the civil service corps is regulated in the Act in a fragmentary manner.[6] This feature plus the reference to the extensive regulations of the Labour Code to the extent that they are not regulated results in certain interpretative doubts related to the application of these provisions. The intention of this article is to clarify them.

2. Concept of Working Time

The concept of working time is defined in Article 128 § 1 of the Labour Code. A key element of this definition is that the employee is at the disposal of the employer. This is not absolutely related to the actual, real performance of work.[7] Instead, it means performing work under the direct leadership of a superior, according to his instructions. The characteristic feature is the restriction of the employee's personal freedom, which results from the obligation to fulfil the purpose of the employment relationship. It is not only the performance of ordinary work activities and the instructions of the management, but also the performance of other activities in the interest of the employer, even without his instructions. In summary, being at disposal in the legal sense is the power of the employer to dispose of the person of the employee resulting from the employee's voluntary commitment to work according to instructions.[8]

---

5 Act of 26 June 1974 Labour Code (Journal of Laws 2022.1510, as amended), hereinafter referred to as the Labour Code.

6 T. Bakalarz, *Status prawny pracowników służby cywilnej i pracowników urzędów państwowych. Specjalne uprawnienia* [w:] red. K. W. Barana, Z. Górala, *System prawa pracy Tom IX Pragmatyki pracownicze pod*, Warszawa 2021, s. 179 [in:] Labour Law System Volume IX Employee pragmatics, ed. K. W. Baran, Z. Góral, Warsaw 2021, p. 179.]

7 K. Rączka, *Czas pracy*, in: red. M. Gersdorf, K. Rączki, *System prawa pracy Tom III Indywidualne prawo pracy*. Część szczegółowa pod, Warszawa 2021, s. 609.

8 Ibid, p. 610.

The concept of working time, working time norms, working time systems, as well as compulsory rest has a very important role related to the implementation of the protective[9] and organisational function of working time.[10] The concept of the function of the law allows us to identify the purpose of the creation of a given regulation.[11] In the case of working time regulations, it will be, on the one hand, the need to protect human health and life in terms of providing the necessary rest from work in order to regulate the mental and physical strength of the employee and, currently, also to ensure the right of the employee to his/her leisure time and the opportunity to pursue his/her family and personal life, to develop his/her passions and interests, which is emphasised by the fact that these needs are classified as second-generation human rights.[12] On the other hand, the rules on working time allow it to be organised by the employer and to define the limits within which he can give instructions so that the employee is at his disposal and to which the latter must obey.

3. Characteristics of the Solutions Adopted in the Act

Turning to the analysis of the detailed solutions concerning working time, it should be pointed out that regarding the members of the civil service corps, certain provisions of the Labour Code apply directly, as they have not been regulated by the Act. In particular, these will be the provisions of a protective nature and pertaining to the obligation to provide the employed with uninterrupted daily and weekly rest, as specified in Articles 132 and 133 of the Labour Code, as well as a break included in the working time (Article 134 of the Labour Code).[13]

In the remaining scope, the Act will have priority in its application excluding the application of the Labour Code regulations, which in particular will concern the issues of working time systems and working time settlement periods. This

---

9 Z. Salwa, *Ochronna funkcja prawa pracy*, [w:] red. K. W. Barana, *System prawa pracy Tom I Część ogólna pod*, Warszawa 2021, s. 477 i n.]

10 Z. Salwa, *Organizacyjna funkcja prawa pracy*, in: red. K. W. Barana, *System prawa pracy Tom I Część ogólna pod*, Warszawa 2021, s. 487

11 B. M. Ćwiertniak, Z. Salwa, *Funkcje prawa pracy*, in: red. K. W. Barana, *System prawa pracy Tom I Część ogólna pod*, Warszawa 2021, s. 459.

12 O. Kucharski, *Swoboda pracodawców w kształtowaniu czasu pracy*, in: red. J. Glumińskiej – Pawlic, B. Przywory *Swoboda działalności gospodarczej. Próba oceny polskich regulacji prawnych pod*, Warsaw 2021, p. 173.

13 Baran Krzysztof W. (red.), Ustawa o służbie cywilnej. Komentarz pod red. K. W. Barana, LEX/el 2021 [Baran Krzysztof W. (ed.), Civil Service Act. Commentary, ed. K. W. Baran, LEX/el 2021]

will result in the application in the civil service of only the basic and equivalent working time system and the maximum settlement periods specified in the Act.[14]

Article 97(1) of the Act indicates the standard of working time for members of the civil service corps (which means both persons employed under a contract of employment and appointed officials). Regarding the working time standard indicated in Article 129 § 1 of the Labour Code, it is noticeable that the expression "in an average five-day working week" has been omitted.[15] As a general rule, however, this should not mean that it is possible to work 6 working days on average per week in the civil service. The legislator's use of the expression in Article 97(1) of the Act that working time may not "*exceed eight hours per day and an average of 40 hours per week in an adopted settlement period not exceeding eight weeks*" should, in practice, result in the adoption of an average five-day working week (which is the accounting consequence of the operation 40:8=5). Exceptions to this may occur if work is scheduled to be shorter on certain days, e.g. 4 hours on Friday and 4 hours on the sixth working day of the week. In such a case, only an appeal to systemic rationale (stemming from the Officials' Working Time Ordinance, which will be characterised below), the need for uninterrupted weekly and daily rest and the protective function of working time regulation,[16] may affect the provision of an average five-day working week to members of the civil service corps. It is quite difficult to identify the arguments underlying the legislator's decision to structure this provision in such a way compared to the Labour Code. Among others, this seems to be the type of case that scholars have in mind when stating that the Act violates the coherence and systematicity of labour law.[17]

---

14 K. Rączka, Working time in the civil service, PiZS 2013/12, pp. 24–25

15 Baran Krzysztof W. (red.), Ustawa o służbie cywilnej. Komentarz pod red. K. W. Barana, LEX/el 2021 [Baran Krzysztof W. (ed.), Civil Service Act. Commentary, ed. K. W. Baran, LEX/el 2021]; W. Drobny, M. Mazuryk, P. Zuzankiewicz, Ustawa o służbie cywilnej. Komentarz, LEX/el2012; J. Jagielski, K. Rączka, Ustawa o służbie cywilnej. Komentarz, LEX/el 2010 [W. Drobny, M. Mazuryk, P. Zuzankiewicz, Civil Service Act. Commentary, LEX/el2012; J. Jagielski, K. Rączka, Ustawa o służbie cywilnej. Commentary, LEX/el 2010]

16 Baran Krzysztof W. (red.), Ustawa o służbie cywilnej. Komentarz pod red. K. W. Barana, LEX/el 2021 [Baran Krzysztof W. (ed.), Civil Service Act. Commentary, ed. K. W. Baran, LEX/el 2021,]

17 W. Sanetra, Pragmatyki zawodowe…, s. 66 [W. Sanetra, Professional pragmatics…, p. 66.]

The provision indicating that members of the civil service work 8 hours per day introduces the standard basic working time system for them as a rule for planning and performing work. Unusual is the settlement period of working time indicated in Article 97, paragraph 1 of the Act, specified as no longer than 8 weeks, while the Labour Code, in Article 129, paragraph 1, provides for the possibility of applying even a 4-month settlement period. This can be explained by the fact that the legislator's intention was, however, that in the civil service, as a rule, the 40-hour working week should be maintained as much as possible, and in this respect the employer's freedom to flexibly shape the working time in longer periods was restricted. This is because the longer the reference period, the greater the employer's freedom to shape working time. The consequence is, of course, an uneven workload for the employee in different weeks. The second argument justifying this solution is the desire for employees to be given days off as soon as possible in exchange for working more than 40 hours per week. It seems that the same effect could be achieved by defining the reference period as two calendar months, which would facilitate the work of HR and payroll departments that settle working time and salaries on a monthly rather than weekly basis. In practice, with an eight-hour working day and the rather exceptional cases of working six working days in some weeks in most offices, the above issue should not cause major problems.

Another solution introduced in the Act and constituting a modification of the provision known from the Labour Code, is the regulation of Article 97(2) of the Act, which stipulates that "*in cases justified by the type of work and its organisation, working time schedules may be used, in which it is permissible to extend the working time to 12 hours per day. In such schedules, however, the working time may not exceed an average of 40 hours per week in the adopted settlement period not longer than 12 weeks*". In labour law, this type of solution is referred to as an equivalent working time system.[18] With regard to the regulation of Article 135 § 1 of the Labour Code, the difference is the omission in the law of the expression: "*The extended daily working time shall be balanced by a shorter daily working time on certain days or by days off*". In practice, there is no other

18 J. Iwulski, W. Sanetra, Kodeks pracy. Komentarz Warszawa 2013, s. 710 [J. Iwulski, W. Sanetra, Labour Code. Commentary Warsaw 2013, p. 710]; K. Jaśkowski, E. Maniewska, Kodeks pracy. Komentarz, Warszawa 2019, s. 779 [K. Jaskowski, E. Maniewska, Labour Code. Commentary, Warsaw 2019, p. 779]; M. Gersdorf, K. Rączka, M. Raczkowski, kodeks pracy. Komentarz, Warszawa 2014 s. 841–842. [M. Gersdorf, K. Rączka, M. Raczkowski, Labour Code. Commentary, Warsaw 2014 pp. 841–842.]

way to ensure an average 40-hour working week during the reference period when working time is extended to 12 hours per day on certain days than to grant additional days off or shorter working hours on certain days.

This provision of the law also introduces an atypical settlement period of no more than 12 weeks, which is a significant modification in relation to the Labour Code, in which the basic settlement period is 1 month, and only in particularly justified cases may be extended to 3 or even 4 months. It thus appears to be another example of a solution underpinning the need to ensure increased availability of the civil service, at the expense of its protective function.

Such a defined pay period – 12 weeks, i.e. other than a calendar month or a multiple thereof – raises questions about the rationality of such an arrangement. After all, remuneration is calculated for the period of a calendar month. Thus, in the event that in the course of a calendar month the working time settlement period ends and a new one begins, it may turn out that a different number of working hours will be worked than the working time of that calendar month. If overtime is involved, having regard to the position of the Legal Department of the Main Labour Inspectorate of 2005 GNP-367–4560/05/PE on time off for overtime,[19] *if time off for overtime work was granted by the employer at the request of the employee in a month other than the month in which the work occurred, the employee shall receive a correspondingly higher remuneration for work in the month in which he/she worked in excess of the norm, while in the month in which he/she took time off he/she shall receive a correspondingly lower remuneration for work". In such a case, the* office's finance department making the salary calculation will have an extremely difficult task to correctly calculate the employee's wages. It seems that the legislator, by deciding on such an atypical formation of the working time settlement periods (no definition in calendar months), introduces unnecessary confusion, without sufficiently strong arguments in favour of such a solution. No thought has been given to all the consequences of a seemingly purely technical solution.

An important element shaping the order and organisation of work in any office is the work regulations. This intra-company act should consider the specific nature of the work of the office in question and even regional demands for its work. In the case of the civil service, the duty to issue work regulations rests with the Director General of the office.[20] Arrangements for the applicable

19 https://sip.lex.pl/orzeczenia-i-pisma-urzedowe/pisma-urzedowe/gnp-367-4560-05-pe-stanowisko-departamentu-prawnego-184562948, accessed 20.10.2022.

20 As evident from Article 25(4)(d) of the Act.

working time system, reference period and working time schedules should be included therein. In this respect, however, the legislative autonomy of the Directors-General is depleted. This follows from Article 97(3) of the Act, which stipulates that working time schedules and, in the week, and their dimensions on particular days of the week shall be determined by the Director General in accordance with the principles set out in the Ordinance by the Prime Minister. Although the President of the Council of Ministers has not issued such an executive act to date, on the basis of transitional provisions, a decree issued under the old Act must be applied, with the result that we use the 2007 act.[21] It follows from this not very extensive regulation that the Director General should determine the schedules and dimensions of the working time of members of the civil service corps in such a way that the work is performed from Monday to Friday between 8:15 a.m. and 4:15 p.m.[22] Thus, the principle of the five-day working week in administration was introduced in the executive regulation to the Act, and not in the Act itself. It seems that such a solution does not demonstrate the highest legislative level and the rationality of the legislator, since it places such an important element of the working time standard in a hierarchically lower act, which may be regarded as depreciating the importance of such a standardisation. However, based on Article 9 of the Labour Code, in connection with the fact that specific acts of labour law may not be less favourable for the employee than acts of general law, such as, inter alia, regulations, it should be acknowledged that a five-day working week should be observed in every office. There is no doubt that it is more beneficial for an employee to work five days a week than six.

In the next part of the ordinance, following the directive contained in Article 97, paragraph 4 of the Act, in which the legislator indicated that the Prime Minister should take into account the need to ensure the efficient work of the office, including the service of the public and the diverse nature of the tasks performed by members of the civil service corps, the possibility of making the office's opening hours more flexible for the public, and thus its working hours, was allowed. In particular, § 3 of the aforementioned regulation stipulates that the Director General of the office:

21 Ordinance of the Council of Ministers of 25 April 2007 on the working time of employees of government administration offices (Journal of Laws 2007, no. 76, item 505).

22 § 2 of the aforementioned Ordinance.

- may determine the schedule and working hours of employees, which include uninterrupted eight hours per day between the hours of 7:00 a.m. and 6:00 p.m., if this is justified by the need to ensure the efficient work of the office and the diverse nature of the tasks performed;
- because of the specific nature of the work performed in a job, the working time schedule of an employee in that job may provide for shift work falling between 6 a.m. one day and 6 a.m. the next day, under the working time system applicable to that employee;
- in offices where tasks related to the service of the public are performed, the timetable and working hours of employees should be established in such a way that, on at least one day of the week, these tasks are performed between 8 a.m. and 6 p.m.;
- due to the specific nature of the work performed in an organisational unit or at a workstation, a day of the week that is not a working day in the office may be set as a working day in the timetable of employees working in that unit or at that workstation if this is justified by the needs of the office;
- when determining the scheduling or working hours on particular days of the week, the Director-General of the Office shall take into account important personal or family reasons of the employees.

In connection with the provisions of the ordinance, a doubt arises as to whether a mobile organisation of working time allowing double work during the working day can be applied in the civil service. Referring to Article 140^1 of the Labour Code, it should be pointed out that this provision does not constitute a separate working time system, but only organisations thereof. Therefore, in order not to perform double work during the working day, defined in Article 128 § 3 para. 1 of the Labour Code resulting in the recognition of such work as overtime work, it would be necessary to introduce this type of solution in the office under the procedure provided for in Article 150 § 3 or 5 of the Labour Code.

Mariusz Paradowski

Violation of the Principle of Dignified Conduct of a Member of the Civil Service as a Basis for Disciplinary Liability

1. Introductory Remarks

The subject of official ethics[1] and axiological rules of state administration is a necessary foundation for the operation of the public authority apparatus. It often becomes the basis of numerous scientific discussions in the plane of shaping the standards of performing official duties by public officials. An important sphere of executive functioning in Poland is the civil service corps. Here, several principles are distinguished that exemplify the manner of performing professional work in public administration. Among the catalogue of norms implementing employee duties is the principle of dignified conduct of a member of the civil service corps in and out of the service, the breach of which is the basis for disciplinary liability. Civil servant practice reveals the complex nature of proceeding in circumstances indicating a breach of the principle in question. For this reason, it is worth looking at the interpretation of the principle in question and drawing attention to the position of the judicature. The views of academics and the jurisprudence are not always sufficiently clear.

2. The Civil Service Corps as an Expression of Professionalism in Executive Action

Normative issues concerning the civil service corps in Poland are an important problematic aspect falling within the area of public law. In legal doctrine, advanced scientific research has been conducted in this area for many years. B. Przywora noted that: "the origins of the establishment of a professional corps of civil servants can already be found in the solutions adopted in the Constitution of 3 May of 1791. The Government Act introduced the foundations for the construction of modern administration"[2]. In his opinion: "the issue of the civil

1 See T. Barankiewicz, *Etyka urzędnicza – funkcje, zasady, postawy* in: *Metryka. Studia z zakresu prawa osobowego i rejestracji stanu cywilnego No* 3, Cracow 2014.

2 B. Przywora, *Transformacje ustrojowe polskiej służby cywilnej*, Cracow 2012, p. 49.

service was the subject of the deliberations of the Constitutional Committee of the National Assembly on 13 March 1997. A positive recommendation was given to the amendment by MP J. Rokita concerning the constitutionalisation of the civil service"[3]. Pursuant to the content of the provision of Article 153(1) of the Constitution of the Republic of Poland of 2 April 1997, to ensure professional, reliable, impartial and politically neutral performance of the tasks of the state, a civil service corps operates in the offices of government administration. B. Banaszak noted that: "from this constitutional provision it is possible to derive what is to be understood by the term civil service corps. It is the entirety of those employed in government administration offices"[4]. The analysed linguistic phrase has experienced a more detailed interpretation paradigm on the grounds of the Act of 21 November 2008 on civil service[5]. Pursuant to the content of Article 2, paragraphs 1 and 2 of the aforementioned legal act, the civil service corps is formed by employees employed in official positions in: the Chancellery of the President of the Council of Ministers, offices of ministers and chairpersons of committees forming the Council of Ministers and offices of central government administration bodies, voivodeship offices and other offices constituting auxiliary apparatus of field government administration bodies subordinate to ministers or central government administration bodies, excluding field executive bodies of the Minister of National Defence, National Fiscal Information and fiscal administration chambers, commands, inspectorates and other organisational units constituting auxiliary apparatus of managers of combined services, provincial services, inspections and guards as well as heads of poviat services, inspections and guards, unless otherwise stipulated by separate acts, the Central Bureau of Investigation of the Police, the Bureau of Internal Affairs of the Police, the Central Bureau for Combating Cybercrime, the Central Forensic Laboratory of the Police, the Internal Affairs Bureau of the Border Guard, the Forest Seed Office and budgetary units servicing state purpose funds whose administrators are government administration bodies – hereinafter referred to as offices. The civil service corps also consists of district and border veterinarians and their deputies. Nevertheless, the legislator includes in the circle of members of the civil service corps: civil servants employed on the basis of appointment, a civil servant employed on the basis of an employment contract and a person employed on a

3 *Ibid*, p. 100.
4 B. Banaszak, *Konstytucja Rzeczypospolitej Polskiej – komentarz*, Warsaw 2012, p. 809.
5 Uniform text: Journal of Laws of 2022, item 1691.

higher position in the civil service. The legal basis is the provision of Article 3 of the aforementioned Act.

3. The Interpretative Paradigm of Human Dignity

There is no doubt that the principle of dignified conduct of a member of the civil service corps has strong philosophical inclinations. This is because its interpretation encounters the paradigm of human dignity. According to an encyclopaedic definition, dignity means: "the property flowing from the structure of being-personal due to the fact that it exists in and for itself as an end, and never as a means of human action"[6]. M. Zdyb, following D. Dudek, in turn pointed out that: "dignity, which has important meanings and implications, is [...] not a legal institution, created by law and strictly normalized [...]. It is a primary phenomenon and independent of the law, related to human existence, possible to reconstruct a philosophical (anthropological and ethical) or philosophical-legal definition rather than a strictly dogmatic-legal one"[7]. An interesting way of understanding dignity comes from the social teaching of the Catholic Church and the teaching of Pope John Paul II[8]. G. Andrzejczuk mentioned that: "the dignity of the person as a value is not similar to other values, i.e. intellectual, vital, aesthetic. Wojtyla refers to dignity as a value of the person himself. He distinguishes from those values that reside in the person. These are innate or acquired values. Dignity is the foundation of freedom. For Karol Wojtyla, this view of dignity is determined by nature, The existence of man as a being of rational nature constitutes a greater good than the existence of many other beings that are not rational"[9]. A similar view of human dignity is presented by other representatives of existential realism. P. Skrzydlewski pointed out that: "the personal vision of man emphasises the reasonableness and freedom of the human person, his inherent dignity, sovereignty and legal subjectivity, which must be affirmed for the good of the human everywhere, also in the field of social

6 See M. Krąpiec, *Powszechna Encyklopedia Filozofii vol.* III, collective work edited by M. A. Krąpiec, Lublin 2002.

7 M. Zdyb, *Standardy służby publicznej. Uwagi ogólne,* in: *Annales Universitatis Mariae Curiae-Sklodowska,* Vol. LXIV, 2, Lublin 2017, p. 17.

8 See K. Wojtyła, *Miłość i odpowiedzialność,* Lublin 1960.

9 Andrzejczuk G., *Godność i wolność w nauczaniu Jana Pawła II,* in: *Dziecko w historii – między godnością a zniewoleniem. vol. 1. Dziecko jako fundament praw człowieka,* collective work edited by Elwira J. Kryńska, Łukasz Kalisz and Agnieszka Suplicka, Białystok 2021, pp. 417–418.

life. This vision includes the social life of the human being, seeing in the human community the natural and necessary niche for the human being to develop his or her personal life[10]. The term dignity has been defined somewhat separately in modern ethics. M. Środka distinguished three types of this concept: "the dignity of the person (human being), as an attribute belonging to every human being by the very fact that he or she is a human being and being the basis of human rights; personal dignity, related to a certain standard of evaluation inherent in a given culture (environment); and the sense of dignity – self-respect and self-esteem"[11] .

4. Principle of Dignified Conduct of a Member of the Civil Service Against the Background of Civil Law Standards

The principle of dignified conduct of a member of the civil service corps is mentioned by the legislator in the content of the provision of Article 76, paragraph 1, point 7 *de lege lata of the* Civil Service Act. Pursuant to the content of the said legal norm, a member of the civil service corps is obliged, in particular, to behave with dignity in and out of the service. The legal definition of this principle is contained in the content of § 14 of the Order No. 70 of the Prime Minister of 6 October 2011 on the guidelines for observance of the principles of civil service and on the principles of ethics of the civil service corps[12], according to which the principle of dignified conduct consists in particular in: performing work with respect for the rules of social coexistence and personal culture, respecting the dignity of others, including subordinates, colleagues and superiors, kindness towards people and preventing the emergence of conflicts at work, in relations with citizens and co-workers and appropriate behaviour also outside work, avoiding undesirable behaviour having a negative impact on the image of the state, the civil service and the office. Similar views are represented by the legal doctrine. K. Oleksy mentioned that: "in the context of the principle of dignified conduct, it is worth emphasising that the welfare of the service and the office as well as the desired image of the state require proper behaviour outside work and avoidance of undesirable behaviour"[13] .

---

10 P. Skrzydlewski, *Osoba w przestrzeni publicznej. Wybrane zagadnienia z filozofii człowieka i polityki,* Cracow 2016, p. 20.

11 See M. Środa, *Etyka dla nauczycieli,* Warsaw 2015.

12 M. P. of 2011, No. 93, item 953.

13 K. Oleksy, *Etyka w służbie cywilnej* [w:] *Studia z zakresu nauk prawnoustrojowych Miscellanea No.* 5, Bydgoszcz 2015, p. 246.

In the context of the above differentiation, it is pertinent to observe that the performance of work with respect for the rules of social coexistence, mentioned by the legislator, is an example of the penetration of civilian values into the plane of shaping the legal status of a member of the civil service corps. It should be borne in mind that in accordance with the content of the provision of Article 5 of the Act of 23 April 1964. – Civil Code[14], one may not make of his/her right a use which would be contrary to the social and economic purpose of this right or to the principles of social coexistence. Such an act or omission by the right holder is not considered an exercise of the right and is not under protection. In other words, the broadly interpreted general clause of principles of social coexistence contained by the legislator in the aforementioned provision has found a slightly modified application on the grounds of interpretation of the principle of dignified conduct of a member of the civil service corps. This normative procedure seems appropriate and rationally justified in view of the ethical and axiological significance of the indicated principle. However, it must not be forgotten that the rule of social coexistence has been shaped in private law. It has a strongly established tradition in the science of civil law. M. Sala-Szczypiński noted that: "the clause of principles of social coexistence was taken from the Soviet law system and introduced in place of the traditional clauses of equity, good faith, honesty in trade"[15]. The author also pointed out that: "such an embracing of the principles of social coexistence as rules of behaviour necessary for the realisation of the goals of socialist society has for a long time weighed on the practical application and theoretical interpretation of this clause"[16]. It was not until the political transformations of the late 20th century that significantly contributed to a change in the interpretative paradigm of the said principle. M. Zaluski mentioned that: "in the case of provisions containing the clause of principles of social coexistence, it is a reference to rules and evaluations of human conduct, which, however, are not legal rules. These principles are born spontaneously in society and are not set by state authorities. The principles of social coexistence are the rules ordering the assessment of a given case according to certain moral or customary rules – such rules which, at a given time and under given social conditions, concern the sphere of people's external behaviour towards others

14 t. j. Dz. U. of 2022, item 1360

15 M. Sala-Szczypiński, *Znaczenie zasad współżycia społecznego w prawie polskim,* in: *Państwo i Prawo No.* 1, Warsaw 2005, p. 56.

16 Ibid., *Zasadność zmiany klauzuli zasady współżycia społecznego,* in: *Studia Prawnicze. Rozprawy i materiały No* 1, Cracow 2007, p. 66

and make it possible to consider such behaviour as good (or bad), justified, appropriate, advisable, generally accepted"[17]. In contemporary legal doctrine, the ethical dimension of rules of social coexistence is emphasised. A. Żurawik, following R. Trzaskowski, noted that: "the criterion of principles of social coexistence has been associated from the very beginning with a plane separate from legal norms, i.e. with morality"[18]. The judicature makes an interesting statement on this subject. Pursuant to the decision of the Supreme Court in Warsaw, principles of social coexistence are an indefinite and vague notion, and referring to the contradiction with the principles of social coexistence should be connected with specific proving of which principles of social coexistence are at stake in a given case and what the contradiction of a given action with these principles consists in[19]. In turn, according to the Regional Court in Świdnica, principles of social coexistence are objective rules of conduct serving as the criterion for assessing what deserves or does not deserve approval from the point of view of society. These principles are norms of human conduct and not legal norms. Thus, there is no sanction for not applying them. The concept of rules of social coexistence also includes moral and customary rules relating to the conduct of one person towards another. Rules of social coexistence are a vague concept. There is no specific catalogue of them and, as societies develop, new ones are created. They perform a very important function in the process of applying the law and are intended to prevent its abuse, and the legislator, by introducing the concept of principles of social coexistence, intended to deform the law by allowing the courts to consider moral criteria and assessments in the process of its application[20] .

Theorising in this way, it should be noted that the principle of social coexistence regulated in civil law significantly influences the understanding of the principle of dignified conduct of a member of the civil service corps. At the basis of the rules of social coexistence referred to in the content of § 14 point 1 of the *de lege lata* Order No. 70 of the Prime Minister on Guidelines for Observing the Rules of Civil Service and on the Ethics of the Civil Service Corps are axiological values

---

17 M. Załucki, *Kodeks cywilny – komentarz,* Warsaw 2022, pp. 1–7

18 A. Żurawik, *Dobre obyczaje a zwyczaje, zasady współżycia społecznego i dobra wiara: ujęcie teoretyczne,* [in:] *Kwartalnik Prawa Publicznego No.* 7/4, Warsaw 2007, p. 206.

19 Order of the Supreme Court of 2 February 2022, I CSK 1036/22, Portal of Judgments of Common Courts

20 Judgment of the Regional Court in Świdnica of 28 February 2013, II Ca 1000/12, **Judgment** Portal of the Regional Court in Świdnica

indicating the need for a member of the civil service corps to observe, in his/her working environment, correct interpersonal relations, the performance of entrusted tasks with due diligence, conscientiousness, impartiality, timeliness, and above all the rule of law. Nonetheless, a feature of the distinctiveness of civilian solutions in relation to the shaped status of a member of the civil service corps still remains the issue of abuse of subjective right, which, as a rule, in relation to the constitutional law does not show coherent meaning. However, the principle of social coexistence retains its axiological dimension permeating the ground of systemic law.

In interpreting the principle of dignified conduct of a member of the civil service corps, the legislator also pointed to the duty of a public servant to maintain personal culture expressed in the standards of adjusting the level of linguistic expression in relation to the social environment, respecting the attitude of broadly conceived benevolence in professional contacts, and a general openness to the existential needs of man. The performance of public tasks in the civil service corps should take place because of respect for the human dignity of persons in the working environment, in contacts with subordinates, superiors and external stakeholders.

When discussing the normative issues in question, it should not escape notice that the interpretation of the principle of dignified conduct of a member of the civil service corps also boils down to the obligation to respect ethical values outside the professional environment, i.e. to respect generally accepted moral norms in private life. Bearing in mind the legal status of this public servant, it is worth mentioning that the criterion for assessing the decent behaviour of a member of the civil service corps outside the work environment consists of the employee's conduct according to the canon of accepted and socially accepted ethical standards. Nevertheless, it should be noted that the formulation against a member of the civil service corps of allegations of a breach of the dignity of the office due to the person's activity in private social contacts should take place in observance of common sense, objectivity, and over-interpretation. Everyone has the right to a private life, to celebrate family and social occasions. In each case, it is important, against the background of the principle under consideration, to weigh the possible allegations against the factual circumstances that may form the basis for liability for its violation.

5. Disciplinary Liability of a Member of the Civil Service Corps

The disciplinary liability of a member of the civil service corps is one of the types of liability regulated by Polish law. P. Skuczyński noted that: "the problem of what disciplinary responsibility is seems today not only to be an issue troubling theorists, but also to have a momentous practical significance. It is easy to observe the growth of its significance in public life and the growth of social expectations to react quickly and decisively to existing pathologies with its help"[21]. P. Ceglarska-Piłat, in turn, following M. Cieślak, pointed out that: "the term disciplinary liability means a set of legal norms regulating the conditions, procedure and principles of incurring negative consequences by persons belonging to certain statutorily defined and distinguished groups, remaining in connection with the violation of specific norms of conduct binding on them"[22]. K. Mroczka, on the other hand, indicated that: "the essence of disciplinary liability is sanctions of the repressive type, i.e. penalties for violation of the duties of a member of the civil service corps, as well as rules of conduct determined by the notion of dignity or solemnity of the office or profession (determined by the norms of the official relationship) and rules of professional performance determined by the norms of professional art and ethics"[23] .

The legal mechanism of the disciplinary proceedings of a member of the civil service corps was regulated under the *de lege lata* norms of the Civil Service Act and under the provisions of the Ordinance of the Prime Minister of 9 April 2009 on the investigation and disciplinary proceedings in the civil service[24]. Pursuant to the provisions of Article 113 et seq. of the analysed Act, a member of the civil service corps is liable to disciplinary action for violation of the duties of a member of the civil service corps. Disciplinary penalties applied to civil servants are: admonition; reprimand; deprivation of the possibility to be promoted to a

---

21 P. Skuczyński, *Granice odpowiedzialności dyscyplinarnej,* in: *Odpowiedzialność dyscyplinarna. Podstawy, procedura i orzecznictwo w sprawach studentów Uniwersytetu Warszawskiego 2000–2005,* collective work edited by P. Skuczyński and P. Zawadzki, Warsaw 2008, p. 7

22 P. Ceglarska-Piłat, *Pojęcie i cechy charakterystyczne odpowiedzialności dyscyplinarnej w prawie polskim,* in: *Studia Prawnicze* z. 2, Warsaw 2015, p. 103.

23 K. Mroczka, *Prawne i organizacyjne uwarunkowania systemu odpowiedzialności członków korpusu służby cywilnej w Polsce,* in: *Polska Polityka i Historia. Politeja No.* 4, Cracow 2016, p. 314.

24 Journal of Laws of 2009, No. 60, item 493.

higher official rank for a period of two years; reduction in basic remuneration, by no more than 25 % – for a period of no more than six months, reduction in civil service rank and expulsion from the civil service. Disciplinary penalties applicable to senior civil servants and civil servants are: warning; reprimand; reduction in basic salary, by no more than 25 % – for a period of no more than six months; and expulsion from the office resulting in termination of the employment relationship and prohibition from applying for employment in the civil service corps for a period of five years. For a minor violation of the duties of a member of the civil service corps, the director general of the office may punish a member of the civil service corps with a written warning. The punishment may be preceded by proceedings aimed at clarifying the circumstances of the case.

The parties may appeal, through the Disciplinary Committee of the first instance, against the decision of the Disciplinary Committee to the Higher Disciplinary Committee within 14 days from the date of delivery of the decision. The Disciplinary Committee of the first instance shall forward the appeal together with the case file to the Higher Disciplinary Committee within 14 days of receipt of the appeal. The rulings of the Higher Disciplinary Committee may be appealed by the parties and the Head of the Civil Service to the Court of Appeal – Labour and Social Security Court with jurisdiction over the place of residence of the accused. The appeal shall be lodged through the Higher Disciplinary Committee. The provisions of the Code of Civil Procedure on appeals shall apply to the examination of the appeal. The decision of the Court of Appeal shall not be subject to cancellation.

It must be mentioned that the legal solutions adopted by the legislator concerning disciplinary proceedings are extremely complex. A detailed research analysis of the procedural provisions applicable to specific facts would require advanced research difficult to present in an academic article. It is worth bearing in mind, however, that a significant breach of the principle of dignified conduct of a member of the civil service corps should constitute grounds for the initiation of disciplinary proceedings preceded by a negative outcome of the investigation resulting in the obligation to present appropriate charges to the member of the civil service corps. Only the discontinuation of the investigation procedure is an expression of the exoneration of that member from the charges made, due to the pointlessness of initiating disciplinary proceedings. It should be noted that the party to the investigation procedure is not the accused, but the subject interested in the outcome of that procedure. The accused is the member of the civil service for whom the disciplinary ombudsman has sent a request to the disciplinary committee to initiate disciplinary proceedings[25] .

6. Summary

A member of the civil service corps is determined by a number of obligations creating the legal status of the entity that is a public servant. One of the key standards existing in the civil service is the need to observe the principle of dignified conduct of a member of the civil service corps. Undoubtedly, its source lies in the normative solutions of private law. It is here that the general clause of the principles of social coexistence was shaped, being the foundation for the development of the legal principle under analysis. Violation of this principle constitutes the basis for disciplinary liability. It is difficult not to notice that the principle of decent behaviour of a member of the civil service corps has strong ethical and axiological inclinations. This argument is supported by the views of legal doctrine, considerations of judicial interpretation and the general understanding of the relations in the professional relations of the civil service. The philosophical and legal analysis undertaken in this paper does not exhaust the problematic scope. Nonetheless, it is a contribution to the conduct of a great deal of detailed scientific research in the plane concerning the creation of standards for the performance of work in the civil service. Officials and civil servants are required not only to comply with the law, but also to maintain a certain social attitude in their official and private relations. For the purposes of the research analysis undertaken, the article used the following research methods: historical-comparative, doctrinal, dogmatic and dedicative method.

25 Office of the Prime Minister, *Method of investigation and disciplinary proceedings in the civil service,* Warsaw 2011, p. 26

Bogusław Przywora

On the Evolution of the Polish Civil Service (1922–2022) and the Directions of Change

1. Introductory Remarks

In 2022, we celebrated the 100th anniversary since the enactment of the Act of 17 February 1922 on the State Civil Service[1] (hereinafter also: the Act on the State Civil Service or ASCS) Like any such occasion, this one also prompts the question about the condition of the Polish civil service law[2], as well as possible directions of changes in which the civil service in particular should evolve in order to strengthen the implementation of the standards stemming from the Polish Constitution? Several events were devoted to this topic. One of them was the 6th Open Academic Seminar "100 years of the Polish Civil Service", which took place on 17 February 2022 in the online format[3]. The seminar was organised by the staff of the Department of Theory and Philosophy of Law of the John Paul II Catholic University of Lublin and the Department of Constitutional and Comparative Law of the Jan Długosz University of Humanities and Sciences in Częstochowa. The seminar was met with considerable interest and generated discussion on the directions of civil service reform. In addition, there was an international conference entitled. "100th Anniversary of the Polish Civil Service", organised by the Faculty of Political Science and International Studies of the University of Warsaw 24-25 February 2022[4] .

This study is a voice in the academic discussion but may also be applied more broadly – if legislative work is undertaken to amend the Civil Service Act. On the other hand, the study is addressed to non-Polish readers and is intended to illustrate the evolution of the Polish Civil Service. Hence, the study takes

1 Journal of Laws No. 21, item 164 as amended.

2 See also: T. Górzyńska, *Polskie prawo urzędnicze – kryzys tożsamości?*, red. W. Drobny, Warszawa 2016.

3 T. Barszcz, VI Otwarte Seminarium Naukowe "100-lecie polskiej służby cywilnej", Lublin–Częstochowa, 17 lutego 2022 r., Studia Prawnicze, KUL 1 (93) 2023, pp. 253–255.

4 On the conference in more detail: https://wnpism.uw.edu.pl/sluzba-cywilna/. See also the issue dedicated to the civil service: "Studia Iuridica" 92/2022 (https://wuw.pl/data/include/cms//SI_2022_92.pdf).

into account the author's thoughts to date from the perspective of several years of dealing with the topic of the civil service[5], the jurisprudence of the Polish Constitutional Tribunal[6], on the other hand, other studies on the civil service and practical aspects of the functioning of the civil service on the basis of the report of the Head of the Civil Service on the state of the civil service and on the implementation of the tasks of the civil service for 2021. The analysis considered the problem of the implementation of the tasks of the civil service in non-standard conditions: on the one hand, the COVID-19 pandemic, on the other hand, the coordination of activities aimed at ensuring the security of persons fleeing Ukraine (as a result of the outbreak of the Russian-Ukrainian war in February/March 2022)[7], as well as in the face of the risk of economic crisis. This allowed for the formulation of final conclusions, including *de lege ferenda* postulates.

---

5 See: B. Przywora, *Transformacje ustrojowe polskiej służby cywilnej,* Kraków 2012; B. Przywora, Kształtowanie *kadr administracji publicznej,* in: ed. R. Hauser, Z. Niewiadomski, A. Wróbel, *Etyka urzędnicza i etyka służby publicznej. System prawa administracyjnego*, Tom XIII, Warszawa 2016; T. Barankiewicz, B. Przywora, *Kształtowanie się etosu służby cywilnej w Polsce – analiza historyczna i systematyczna*, Studia Iuridica 92 (2022), pp. 104–110.

6 Jurisprudence of the Constitutional Tribunal: judgment of the CT of 28.04.1999, K 3/99, OTK 1999, no. 4, item Journal of Laws No. 21, item 164 as amended; See also: T. Górzyńska, *Polskie prawo urzędnicze – kryzys tożsamości?*, red. W. Drobny, Warszawa 2016; T. Barszcz, VI Otwarte Seminarium Naukowe "100-lecie polskiej służby cywilnej", Lublin–Częstochowa, 17 lutego 2022 r., Studia Prawnicze, KUL 1 (93) 2023, pp. 253–255; On the conference in more detail: https://wnpism.uw.edu.pl/sluzba-cywilna/. See also the issue dedicated to the civil service: "Studia Iuridica" 92 (2022) (https://wuw.pl/data/include/cms//SI_2022_92.pdf); See: B. Przywora, *Transformacje ustrojowe polskiej służby cywilnej,* Kraków 2012; B. Przywora, Kształtowanie *kadr administracji publicznej*, in: ed. R. Hauser, Z. Niewiadomski, A. Wróbel, *Etyka urzędnicza i etyka służby publicznej. System prawa administracyjnego*, Tom XIII, Warszawa 2016; T. Barankiewicz, B. Przywora, *Kształtowanie się etosu służby cywilnej w Polsce – analiza historyczna i systematyczna*, Studia Iuridica 92 (2022), pp 73; judgment of the CT of 12.12.2002, K 9/02, OTK-A 2002, no. 7, item 94; judgment of the CT of 13.11.2003, K 51/02, OTK-A 2003, no 8, item 86; judgment of the CT of 15.06.2011, K 2/09, OTK-A 2011, no 5, item 42; judgment of the CT of 14.06.2011, Kp 1/11, OTK-A 2011, no 5, item 41.

7 Report of the Head of the Civil Service on the state of the civil service and on the implementation of the tasks of the civil service for 2021, pp. 11–12.

2. Comparative and Historical Notes

The civil service is a separate corps within the public administration, and, at the same time, the main part of the executive apparatus of the state by assumption established to carry out the entrusted tasks in a reliable, professional, and politically neutral manner[8] .

When looking for a model for thinking about professional civil servant (civil service) corps, we reach back to various concepts, including European administrative thought, and this in particular to French administrative thought (especially the period of the French Third Republic), but also to experiences: German (including especially in the legal solutions of the late 18th century) and British (in 1855 the Civil Service Commission was established)[9]. Nowadays, the following models stemming from general concepts of public (civil) administration are distinguished:

(a) career model (referred to as the *career system* in the English-language literature and the promotion or closed model in Poland),
(b) the position model (called the *position system* in the English-language literature and the position or open model in Poland),
(c) mixed model[10] .

Most often, elements of the models indicated are combined (i.e. on the one hand, classical solutions derived from M. Weber's concept of bureaucracy and on the other hand, a modern organisation oriented towards social, economic, business and technological challenges). This applies to the different stages of the service: recruitment, training, as well as the status of civil servants, their remuneration and pension benefits[11]. The mixed model is found in, among

---

8 See also: D. Dudek, *Komentarz do art. 153*, in: ed. M. Safjan, L. Bosek, *Konstytucja RP. Tom II. Komentarz do art. 87–243*, Warszawa 2016, p. 812; see also: P. Czarny, *Komentarz do art. 153…*, p. 463; A. Banaszkiewicz, *Nowelizacja ustawy o służbie cywilnej z dnia 30 grudnia 2015 r. w kontekście wymogu neutralności politycznej członków korpusu służby cywilnej,* Studia Iuridica Lublinensia, XXV, No. 4 (2016), pp. 10–11.

9 G. Rydlewski, *Służba cywilna w Polsce. Przegląd rozwiązań na tle doświadczeń innych państw i podstawowe akty prawne*, Warszawa 2001, pp. 15–16.

10 B. Przywora, Kształtowanie *kadr administracji publicznej…*, p. 51; H. Szewczyk, *Modele służby publicznej i ich przydatność dla polskiego porządku prawnego,* in: red. M. Stec, S. Płażek, *Służba publiczna. Stan obecny, wyzwania i oczekiwania*, Warszawa 2013, pp. 271–274; J. Itrich-Drabarek, *Uwarunkowania standardy i kierunki zmian funkcjonowania służby cywilnej w Polsce na tle europejskim*, Warszawa 2010, pp. 49–50.

11 D. Bossaert, C. Demmke, Służba…, op.cit.

others: Czech Republic, Lithuania, Latvia, Poland, Switzerland, Hungary[12]. The choice of a particular model of service is most often influenced by the following factors: the history and tradition of a given country, or the political system[13].

It is also important to note the process of different approaches to change in public administration. This was the case in Anglo-Saxon administrative culture (from the idea of *new public management* to different varieties of the concept of *governance*), while in continental Europe, attention was paid to new ways of thinking about public administration, which were linked in particular to the renaissance of economic and political liberalism and the critique of the established idea of the state. Hence, the transformation of thinking about public administration from the classical model of Max Weber, through managerial and participatory approaches, to some of M. Weber's ideas and a model that can be described as neo-Weberian[14]. Thus, we are not only dealing with a process of constant modernisation, but with the emergence of a model which reaffirms the ideas of M. Weber. Attention is drawn to the following theses:

1. a return to the special role and position of the state in the social communication process;
2. maintaining a system of representative democracy in the emergence of power with its social and rational-legal justification (legitimacy);
3. maintaining the role and importance of administrative law;
4. maintaining the role and importance of the professional civil service[15] .

---

12 Cf. J. Itrich-Drabarek, *Uwarunkowania…*, pp. 52–54.

13 Cf. G. Rydlewski, *op. cit.*, p. 17.

14 See also: T. Barankiewicz, B. Przywora, *Kształtowanie się etosu służby cywilnej…*, pp. 104–110; see also: J. Czaputowicz, *Modele administracji publicznej i ich przydatność dla konceptualizacji administracji publicznej w państwach Europy Środkowej*, [w:] ed. A. Mednis, *Misja publiczna, wspólnota, państwo. Studia z prawa i administracji. Księga dedykowana pamięci profesora Michała Kuleszy*, Wrocław 2016, Vol. 2, pp. 363–364; see also: Ch. Pollitt, G. Bouckaert, *Public Management Reform. A comparative Analysis*, Oxford-New York 2000; W. Drechsler, *Max Weber (1864–1920) and Public Administration Today*, The Estonian Journal of Administrative Culture and Digital Governance, 1 (2020); H. G. Frederickson, *Whatever Happened to Public Administration? Governance, Governance Everywhere*, Working Paper. Queen's University Belfast, 2004, Vol. 3, p. 3, https://citeseerx. ist.psu.edu/viewdoc/download?doi=10.1.1.537.8624&rep=rep1 &type=pdf. (accessed 20.12.2022); D. F. Kettel, *The Global Public Management Revolution,* Washington 2005.

15 For a broader discussion, see T. Barankiewicz, *Neoweberyzm. Etos służby publicznej. Analiza krytyczna i perspektywy*, Lublin 2020.

3. On Poland's Civil Service Arrangements – Some Reflections

Looking at the Polish civil service, we reach back to the beautiful traditions associated with the of the creation of a professional civil service, i.e. the Act of 17 February 1922 on the State Civil Service, which constituted the foundation for the functioning of the civil service corps in the years 1922–1974. The significance of this regulation for the then newly amalgamating state (after the period of the Partitions of Poland) is best evidenced by the text of the Stenographic Report of the 263rd Session of the Legislative Parliament of 22 November 1921 on the draft law on the state civil service, from the content of which the idea of the necessity of building an efficient administrative personnel for the rebuilding of statehood in the full sense of the word emerges convincingly. It should be emphasised that this law contained a number of interesting solutions (e.g. regarding formal requirements for civil servants). It is worth noting the use of the adjective "state" civil service in the 1922 Act. The Act covered only persons defined as "state civil servants", employed in the state administration. This constituted a distinction from the draft laws developed in France since 1871 defining the status of public servants and thus normalizing the "public function" (*fonction publique*), which also included those employed on the basis of a public-law relationship in local government[16]. In the Second Republic, a model of civil servant law was formed, as a public service of the individual, subordinated to the interests of the state[17]. In the state civil service, a classical model of service (so-called career) was adopted, based – to a large extent – on Western experience (German and Austrian). The distinguishing element of this model was the assumption of binding an officer to the service for the entire period of professional activity[18]. This was associated, on the one hand, with high availability, on the other hand, with professional stability and certain privileges and benefits[19]. Two categories of officers were distinguished: civil servants and lower officials (art. 3 ASCS). The State Civil Service Act after 1926 did not function fully. In particular, the principle of stabilising the service relationship of permanent appointees was violated[20] .

After the Second World War, the civil service was gradually adapted to the requirements of the new political system. The final result was the replacement of

---

16 H. Izdebski, *Wpływ rozwiązań prawnych i tradycji służby cywilnej RP na obecny model służby cywilnej*, Studia Iuridica, No. 92 (2022), p. 86.

17 Z. Leoński, *Zarys prawa administracyjnego*, Warszawa 2006, p. 221.

18 H. Izdebski, *Wpływ rozwiązań prawnych...*, p. 88.

19 Z. Leoński, *Zarys...*, p. 221.

20 H. Izdebski, *Wpływ rozwiązań prawnych....*, pp. 88 i 90.

the Act on the State Civil Service by the Act of 26 June 1974. – Labour Code[21], departing from the standards of the civil service of the Second Republic (and especially from one of its basic pillars – the political neutrality of officials)[22]. After regaining sovereignty there was a return to thinking about a professional civil service, which was reflected in the establishment, following the example of French solutions, of the National School of Public Administration, and then in the enactment of the first Civil Service Act of 1996. Since then, the pragmatics of the civil service has been subject to many statutory changes (especially in 1998, 2006, 2008), which significantly influenced the shape of the civil service.[23]

Polish legislation on the civil service after 1997 was significantly influenced by the jurisprudence of the Constitutional Tribunal (Article 153 of the Polish Constitution)[24]. The Court's jurisprudence shows that the civil service is an essential element of government administration under the authority of the Prime Minister to ensure professional, reliable, impartial, and politically neutral performance of the tasks of the state[25]. The civil service is a special constitutional

21 Journal of Laws 1974, No. 24, item 142, as amended.

22 Also: J. Itrich-Drabarek, *The Evolution of the Polish Civil Service since 1989*, Studia Politologiczne, No. 57 (2006), pp. 92–112; Z. Góral, *Artykuł 1 ustawy o służbie cywilnej*, in: ed. K. W. Baran, *Prawo urzędnicze. Komentarz*, Warszawa 2014, p. 26.

23 See, e.g., H. Izdebski, *Wpływ rozwiązań prawnych…*, s. 85–94; J. Korczak, *Refleksje nad polską służbą cywilną z perspektywy setnej rocznicy uchwalenia ustawy o państwowej służbie cywilnej*, [in:] ed. A. Górnicz-Mulcahy, M. Lewandowicz-Machnikowka, A. Tomanek, *Pro Opere Perfecto Gratias Agimus. Księga jubileuszowa dedykowana Profesorowi Tadeuszowi Kuczyńskiemu*, Wrocław 2022, pp. 167–173; also: B. Przywora, *Komentarz do art. 1…*, pp. 35–36; see also: K. Rączka, J. Jagielski, *Ustawa o służbie cywilnej. Komentarz*, Warszawa 2010, pp. 21–23; W. Drobny, *Kierunki zmian tożsamości polskiego prawa urzędniczego*, Annales Universitatis Mariae Curie-Skłodowska, Sectio G, 64, z. 2 (2017), pp. 76–80.

24 CT jurisprudence: CT judgment of 28.04.1999, K 3/99; CT judgment of 12.12.2002, K 9/02; CT judgment of 13.11.2003, K 51/02, OTK-A 2003, no. 8, item 86; CT judgment of 15.06.2011, K 2/09; CT judgment of 14.06.2011, Kp 1/11.

25 K. Działocha, A. Łukaszczuk, *Nowa ustawa o służbie cywilnej (aspekt prawno-konstytucyjny)*, Państwo i Prawo, nr 11 (2006), s. 6; W. Sokolewicz, *Komentarz do art. 153*, in: ed. L. Garlicki, *Konstytucja Rzeczypospolitej Polskiej. Komentarz*, Warszawa 2005; R. Balicki, *Komentarz do art. 153*, in: ed. M. Haczkowska, *Konstytucja Rzeczypospolitej Polskiej. Komentarz,* Warszawa 2014; T. Górzyńska, *Konstytucyjne podstawy służby cywilnej*, w: red. R. Hauser, Z. Niewiadomski, A. Wróbel, *System Prawa Administracyjnego. Tom 2. Konstytucyjne podstawy funkcjonowania administracji publicznej*, Warszawa 2012; B. M. Ćwiertniak, *O zasadach prawa urzędniczego (podstawowe problemy)*, Studia Iuridica Lublinensia 24, No. 3 (2015), pp. 331–344.

value, and the creation of the corps is a common good[26]. The service is not a private domain of a political party, but its purpose is to serve the common good Poland understood as a value uniting opposing political groups[27] .

At this point it can be appreciated that the Polish constitutional solutions – compared to other countries – are quite elaborate. In most countries, one sees only a signalling reference to the role of the administration. For example, in the Swedish Constitution[28] employees of administrative bodies under the government are employed by the government or a body designated by the government, and only objective considerations such as merit and qualifications are to be taken into account in the employment of public servants (Chapter 12 "Administration", § 5)[29] .

In comparison, the solutions arising from the Constitution of the Kingdom of Spain are more elaborate[30], where the public administration's role of serving the general interest in a spirit of impartiality and operating in the light of the principles of: efficiency, hierarchy, decentralisation, deconcentration and coordination, with full submission to laws and legislation[31]. Similarly, the Portuguese Constitution[32] emphasises the importance of public administration employees and other officers of the state serving only the public interest under

26 Judgment of the CT of 14.06.2011, Kp 1/11.

27 R. Piotrowski, *Polityka zagraniczna a dobro wspólne. Uwagi o zgodności z Konstytucją RP projektu ustawowej regulacji służby zagranicznej*, Gdańskie Studia Prawnicze, No. 2 (2018) p. 538.

28 Constitution of the Kingdom of Sweden Grundlagarna. Act on the form of Government (Regeringsformen); Translation: Krzysztof Dembinski, Marian Grzybowski https://biblioteka.sejm.gov.pl/wp-content/uploads/2016/04/Szwecja_pol_010711.pdf (accessed 15.10.2022).

29 See also: E. Holmberg, N. Stjernquist, G. Regner, M. Eliasson, M. Isberg, Grundlagarna RF, RO, SO, Stockholm 2012, pp. 477 – 524.

30 Spanish Constitution of 27 December 1978 translated by Tadeusz Moldova: https://biblioteka.sejm.gov.pl/wp-content/uploads/2015/10/Hiszpania_pol_300612.pdf (accessed 15.10.2022).

31 See also: Gema SÁNCHEZ MEDERO, Rubén SÁNCHEZ MEDERO EL SISTEMA CIVIL DE CARRERA EN ESPAÑA. Desde el franquismo hasta la democracia, The Career Civil Service in Spain: From Franco to democracy, Revista Enfoques, vol. IX, N°14, 2010, pp. 177–193; Cadena Inostroza, Cecilia Servicio civil de carrera: lecciones para el futuro, Economía, Sociedad y Territorio, IV, núm. 14, julio-diciembre, 2003, pp. 365–387.

32 Constitution of the Portuguese Republic of 2 April 1976 Translation: Agnieszka Wojtyczek-Bonnand; https://biblioteka.sejm.gov.pl/wp-content/uploads/2016/03/Portugalia_pol_010116.pdf (accessed 15.10.2022).

the law by the competent administrative bodies. In addition, employees and officers may not be discriminated against or privileged for exercising any of their political rights, and in disciplinary proceedings against them, the right to be heard and the right to defence are guaranteed. In addition, it should be pointed out that there is a prohibition on the combination of positions or public offices, except in cases expressly permitted by law (art. 269).

Italian constitutional arrangements are also quite elaborate[33]. In particular, this concerns ensuring the proper functioning and impartiality of the administration. Positions are filled by means of competitions, except as provided by law (Article 97). The Constitution allows for statutory restrictions on the right to join political parties for several categories of public officials: judges, professional military officers in active service, police officers and officers, diplomatic and consular representatives abroad (Article 98)[34] .

4. Concluding Remarks

There have been successive attempts in Poland to implement the constitutional principles of the civil service[35]. However, an analysis of these experiences leads to the reflection that the idea of civil service anchored in the Polish Constitution has not been fully realised. This is reflected in the jurisprudence of the Constitutional Tribunal cited in the study. We have been on the road to building a civil service corps for many years. Every political change has been associated with a change

---

33 *Costituzione Italiana. Testo vigente aggiornato alla legge costituzionale 11 febbraio 2022, n. 1.* [Italian Constitution. Text of the current Fundamental Law updated to Constitutional Law No. 1 of 11 February 2022], https://www.senato.it/sites/default/files/media-documents/Costituzione.pdf (accessed 15.10.2022).

34 Constitution of the Italian Republic of 27 December 1947, source: Constitution of Italy, transl. Z. Witkowski, Warsaw 2004, http://libr.sejm.gov.pl/tek01/txt/konst/wlochy.html (accessed 15.10.2022); see in more detail P. Caretti [*et al.*] *Art. 97–98: La pubblica amministrazione*, in: a cura di G. Branca, *Commentario alla Costituzione*, Bologna-Roma 1994.

35 See also: W. Sanetra (ed.), *Stosunki pracy w służbie cywilnej i samorządzie terytorialnym*, Białystok 2001; T. Liszcz (red.), *Prawo urzędnicze*, Lublin 2010; A. Dubowik, Ł. Pisarczyk, *Prawo urzędnicze*, Warszawa 2011; T. Górzyńska, *Konstytucyjne podstawy…*, s. 415–453; M. Mazuryk, P. Zuzankiewicz, W. Drobny, *Ustawa o służbie cywilnej. Komentarz*, Warszawa 2012; J. Stelina *Prawo urzędnicze*, Warszawa 2013; W. Drobny, *Przekształcenia pragmatyk urzędniczych członków korpusu służby cywilnej i pracowników samorządowych w prawie polskim po 1989 r.*, Warszawa 2015; CT jurisprudence: Judgment in case K 9/02, judgment in case Kp 1/11.

in civil service solutions. Lack of stability does not serve its professionalisation or build trust in public institutions. However, regardless of this, the activities of the Polish administration, including the civil service, should be appreciated. This was demonstrated by the epidemic period, which forced the introduction of a number of changes in the organisation of work in administration offices (also in the area of government administration). This often involved the need to switch to remote work, and thus to provide members of the civil service corps with the appropriate tools to do so. According to a report by the Head of the Civil Service, at the height of the COVID-10 pandemic, as many as 42 % of civil service corps members were working remotely[36]. The public administration was also challenged to coordinate activities aimed at providing security, shelter, healthcare and education for children and young people to the several million people fleeing Ukraine (as a result of the outbreak of the Russian-Ukrainian war in February/March 2022)[37]. Add to this the performance of state tasks in the face of the risk of economic crisis. All these circumstances lead to the conclusion that the civil service must act in a non-standard way, skilfully adapting to changing political and economic conditions. This is hampered by the public's attitude towards civil servants – faced with constant pressure, complaints, resentment – they are often undervalued and often criticised. The notion of bureaucracy, which is often pejoratively perceived, has also lost its meaning[38] .

It should be borne in mind that it is not possible nowadays to shape the service relationship in the way it was under the 1922 Act on the State Civil Service. It is noticeable – throughout the public service and to an increasing extent – a phenomenon of the so-called "laborisation", i.e. the inclusion in the legal status of public officials of elements directly modelled on those of employees (this concerns issues of: maternity, labour protection or freedom of association in trade unions). However – and this should be noted – official relations show categorical differences in relation to the employment relationship, consisting in

36 Report of the Head of the Civil Service on the state of the civil service and on the implementation of the tasks of the civil service for 2021, s. 11 (accessed: https://www.bing.com/search?q=sprawozdanie+szefa+służby+cywilnej+za+2021&cvid=e7f8074fd2714d1193c660abb932e9f7&aqs=edge.0.69i59i450l8...8.704212j0j4&FORM=ANAB01&PC=DCTS, 19.10.2022).

37 Report of the Head of the Civil Service on the state of the civil service and on the implementation of the tasks of the civil service for 2021, pp. 11–12.

38 See also: E. Łętowska, J. Łętowski, *O państwie prawa, administrowaniu i sądach w okresie przekształceń ustrojowych*, Warszawa 1995, pp. 167–171.

particular of an increased degree of availability and increased requirements in terms of the conditions of performing duties[39] .

Within the framework of this study, several directions for change should be indicated. The construction of a professional and politically neutral civil service corps requires a precise specification of the catalogue of positions appointed under a political "key", and their separation from those that will be filled through open and competitive recruitment. As regards managerial positions in the civil service, consideration could be given to filling them from among civil servants (i.e. persons employed on the basis of nomination). Achieving this civil servant classification is undoubtedly a difficult challenge. The creation of a professional corps of civil servants should be in the interest of all the political elite, as the quality of the tasks they perform, which are ultimately under the control of the political leadership, depends primarily on the level of qualification of the civil servants[40]. However – according to the report of the Head of the Civil Service in "2021 – the qualification procedure for civil servants applying for nomination was not held for the second time in a row", resulting in the appointment this year of only graduates of the National School of Public Administration who had applied for nomination[41]. As the Head of the Civil Service points out, this is one of the reasons for the decrease in the number of civil servants, which slows down the "process of professionalisation of the civil service"[42]. The Constitution of the Republic of Poland provides for a civil service corps, without excluding managerial positions from it. So, it should be considered that they are an important part of the constitutional reasoning of the civil service. In addition, it is still possible to consider raising the formal requirements directed at persons for senior positions in the civil service. This involves in particular the introduction of so-called "fuses" to guarantee the constitutional standards of the civil service:

---

39 J. Stelina, *Stosunki pracy osób pełniących funkcje organów państwa*, Warszawa 2016, s. 114–115.

40 Similar position: W. Brzozowski, *Rec.: A. Łukaszczuk, Kształtowanie się modelu ustrojowego służby cywilnej w Polsce,* Warszawa 2014, Państwo i Prawo No. 4 (2015), p. 116.

41 Report of the Head of the Civil Service on the state of the civil service and on the implementation of the tasks of the civil service for 2021, p. 12.

42 Ibid.

1. a ban on political party affiliation (e.g. at least 5 years before taking up office, which would be conducive to guaranteeing constitutional political neutrality).
2. in terms of experience and professional education in the field (e.g. at least 5 years of experience in a managerial position, which in turn serves to reinforce the professional nature of the service).

It is important to verify the employee's (civil servant's) skills in terms of qualifications and professional preparation and to create appropriate conditions to guarantee the stability of the employment relationship, the acquisition (upgrading) of skills, as well as mechanisms for the assessment of professional preparation (e.g. through preparatory service or periodic appraisals). Changes are needed to make the process of selecting officials and their working time more flexible, to indicate – in a clear and convincing way to the candidates for officials – the paths of promotion and professional development, as well as changes to remuneration rules. To a certain extent, this will serve to rebuild the thinking of public administration in terms of firstly serving, and secondly, naturally, a place creating a transparent – and importantly real in practice – career path[43] .

The draft law on amending the Civil Service Act and certain other acts[44] may serve as a stimulus for these considerations. It is reasonable to establish a team of a wide range of specialists (theoreticians and practicing administrators) in order to create a single civil servants' code, which would contain, on the one hand, principles concerning all employees (civil servants) employed in public administration, and, on the other hand, distinctiveness concerning particular employee pragmatics.

43 See also: J. Korczak, *Refleksje…*, s. 173 [J. Korczak, *Thoughts on…*, p. 173].
44 https://legislacja.rcl.gov.pl/projekt/12352552 (date of access, 4.02.2023).

Aleksandra Syryt

The Constitutional Features of the Civil Service: Some Observations in the Light of the Case Law of the Constitutional Tribunal

1. Introduction

The centenary of the Polish Civil Service provides an opportunity to reflect on this institution from different perspectives. Undoubtedly, from the point of view of the hierarchical structure of the legal system, the constitutional aspect is essential since it sets the framework for the formulation of legal solutions and creates a certain standard for the bodies that create and apply the law. This article aims to recall the constitutional provisions on the Civil Service and to explain, based on the case law of the Constitutional Tribunal, what the constitutional functions of the Civil Service are and how they are to be understood in the context of the functioning of a particular institution, as well as what characteristics the Civil Service should have in order to fulfil the norm enshrined in the Constitution of the Republic of Poland. With this in mind, it should be stressed that the purpose of this paper is not to analyse the legal provisions on the Civil Service and, thus, to check whether the legislator has developed the constitutional provisions correctly. This paper aims to identify and recall the constitutional norms governing the Constitution and functioning of the Polish Civil Service, taking into account the characteristics of the Civil Service and its functions.

2. The Constitutional Basis of the Civil Service and the Right to Good Administration

Art. 153 sec. 1 of the Constitution of the Republic of Poland[1] states that "In order to ensure the professional, reliable, impartial and politically neutral performance of the functions of the State, there shall be a body of civil servants in the offices of the State administration." Pursuant to sec. 2 of that article, the Prime Minister heads the Civil Service[2].

---

1 Constitution of the Republic of Poland of 2 April 1997 (Journal of Laws No. 78, item 483, as amended).

2 See more, e.g., D. Dudek, *Komentarz do art. 153*, in: ed. M. Safjan, L. Bosek, *Konstytucja RP. Komentarz. T. II*, Warszawa 2016, Legalis.

The Civil Service is part of the constitutional system of government administration. It is a separate structure under the authority of the President of the Council of Ministers to ensure the proper performance of state tasks in government offices. The constitutionalisation of the Civil Service develops the programmatic norm derived from the Preamble to the Constitution of the Republic of Poland, which obliges it to ensure the reliable and efficient functioning of public institutions. It is linked to the concept of the state as a common good. It also has to do with the right to good administration[3]. The Constitutional Tribunal has confirmed this, explaining that the primary objective of the stability of employment in the Civil Service is to guarantee citizens the right to good administration[4].

The right to good administration can be considered a legal category that defines a right of citizens, the subject of which is the public administration[5]. These powers are designed to protect individual rights and relate to administrative procedures' regularity, fairness and efficiency. The right to good administration can also be defined as a para-legal category by considering the right to good administration as a non-binding legal principle[6]. Although the right to good administration is

---

3 See more about the right to good administration, e.g., Z. Niewiadomski, *Prawo do dobrej administracji – aspekty procesowe, ustrojowe i materialne*, in: *Prawo do dobrej administracji*, Warszawa 2003; I. Lipowicz, *Prawo obywatela do dobrej administracji*, in: ed. R. Hauser, L. Nawacki, Księga Jubileuszowa Jerzego Świątkiewicza. Państwo w służbie obywateli, Warszawa 2005, p. 2; A. I. Jackiewicz, *Prawo do dobrej administracji jako standard europejski*, Toruń 2008; M. Krzyżanowska-Mierzewska, *Dobra administracja a orzecznictwo Europejskiego Trybunału Praw Człowieka*, Warszawa 2007; K. Rożek, *Prawo do dobrej administracji w orzecznictwie Europejskiego Trybunału Praw Człowieka*, Roczniki Administracji i Prawa, nr XVIII (1), pp. 29–47.

4 See judgment of the Constitutional Tribunal of 14 June 2011, ref. Kp 1/11, OTK ZU No. 5/A/2011, item 41.

5 In the judgment of 18 December 2007, ref. SK 54/05 (OTK ZU No. 11/A/2007, item 158), the Constitutional Tribunal pointed out, however, that "the duties of public authorities resulting from the constitutional principle of a democratic state ruled by law and the rule of law should be considered the basis and standard of "good administration", however, this is not tantamount to granting (to each) individual the constitutional, subjective "right to good administration", understood as a set of procedural rights similar to administrative proceedings to a court trial, in which the parties are entitled to far-reaching guarantees".

6 P. Żuradzki, *Prawo do dobrej administracji w polskim porządku prawnym na tle Europejskiego kodeksu dobrej administracji*, in: ed. M. Kępa. M. Marszał, *Duch praw w krajach Europy Środkowo-Wschodniej*, Wrocław 2016, p. 53; D. Tykwińska-Rutkowska, [in:] *Leksykon prawa administracyjnego*, eds. E. Bojanowski, K. Żukowski, Warszawa 2009, pp. 285–286.

not explicitly expressed in the Polish Constitution, it can be reconstructed from constitutional provisions, notably Article 2 of the Constitution (the principle of a democratic state of law, including the order to build citizens' trust in the state and its laws) and Article 7 of the Constitution (principle of legalism requiring public authorities to act on the basis and within the limits of the law).

The case law of the Constitutional Tribunal shows that the right to good administration should be understood as the right to an effective administration, acting solely based on the law and within its limits, without undue pressure. The administration has a role to play in serving the citizen. In situations where the completion of the document verification process is prevented for reasons beyond the control of the party concerned, it must provide professional and reliable assistance. The lack of such assistance, which results in the parties to the procedure being deprived of the opportunity to defend their rights, is highly unacceptable and cannot violate the human dignity protected by the Constitution, which the public administration also upholds[7]. The rule of law governs the right to good administration, the principles of non-discrimination and equal treatment, proportionality, impartiality, consistency and legitimate expectations, fairness, openness (transparency), effectiveness, utility and privacy.

The Civil Service, as defined in Article 153 of the Constitution, is vital for realising the right to good administration, and it is one of the guarantors of good administration. The right of citizens to equal access to public services can be linked to the requirements imposed on the Civil Service (Article 60 of the Constitution of the Republic of Poland).

In this context, it should be noted that the concept of the Civil Service can be understood in different ways. Firstly, it can be understood as a system of values, institutions and procedures designed to ensure state functions' professional and non-political performance. Secondly, from the staff's point of view, the Civil Service can be understood as a Civil Service comprised of employees and civil servants[8].

---

7 See e.g, judgments of the Constitutional Tribunal of 15 November 2010, ref. P 32/09, OTK ZU No. 9/A/2010, item 100; 15 April 2003, ref. SK 4/02, OTK ZU No. 4/A/2003, item 31.

8 See e.g., J. Itrich-Drabarek, who believes that "civil service is a separate team of people employed under public or private law in order to perform tasks specified in law, guided by a specific system of norms, values and procedures designed to serve the society and maintain essential functions of the state", J. Itrich-Drabarek, *Służba cywilna w Europie Środkowo-Wschodniej. Implementacja norm, procedur i wartości europejskiej służby cywilnej*, Warszawa 2013, p. 17.

Therefore, it is possible to analyse the characteristics of the Civil Service and the values to which it must adhere.

3. Constitutional Objectives for the Establishment of the Civil Service and the Principles for Achieving Them

Art 153 sec. 1 states the purpose for which the Civil Service is established. The primary purpose of this provision is to indicate how a specific group of persons forming the Civil Service will perform the functions of the State. The activities concerned must be professional, reliable, impartial and politically neutral.

Interestingly, however, the legislator has not given the Civil Service any guarantees as to its organisational independence and the independence of its staff. On the contrary, it has placed the Civil Service within the agencies of the State administration, thus making it part of the system of that administration. The fact that the Civil Service is headed by the President of the Council of Ministers is also characteristic of the structure of this unit in relation to the public administration. This makes it possible to regulate the civil service model in a way that takes account of its hierarchical structure and the subordination of the individual to the civil servant.

From the point of view of the characteristics of the civil service, one may wonder what the list of "professional competence, integrity, impartiality and political neutrality" in Article 153 sec. 1 of the Constitution refers to. A linguistic analysis shows that it is a question of the qualities that relate to the performance of State functions in State agencies. However, it should not be forgotten that those who perform these tasks are specific actors who must act in a certain way. This makes it possible to transfer the characteristics of the activities to the characteristics of the entities.

With this in mind, it must be recognised that the civil service must be professional, reliable, impartial and politically neutral.

3.1. Professional Nature

The professional nature of the Civil Service is intended to ensure professionalism in the performance of State duties. The doctrine recognises that this characteristic is linked to the organisation of the unit as an organised and permanent structure within the system of public authority and to the recruitment and status of its members. The primary criteria, in this case, are relevant education and qualifications. This results from the assumption that qualified civil servants in charge of public functions should be free from political influence[9]. The Constitutional Tribunal has confirmed this approach, stating that the professional performance of duties requires, above all, appropriate qualifications and professional preparation. In order to implement a particular constitutional norm, it is necessary to establish proper conditions to ensure that candidates for public office are suitably qualified, as well as a mechanism to verify their professional preparation and to recruit them for specific vacancies in government agencies. The Tribunal explained that "professional competence thus refers to the professional skills required by law of employees or civil servants in general, whereas the performance of a particular post requires a specific qualification. For this reason, above all, 'professional qualifications' cannot be understood as a mere formal condition for the acceptance or appointment to a particular post. The acquisition of appropriate qualifications should be verified before admission to the service and subsequently during the performance of the duties of a service member, when they reliably carry out the tasks entrusted to them. The so-called competition provided for by the law is also intended to verify qualifications in relation to the requirements of a particular post"[10].

The Tribunal also pointed out that the professional performance of State duties requires the recruitment of persons who consider the performance of those duties to be a profession. The civil service must, therefore, not be a purely temporary occupation but a permanent source of income and a job which offers qualified persons the opportunity to pursue a career. However, professional preparation should not be confined to the entry phase but should be developed later through continuous improvement and updating of skills[11].

The professionalism of public service must be guaranteed by ensuring professional stability and by establishing transparent rules for recruitment and the validation of acquired knowledge and experience[12].

3.2. Reliability

The concept of fairness in Art. 153 sec. 1 of the Constitution of the Republic of Poland, is not explicitly addressed in the case law of the Constitutional Tribunal.

---

9 See more L. Sinkowska, *Status prawny członka korpusu służby cywilnej*, Toruń 2002, p. 9.

10 See judgment of the Constitutional Tribunal of 12 December 2002, ref. K 9/02, OTK ZU No. 7/A/2002, item 94.

11 Ibidem.

12 J. Jagielski, K. Rączka, *Komentarz do ustawy o służbie cywilnej*, Warszawa 2001, pp. 15–16.

The Tribunal treats it as a constitutional value referring to public authorities' activities and state bodies' powers[13]. The case law of the Constitutional Tribunal repeatedly refers to the norm of a fair trial or due process. The term "fair" itself is not explained; it should be given a colloquial meaning. Synonyms for this term include caring, good, skilled, competent, impeccable, conscientious, responsible, hard-working, decent, exemplary, verbal, firm, honest and reliable[14]. Reliability means the performance of activities in a good, conscientious and competent manner, in accordance with accepted rules and principles of conduct.

3.3. Impartiality

The functions of the State shall be performed impartially. Impartiality in this context is to be understood as an attitude and approach that is objective, unbiased, fair and impartial, respectful of the rule of equity and objective justice, non-favourable and non-discriminatory. On the other hand, impartiality is the internal attitude of a public officeholder, who is not an advocate of any party or interest.

As regards public administration, the Constitutional Tribunal states that impartiality implies the duty to consider and decide on the interests of the various actors objectively, without pressure or personal views or sympathies. The Tribunal also affirms that "the permanent structure of the executive - constituted by the agencies of the State administration - which is at the interface with the citizens, must not show sensitivity and susceptibility to the influences of different political forces (…) but must be guided by a properly understood common and general interest, which prevails over individual and particular interests"[15].

As the doctrine maintains, in terms of impartiality, no public authority or official acting properly in the public interest can assume *a priori* that certain beliefs are merely correct, accurate, just and acceptable or objectionable, especially when they are compatible or incompatible with the personal beliefs and views or attitudes of the person exercising the public function in question[16].

---

13 See instead of many, e.g., the judgment of the Constitutional Tribunal of 30 May 2007, ref. SK 68/06, OTK ZU No. 6/A/2007, item 53.

14 See instead of many, e.g., the judgment of the Constitutional Tribunal of 30 May 2007, ref. SK 68/06, OTK ZU No. 6/A/2007, item 53.

15 See judgment of the Constitutional Tribunal of 12 December 2002, ref. K 9/02, OTK ZU No. 7/A/2002, item 94.

16 Zob. D. Dudek, *Zasada bezstronności władz publicznych w sprawach przekonań i wolność ich wyrażania w życiu publicznym*, in: ed. J. Krukowski, M. Sitarz, H. Stawniak, *Katolickie zasady relacji Państwo-Kościół a prawo polskie*, Lublin 2015, pp. 142 i n.

This means that impartiality is linked to the principle of equality before the law (Article 31 sec. 1 of the Constitution) and the prohibition of discrimination (Article 32 sec. 2 of the Constitution).

The requirement of impartiality is not the same as the imperative of absolute independence of a member of the civil service. However, any dependence can only be internal, linked to the civil service structure. It is, therefore, a question of organisational and departmental issues and not of substantive measures.

In the Tribunal's case-law, the issue of impartial performance of the State's tasks has not been overly developed, unlike another feature of the corps' activities, which is political neutrality. The legislature in the Constitution made it clear that the civil service is to be based on professionalism, integrity, impartiality and apoliticality. This is because it aims to ensure the highest substantive, legal and ethical level in performing public tasks. In this way, it is possible to ensure continuity and stability in the performance of public authority functions, regardless of the changing balance of political forces as a result of elections, which have a leading influence on the staffing of leadership positions in government administration.

3.4. Political Neutrality

The concepts of neutrality and impartiality, although *prima facie* seem synonymous, have different meanings in Polish constitutional law. This difference is particularly clearly explained when interpreting Article 25 sec. 2 of the Constitution concerning impartiality in matters of religious, philosophical and ideological beliefs[17].

Turning to the issue of political neutrality, it should be noted that in its previous case-law, the Constitutional Tribunal has recognised neutrality as an element of impartiality. However, it clarified that political neutrality does not mean the absence of holding political views but only the renunciation of their manifestation in official activities[18].

The Constitutional Tribunal also stressed that political neutrality in the performance of state tasks can be ensured by such a statutory formation of the mechanism for the appointment and operation of the civil service that will guarantee the absence of any, even temporary, possibility of interference in this

---

17 Zob. M. Olszówka, *Komentarz do art. 25*, in: ed. M. Safajan, L. Bosek, *Konstytucja RP. Komentarz, T. I*, Warszawa 2016 i przywołana tam literatura.

18 See judgment of the Constitutional Tribunal of 17 November 1998, file ref. K 42/97, OTK No. 7/1998, item 113.

regard by politicians in power. Therefore, this mechanism should be free from any interference from politics or attempts to impose specific solutions[19].

The Constitution does not define the term "political neutrality," although this requirement applies to various public positions. As a rule, it refers to institutionalised political relations. Political neutrality is expressed through the prohibition of membership in a political party and the rule prohibiting public activities that are incompatible with the constitutional position or dignity of the office in question.

This issue develops the case-law of the Constitutional Tribunal, from which it follows that political neutrality (apoliticality) implies, first of all, that civil servants must not be determined in any way in their actions by their own political, religious, ideological beliefs, party or group interests. That is, the official's attitude and action is to be objectified and distanced. According to the CT, the apolitical nature of a civil servant should be understood in such a way that they do not take part in the widely understood political game and are free in their functioning from the "peculiar 'complex' of any party, political option, ideology, religion, determinants and conditions." Political neutrality of the civil service should be seen not only as independence from parties, political parties but also independence from the influence of other organisations"[20].

It should be noted that the requirement of political neutrality of the civil service applies both to the attitudes and conduct of a member of the service corps, as well as to the purpose and manner of the structure in carrying out the tasks of the State. Although the head of the civil service corps is the Prime Minister of the Council of Ministers, the civil service cannot be the implementer of the interests of political groups. It should pursue the public interest[21]. The Constitutional Tribunal indicates that the order of political neutrality in the performance of state tasks applies to members of the Civil Service. In particular, it applies to neutrality towards the interests of political groupings and disputes waged by these groupings or individual politicians. Article 153 sec. 1 of the Constitution states that politicians are excluded from shaping the organisational framework, control and evaluation of the Civil Service since the politician is the Prime Minister, who exercises executive authority over the civil service

19 Judgment of the Constitutional Tribunal of 12 December 2002, ref. K 9/02, OTK ZU No. 7/A/2002, item 94.

20 See judgment of the Constitutional Tribunal of 10 April 2002, ref. K 26/00, OTK ZU No. 2/A/2002, item 18.

21 See in more detail, the judgment of the Constitutional Tribunal of 28 April 1999, ref. K 3/99, OTK ZU No. 4/1999, item 73.

and official authority over members of its corps. From this, it follows that the law can facilitate insight into civil service matters for politicians of different options, including those from opposition groups, and balance the influence of democratically legitimised political orientations on systemic solutions in the civil service[22].

4. Summary

These findings recalled that the creation of a civil service corps which meets constitutional requirements facilitates the realisation of the right to good administration and is thus able to realise the principle of the common good (Art. 1 of the Constitution) and to protect the freedoms and rights of individuals within the territory of the Republic of Poland.

The constitutional legislator has made it clear in the Constitution that the civil service is to be based on professionalism, integrity, impartiality and apoliticality since its purpose is to ensure the highest substantive, legal, and ethical standards in performing public duties. This will ensure continuity and stability in the exercise of public authority, irrespective of the changing balance of political power resulting from elections, which is a critical factor in the performance of the functions of public administration. This approach is confirmed by the Constitutional Tribunal, which has held that all objectives indicated in Art. 153, section 1 of the Constitution, are to be pursued together, and their achievement is guaranteed by law. Their implementation is only possible through the creation of an appropriate statutory mechanism which will ensure that these tasks are carried out by civil servants who are adequately prepared to do so[23].

The CT judicial practice regarding the civil service covers a variety of issues. There is no shortage of references to the characteristics of the activities of the civil service corps and, thus, the characteristics of the corps itself.

A review of the judgments of the Constitutional Tribunal allows us to confirm that the justifications of the tribunal's judgments in the field of the civil service focus – as far as the characteristics of the civil service are concerned – on two values derived from the Art. 153, section 1 of the Polish Constitution. Firstly, it is the professional nature of the corps, and secondly, its political neutrality. Although mentioned in the rulings, reliability and impartiality do not have any particular development, which can be explained by the fact that these concepts

---

22 Ibidem.

23 See judgment of the Constitutional Tribunal of 12 December 2002, ref. K 9/02, OTK ZU No. 7/A/2002, item 94.

have such an established meaning in the jurisprudence of the CT and in law that there is no need for further clarification on these aspects. By making only a linguistic interpretation, one can understand what the reliable and impartial actions of the corps in connection with the performance of the tasks of the state should consist of.

It seems that the Constitutional Tribunal, when discussing the civil service, attributes a large role to the issue of the political neutrality of the civil service corps. This is confirmed by the fact that in the justifications of the Tribunal's judgments on this matter, it is repeated that political neutrality is the foundation of the civil service on which the institution should be developed. It means the civil service system must create objective, clear, and precise criteria limiting political decisions' discretionary nature.

Although the jurisprudence of the CT relates primarily to political neutrality, other characteristics listed in Art. 153, section 1 of the Constitution cannot be forgotten when shaping a system. It must not be forgotten that, for the proper implementation of the constitutional norm, all of indicated in Art. 153, section 1 of the Constitution, objectives are to be pursued together, and their achievement is guaranteed by law. Only in such a systemic and holistic approach will it be possible to shape a civil service corps system that meets the conditions set by the legislator.

Adam Wróbel

Final Conviction for an Intentional Crime or an Intentional Fiscal Crime as Grounds for Ineligibility for Employment in the Civil Service

1. Introduction

The research subject under consideration is the issue of a final conviction for an intentional crime and an intentional fiscal crime as a basis for inability to be employed in the civil service – included in the provisions of the statute of 21 November 2008 on the civil service[1]. It is important from the point of view of strengthening the rule of law, as well as civil servant integrity-reliability. The scientific analysis-narrative leads through the issues of employment in the civil service, intentional crime or intentional fiscal crime, final conviction. In the conclusions, the *de lege ferenda* postulate is presented.

A final conviction for an intentional crime or an intentional fiscal crime has negative consequences in the context of employment in the civil service. I.e:

- a person may not be employed in the civil service if he has been convicted of an intentional crime or an intentional fiscal crime by a final judgment[2] (which follows from art. 4 pt. 3 S.C.S.);
- the Head of the Civil Service may not be a person who has been convicted by a final judgment of an intentional crime or an intentional fiscal crime (which follows from art. 11 par. 1 pt. 3 S.C.S.);
- the employment relationship of a civil servant terminates in the event of a final conviction for an intentional crime or an intentional fiscal crime (art. 70 pt. 4 S.C.S.).

The view should be shared that this attribute of "no criminal record" of a member of the civil service corps must be in evidence not only at the stage of

---

1 Journal of Laws 2021, item 1233 unified text, as amended (hereinafter: S.C.S.).

2 This is also recalled in the judicature; verdict of the Supreme Court of 18 December 2003, I PK 157/03, LEX No. 127823.

recruitment to the civil service, but also while remaining in its structures[3]. Thus, not having been convicted of an intentional crime or an intentional fiscal crime is – firstly – an absolute selection limit[4], and – secondly – an impassable obstacle to continuing employment in the civil service. In the second case, it is essential that the civil servant's conviction occurs during the course of employment[5] .

2. Employment in the Civil Service

A person employed in the civil service is:

- a civil service employee, i.e. a person employed on the basis of an employment contract in accordance with the principles set out in the statute of civil service (art. 3 pt. 1 S.C.S.);
- a civil servant, i.e. a person employed on the basis of nomination in accordance with the rules laid down in the statute of civil service (art. 3 pt. 2 S.C.S.);
- a member of the civil service corps, i.e. a civil service employee and also a civil servant (as in art. 3 pt. 1 and 2 S.C.S.), and a person employed in a senior position in the civil service (art. 3 pt. 3 S.C.S.).

Pursuant to art. 10 par. 3 S.C.S., the Head of the Civil Service is appointed – and dismissed – by the Prime Minister.

In matters concerning the employment relationship in the civil service, not regulated in the CSA, the provisions of the Labour Code, as well as other provisions of the labour law, apply (art. 9 par. 1 S.C.S.). It should been remember that in Polish law the employment relationship is regulated by the provisions of the Labour Code and other labour law provisions. Accordingly, employment in the civil service has the nature of an employment relationship, taking as its formal basis:

---

3 W. Drobny, [in:] M. Mazuryk, P. Zuzankiewicz, W. Drobny, *Ustawa o służbie cywilnej. Komentarz*, Warszawa 2012, LEX/el., commentary to. 4, pt 13.

4 See the verdict of the Supreme Court of 15 March 2011, I PK 192/10, LEX No. 1162172.

5 W. Witoszko, [in:] *Ustawa o służbie cywilnej. Komentarz*, K. W. Baran (ed.), Warszawa 2021, LEX/el., commentary to art. 70, pt 5. As aptly indicates K. Rączka, a flagrant manifestation of an infringement of the legal order, consisting of the commission of an intentional crime, should result the absolute, automatic termination of the employment relationship; K. Rączka, [in:] J. Jagielski, K. Rączka, *Ustawa o służbie cywilnej. Komentarz*, Warszawa 2010, LEX/el. commentary to art. 70, pt. 7.

- employment contract, in the case of civil service employees (which follows from art. 3 pt. 1 S.C.S.)[6],
- nomination, with regard to civil servants (as follows from art. 3 pt. 2 S.C.S.),
- appointment, in the case of persons employed in a senior position in the civil service (which follows from art. 53a par. 1 – 4a S.C.S.), which also applies to the Head of the Civil Service (*vide* art. 10 par. 3 S.C.S.).

In conjunction with art. 9 par. 1 S.C.S. – as above – the employment relationship should be understood as it is defined in art. 22 § 1 of the Labour Code[7], i.e. the relationship in which the employee undertakes to perform work of a specified kind for the employer and under its direction, and at a place and time designated by the employer, and the employer – to employ the employee for remuneration. An employee is – according to art. 2 L.C. – a person employed on the basis of (1) an employment contract, (2) an appointment, (3) an election, (4) a nomination or, (5) a cooperative employment contract. The first, second and fourth grounds of employment set out in the article directly quoted above refer to an employee's employment in the civil service. Therefore, a person employed on the basis of a civil law contract is not *de lege lata* employed in the civil service according to the Civil Service Statute. As it is indicated in the judicature, in order to determine whether in a given situation the prerequisites constituting the code term „employee" have occurred, the statutory definitions from art. 2 and art. 22 § 1 L.C. should be treated jointly. The juxtaposition of the content of both provisions orders to assume that an employee is a person who, by means of one of the legal actions listed in art. 2 L.C., has established an employment relationship characterized by the features indicated in art. 22 § 1 L.C.[8].

3. A Final Conviction for a Prohibited Act That Is an Obstacle to Employment

The legislator specifies the prohibited act for which conviction is an obstacle to the perpetrator's employment in the civil service. It is a intentional crime or an intentional fiscal crime; that is, a prohibited act:

---

6 Cf. the verdict of the Supreme Court of 25 May 2016. II PK 185/15, LEX No. 2069441.

7 Journal of Laws 2022, item 1510 unified text, as amended (hereinafter: L.C.).

8 Verdict of the Supreme Administrative Court of 13 March 2007, I OSK 630/06, LEX No. 330453. Cf. verdict of the Supreme Court of 18 May 2006, II UK 164/05, LEX No. 192462 and verdict of the Court of Appeals in Łódź of 3 September 2014, III AUa 2070/ 13, LEX No. 1511671.

- committed by a human; a perpetrator who is at least 17 years of age (in the case of crimes – art. 10 § 1 of the Criminal Code[9], fiscal crimes – art. 5 § 1 of the Fiscal Criminal Code[10]), or *in extremis* 15 or 14 years of age (optionally in specific situations when specific crimes are committed, as defined by art. 10 § 2 or appropriately 2a C.C.);
- the elements of which are defined in a criminal statute (art. 115 § 1 C.C.); in the case of fiscal crimes in the Fiscal Criminal Code (art. 53 § 1 of the F.C.C.);
- of social harmfulness higher than negligible (art. 1 § 2 C.C, art. 1 § 2 F.C.C.);
- by the statute in force at the time it was committed (art. 1 § 1 C.C, art. 1 § 1 F.C.C.);
- culpable, the core of which, in addition to the chargeability of the act, are the elements of the act on the subjective side; in the case under consideration, these relate solely and exclusively to the intentional form of the act; in the case of crimes, a felony may be committed only intentionally (art. 8 C.C.), a misdemeanour may be committed intentionally as well as unintentionally if the statute so provides (art. 8 C.C.); while a fiscal crime may be committed intentionally as well as unintentionally if the Fiscal Criminal Code so provides (art. 4 § 1 F.C.C.). The intentional commission of a prohibited act fulfilling the elements of a crime or a fiscal crime means that the perpetrator has the intention to commit it, i.e. he wants to commit it, or anticipating the possibility of committing it, accepts it (respectively art. 9 § 1 C.C. or art. 4 § 2 F.C.C.);
- unlawful-illegal; for it may turn out in a specific situation, that an act fulfilling the elements of a crime, or a fiscal crime is not a prohibited act[11].

An obstacle for employment in the civil service (as follows from art. 4, pt. 3 and art. 11, par. 1, point 3 S.C.S.) or continuation of employment (as follows from art. 70, pt. 4 S.C.S.) is therefore not an offence or a fiscal offence, or a disciplinary offense, or even a conviction for an intentional crime or an intentional fiscal crime, but not final, or a final conviction for a crime or a fiscal crime, but

9 Journal of Laws 2022, item 1138 unified text, as amended (hereinafter: C.C.).

10 Journal of Laws 2022, item 859 unified text, as amended (hereinafter: F.C.C.).

11 Cf. A. Wróbel, *Przedawnienie przestępstw funkcjonariuszy publicznych nieściganych z przyczyn politycznych (art. 44 Konstytucji Rzeczypospolitej Polskiej)* [in:] ed. B. Przywora, A. Rogacka-Łukasik, K. Skotnicki *Z, prawem ustrojowym porównawczym przez ponad półwiecze. Księga Jubileuszowa dedykowana Profesorowi Marianowi Grzybowskiemu z okazji 55-lecia pracy naukowej*, Częstochowa 2022, p. 657.

unintentional[12]. However, as M. Lekston rightly points out, committing a offence or a fiscal offence may have an impact on the ascertainment whether a candidate for the civil service corps meets the condition of good repute[13], referred to in art. 4 pt. 5 S.C.S. Also H. Szewczyk notes in a similar context, that although committing an unintentional crime is not an obstacle to employment in the civil service, *De lege lata,* however, persons who have committed an unintentional crime, do not usually fulfil another statutory requirement – in the form of having an unblemished opinion and therefore should not be members of the civil service[14].

The legislator also stipulates the impossibility of employment in a specific position – in the event of a final conviction for an intentional crime or a fiscal crime – in several other statuses. Just to give an example, it could be to mention the impossibility of employment in the position of: professional diplomat (art. 14 pt. 3 and art. 16 par. 3 pt. 2 of the statute of 21 January 2021 on foreign service[15]), foreign employee of the foreign service (art. 18 pt. 3 F.S.A.), domestic employee of the foreign service (art. 20 pt. 3 F.S.A.), Head of the Foreign Service (art. 11 par. 1 pt. 3 F.S.A.), President of the Government Agency for Strategic Reserves (art. 35 par. 1 pt. 4 of the statute of 17 December 2020 on Strategic Reserves[16]), the President of the Military Property Agency (art. 5 pt. 4 of the statute of 10 July 2015 on the Military Property Agency[17]), the President of the Polish Space Agency (art. 9 par. 1 pt. 3 of the statute of 26 September 2014 on the Polish Space Agency[18]), the Vice-President of the Polish Space Agency (art. 10 par. 4 pt.

---

12 As M. Lekston aptly claims, the rigour of non-criminal record is related to crimes and fiscal crimes of an intentional nature, which *a contrario* means that these acts committed unintentionally will not exclude the possibility of employment in the structures of the civil service corps; M. Lekston, [in:] *Ustawa o służbie cywilnej. Komentarz,* K. W. Baran (ed.), Warszawa 2021, LEX/el., commentary to art. 4, pt 2.3.4. Similarly J. Jagielski, [in:] K. Rączka, J. Jagielski, *Ustawa o służbie cywilnej. Komentarz,* Warszawa 2010, LEX/el., commentary to art. 4, pt 4 and H. Szewczyk, *Stosunki pracy w służbie cywilnej,* Warszawa 2010, LEX/el., chapter 3, pt 3.4 and A. Jezierska-Markocka, [in:] A. Jezierska-Markocka, M. Markocki, *Służba cywilna. Stosunek pracy. Zarządzanie zasobami ludzkimi,* Warszawa 2016, Legalis/el., chapter 3, pt 1.3.

13 M. Lekston, *op. cit.*, commentary to art. 4, pt 2.3.2. [M. Lexton, *op. cit.*, commentary to art. 4, pt. 2.3.2.].

14 H. Szewczyk, *op. cit.*, chapter 3, pt 3.4. [H. Szewczyk, *op. cit*, chapter 3, pt. 3.4.].

15 Journal of Laws 2022, item 1076 unified text, as amended (hereinafter: F.S.A.).

16 Journal of Laws 2022, item 637 unified text, as amended.

17 Journal of Laws 2021, item 303 unified text, as amended.

18 Journal of Laws 2020, 1957 unified text (hereinafter: P.S.A.).

3 P.S.A.), the director of the field branch of the Polish Space Agency (art. 11 par. 2 pt. 4 P.S.A.), the President of the Agency and the Deputy President of the Agency for the Restructuring and Modernisation of Agriculture (art. 8 par. 4 pt. 4 of the statute of 9 May 2008 on the Agency for the Restructuring and Modernisation of Agriculture[19]), the head of an organisational unit at the Head Office of the Agency for the Restructuring and Modernisation of Agriculture and his deputy, the director of a regional branch and his deputy, the advisor to the President of the Agency for the Restructuring and Modernisation of Agriculture and the head of a district office (art. 9 par. 4 pt. 4 R.M.A.A.), the Chief Inspector of Environmental Protection (art. 4 par. 4a pt. 4 of the statute of 20 July 1991 on Environmental Protection Inspection[20]), the voivodal environmental inspector (art. 3 par. 3 pt. 3 E.P.I.), the Inspector of Environmental Protection Inspection (art. 8e par. 1 pt. 4 E.P.I.), the commander of the State Protection Service or his deputy (art. 11 par. 4 pt. 5 of the statute of 8 December 2017 on the State Protection Service[21], art. 107 par. 1 pt. 5 S.P.S.), in the State Protection Service (art. 68, art. 107 par. 1 pt. 5 S.P.S.), the President of the Higher Mining Authority (art. 165 par. 3 pt. 4 of the statute of 9 June 2011, Geological and Mining Law[22]), President of the Management Board of the National Fund for Environmental Protection and Water Management (art. 400i par. 4 pt. 4 of the statute of 27 April 2001, Environmental Protection Law[23]), President of the State Atomic Energy Agency (art. 109 par. 3a pt. 4 of the statute of 29 November 2000, Atomic Law[24]), Chief Pharmaceutical Inspector (art. 111 par. 3 pt. 4 of the statute of 6 September 2001, Pharmaceutical Law[25]), President of the Civil Aviation Authority (art. 20 par. 4 pt. 4 of the statute of 3 July 2002, Aviation Law[26]), President of the Polish Committee for Standardisation (art. 16 par. 3 pt. 4 of the statute of 12 September 2002 on standardisation[27]), the President of the Government Legislation Centre (art. 14e par. 2a pt. 4 of the statute of 8 August 1996 on the Council of Ministers[28]), the Chief Sanitary Inspector (art. 8 par. 6 pt. 4 of the statute of

19 Journal of Laws 2019, item 1505 unified text, as amended (hereinafter: R.M.A.A.).
20 Journal of Laws 2020, item 995 unified text, as amended (hereinafter: E.P.I.).
21 Journal of Laws 2021, item 575 unified text, as amended (hereinafter: S.P.S.).
22 Journal of Laws 2022, item 1072 unified text, as amended.
23 Journal of Laws 2021, item 1973 unified text, as amended.
24 Journal of Laws 2021, item 1941 unified text, as amended.
25 Journal of Laws 2021, item 1977 unified text, as amended.
26 Journal of Laws 2022, item 1235 unified text.
27 Journal of Laws 2015, item 1483 unified text.
28 Journal of Laws 2022, item 1188 unified text.

14 March 1985 on the State Sanitary Inspection[29]), the President of the Office of Technical Inspection (art. 38 par. 1a pt. 4 of the statute of 21 December 2000 on technical inspection).[30]

A final conviction for a crime or a fiscal crime takes place when the guilt of its perpetrator, the accused, is established by a final court verdict – as indicated in the principle of the presumption of innocence in art. 42 par. 3 of the Constitution of the Republic of Poland[31] and art. 5 § 1 of the Code of Criminal Procedure[32]. As the doctrine rightly notes, a verdict is final if no ordinary means of appeal, e.g. an appeal, is available against it[33]; in other words, as noted in the judicature, when there is no longer any legal possibility to challenge it with an ordinary means of appeal[34] .

Therefore, a final conviction of an perpetrator-accused lasts from the day following the day on which the time limit for challenging the conviction with an ordinary appeal expires, until the conviction is expunged – a convicted person whose conviction has been expunged may be employed in the civil service,

---

29 Journal of Laws 2021, item 195 unified text, as amended.

30 Journal of Laws 2021, item 272 unified text, as amended.

31 Journal of Laws 1997, No. 78, item 483, as amended.

32 Journal of Laws 2022, item 1375 unified text, as amended.

33 J. Lang, [in:] *Prawo geodezyjne i kartograficzne. Komentarz*, ed. J. Maćkowiak, T. Myśliński, E. Stefańska, Warszawa 2018, LEX/el., commentary to art. 44, pt 2.

34 Judgment of the Court of Appeals in Warsaw of 19 December 2014, II AKa 441/14, LEX No. 1621228. As the Court of Appeals in Warsaw notes there: thus, a verdict becomes final when: (a) there is no appeal against to it, due to the fact that it was issued by the appellate court as a result of an appeal (art. 426 § 1 of the Code of Criminal Procedure); (b) the time limit for filing a motion for written preparation and service of a justification of the judgment has expired (art. 422 § 1 and 2 of the Code of Criminal Procedure); (c) the time limit for filing an appeal has expired (art. 445 § 1 of the Code of Criminal Procedure); (d) the time limit for appealing against the order of the president of the court to refuse the request for justification of the judgment has expired (art. 422 § 3 of the Code of Criminal Procedure) or on the refusal to accept the means of appeal (art. 429 § 1 of the Code of Criminal Procedure) or the complaint against this ordinance was not upheld; (e) the time limit for lodging a complaint against the decision of the appellate court leaving the mean of appeal unprocessed has expired (art. 430 § 1 of the Code of Criminal Procedure) or the complaint against this decision has not been taken into account; (f) the appellate court has issued a (non-appealable) decision to leave the mean of appeal unprocessed in the event of its withdrawal (art. 432 of the Code of Criminal Procedure). The judgement becomes final after the day on which the time limit for the given procedural action has expired, or, on which the non-appealable judgement of the court has been issued.

as J. Jagielski rightly notes[35]. H. Szewczyk is equally correct in stating that the requirement of not having a criminal record for an intentional crime will be preserved if the punishment for the intentional crime has been expunged[36]. The expungement of a conviction may take place by force of law or by court judgement[37]. As W. Drobny argues, no legal consequences may be drawn from an expunged conviction, and no one has the right to make a charge on this account[38]. B. Przywora also accurately argues that in the event of expungement, there are no formal grounds for refusal to accept or exclusion of persons from the civil service corps[39]. At the moment as a conviction is expunged, it is considered to be non-existent; the entry on the conviction is removed from the register of convicted persons (art. 106 C.C., also in connection with art. 20 § 2 F.C.C.). The expungement of a conviction is a kind of abstraction, a legal fiction which results, that not only the conviction, but also the commission of the crime itself is deemed to have been expunged[40] .

Regarding a conviction for a crime, if under the new statute the act covered by the verdict is no longer prohibited under penalty, the conviction is expunged by operation of law (art. 4 § 4 of C.C.). With regard to a conviction for a fiscal crime, if, under the new statute, the prohibited act covered by the judgment is no longer prohibited under penalty, the conviction is expunged by the power of law and the punishment is deemed to be null and void (art.. 2 § 6 F.C.C.).

The provisions of the Criminal Code concerning the expungement of a conviction apply to crimes defined in the Criminal Code, specific statuses – which also follows from art. 116 C.C. – and, moreover, an overwhelming part of them, respectively[41] to fiscal crimes, as indicated by the content of art. 20 § 2 F.C.C. This is in the case:

35 J. Jagielski, *op. cit.*, commentary to art. 4, pt 4.

36 H. Szewczyk, *op. cit.*, chapter 3, pt 3.4.

37 See W. Drobny, *op. cit.*, LEX/el., commentary to art. 4, pt 14.

38 W. Drobny, [in:] W. Drobny, M. Mazuryk, P. Zuzankiewicz, *Ustawa o służbie cywilnej. Komentarz*, Warszawa 2012, p. 83.

39 Yes, and more extensively, B. Przywora, *Transformacje ustrojowe polskiej służby cywilnej*, Kraków 2012, p. 82.

40 See M. Lekston, *op. cit.*, commentary to art. 4, pt 2.3.6.

41 Appropriate application – as Ł. Chojniak observes – may mean either the application of the provisions of a statute directly, or with modifications resulting from the essence of the institution for the purposes of which the given provisions are applied or, finally, on not applying certain provisions at all; Ł. Chojniak, [in:] *System Prawa Karnego Procesowego. Tom VI. Strony i inni uczestnicy postępowania karnego*, ed. P. Hofmański, C. Kulesza, Warszawa 2016, LEX/el. chapter 6, pt 6.

(a) of expungement of the conviction by operation of law:
- in the event of a sentence to an "ordinary" penalty of deprivation of liberty (i.e. one listed in art. 32 pt. 3 C.C.), the conviction is expunged by operation of law upon the lapse of 10 years from the execution or remission of the penalty or from the prescription of its enforcement (art. 107 § 1 C.C.);
- in the event of a sentence of penalty of deprivation of liberty for life, the sentence shall be expunged by operation of law upon the lapse of 10 years, from the date the penalty is remitted or from the prescription of its enforcement (art. 107 § 3 C.C.);
- in the event of a sentence of limitation of liberty, the conviction is expunged by operation of law upon the lapse of 3 years from the execution or remission of the penalty or from the prescription of its enforcement (art. 107 § 4 C.C.);
- in the event of a fine conviction, the conviction is expunged by operation of law on the lapse of one year from the execution or remission of the penalty or from the prescription of its enforcement (art. 107 § 4a C.C.);
- in the event of waiving from imposing a penalty, the conviction is expunged by operation of law with the lapse of one year from the final judgement (art. 107 § 5 C.C.);
- the conviction is expunged by operation of law with the lapse of year after the end of the probation period (art. 76 § 1 C.C.). In the case referred to in art. 76 § 1 C.C., the provision of art. 108 C.C. (expungement at the concurrence of convictions) shall be applied (art. 76 § 1b C.C.). Pursuant to the mentioned art. 108 C.C., if the perpetrator has been convicted of two or more non-concurrent crimes, as well as if the convicted person, after the commencement, but before the expiry, of the period required for the expungement of the conviction, has again committed an crime, it is only permissible to expunge all convictions at the same time;

(b) of an application by the convicted person for a conviction to be expunged
- the submission of which gives the court the optional possibility to order the expungement of a conviction already after the lapse of 5 years, if the convicted person has respected the legal order during that period and the imposed deprivation of liberty did not exceed 3 years (art. 107 § 2 C.C.);

(c) of a soldier or, as the case may be, a person called up for military service,

- exoneration from penalty – pursuant to art. 336 § 3 or 4 C.C. – entails the expungement of the conviction by operation of law; if a fine or a penal measure has been imposed on the convicted person; however, the expungement of the conviction cannot take place before the execution of the fine or penal measure (art. 336 § 5 C.C.).

Moreover – generally speaking – if a penal measure, forfeiture, or compensatory measure has been adjudicated, the expungement of the conviction cannot take place before its execution, remission or from the prescription of its enforcement; the expungement of the conviction also cannot take place before the execution of a security measure (art. 107 § 6 C.C). Art. 107 § 6 C.C. applies mutatis mutandis to the expungement of a conviction in relation to the penal measures listed in art. 22 § 2 pt. 2–7 of the Fiscal Criminal Code[42] (art. 45 § 2 F.C.C.). In the case of expungement of a conviction when the perpetrator is sentenced on probation, if a fine, a penal measure, a forfeiture or a compensatory measure has been imposed on the convicted person, the expungement of the conviction may not take place before their execution, remission or statute of limitations of their execution. A conviction may also not be expunged prior to the enforcement of a protective measure (art. 76 § 2 C.C.). Art. 107 § 6 as well as art. 76 § 2 C.C. should also be applied mutatis mutandis to fiscal crimes, as follows from art. 20 § 2 F.C.C.

It should also be mentioned, that in the event of a conviction by the court, referred to in art. 114a § 1 C.C.[43], in matters of expungement of conviction, the statute in force at the place of conviction shall apply; the provision of art. 108 C.C. does not apply (art. 114a § 2 pt. 2). Also art. 114a and 114 C.C. shall apply mutatis mutandis to fiscal crimes, in accordance with art. 22 § 2 F.C.C.

In addition to this, but with regard to crimes perpetrators only, i.e. excluding perpetrators of fiscal crimes:

---

42 These are the following criminal measures: forfeiture of objects, recovery of the monetary equivalent of the forfeiture of objects, forfeiture of pecuniary gain, recovery of the monetary equivalent of the forfeiture of pecuniary gain, prohibition to carry out a certain business activity, to performing a certain profession or to holding a certain position, making a verdict public, deprivation of public rights.

43 According this prescription, a verdict of conviction is also a final judgment of conviction for committing a crime issued by a court competent in criminal matters in a Member State of the European Union, unless, according to the Polish criminal statute, the act does not constitute a crime, the perpetrator is not subject to a penalty, or a penalty unknown to the statute has been judged.

- with regard to a soldier in basic service who has been convicted, for an crime specified in the military section of Criminal Code committed during such service, of a fine, a penalty of limitation of liberty or deprivation of liberty not exceeding one year, the court may order that the conviction be expunged after his transfer to the reserve, if the penalty or the adjudicated penal measure were been executed (art. 337 C.C.);
- a sentence to deprivation of liberty without conditional suspension of sentence for a crime against sexual freedom and decency is not expunged if the victim was a minor under 15 years of age (art. 106a C.C.).

The expungement of a conviction may furthermore take place in the case of:

- individual amnesty, applied by the President of the Republic of Poland and understood as his „law of grace"[44]; however, the law of grace is not applied to persons convicted by the State Tribunal (art. 139 of the Constitution of the Republic of Poland)[45];
- general (statutory) amnesty; as aptly stated by T. Grzegorczyk, the expungement of a conviction may also occur as a result of amnesty itself, i.e. the remission of judgemented penalties, if an amnesty act so provides. The remission of penalty in amnesty mode and here because only accelerates the course of this expungement, but it is also possible to separately assume, that in such case the conviction is deemed to have been expunged, although this does not always apply to all situations covered by the amnestious remission of penalty[46]. A general amnesty usually specifies that the prohibited acts concretised in the amnesty statute are „forgiven and forgotten"[47] .

44 Cf. the judgment of the Constitutional Tribunal of 17 July 2018. K 9/17, LEX No. 2518248.

45 Journal of Laws of 1997, No. 78, item 483, as amended.

46 T. Grzegorczyk, [in:] *System Prawa Karnego Procesowego. Tom IV. Dopuszczalność procesu*, ed. P. Hofmański, M. Jeż-Ludwichowska, A. Lach, Warszawa 2015, LEX/el., chapter 5, pt 2.1.2. As submits C. Kulesza, the basic difference between an abolition and an amnesty is that while an abolition constitutes the inadmissibility of the initiation of a trial, an amnesty has an impact on the executive proceeding; C. Kulesza, [in:] *Kodeks postępowania karnego. Komentarz*, red. K. Dudka, Warszawa 2020, LEX/el., commentary to art. 17, pt 94.

47 As for example: offenses committed before 21 July 1984 for political reasons or against the background of social conflicts are forgiven and forgotten, and penalties not executed – are forgiven (art. 7 par. 1 of the statute of 21 July 1984 on amnesty, Journal of Laws 1984, No. 36, item 192); offenses and fiscal offenses are forgiven and forgotten, and penalties not executed are forgiven (art. 10, par. 1, of the statute of 7 December

4. Conclusions

As a rule there is no doubts, that persons who have committed an intentional crime or an intentional fiscal crime should not be employed in the civil service[48]. However, the question arises as to whether the prohibition in question should not be broadened *de lege ferenda* – in the subjective perspective. Therefore, it is worth considering the question of whether certain unintentional crimes that constitute an attack on legal goods which are extremely important from the point of view of the tasks of the civil service, the rule of law and official integrity-reliability associated with it – such as the activities of state and local government institutions, the justice system, the protection of information, *etc.*; although those that take an unintentional form are not currently defined by the legislator in large numbers, but are rather rare – should not also constitute some kind of disqualification in employment in the civil service(?). A partial example is the solution adopted in art. 18 § 2 of the Commercial Companies Code[49], which states that: a person may not be a member of the management board, supervisory board, audit committee, liquidator or proxy, a person who has been convicted by a final judgment of crimes specified in the provisions of chapters XXXIII–XXXVII of the Criminal Code and in art. 587, 590 and 591 of the statute. Thus, employment in the civil service, whether in the context of selection or continuation of employment, could be conditional on a person having been convicted by a final judgment of an intentional crime or an intentional fiscal crime or of crimes specified in the provisions of chapters XVII, XXIX, XXX, XXXIII, XXXIV of the Criminal Code.

Abstract: The subject of the research is the issue of a final conviction for an intentional crime or an intentional fiscal crime as the basis for the inability to be employed in the civil service. The following issues are under consideration: employment in the civil service, intentional crime or intentional fiscal crime, final conviction. In the conclusions, has been shown – for consideration – the de lege ferenda postulate, extending the operation of the prohibition also to other subjective spheres.

1989 on amnesty, Journal of Laws 1989, No. 64, item 390); offences committed before the date of lifting martial state-law for political reasons or against the background of social conflicts are forgiven and forgotten, and penalties not executed – are forgiven (art. 8 of the statute of 21 July 1983 on amnesty, Journal of Laws 1983, No. 39, item 177).

48 Cf. E. Włodkowska, *Wygaśnięcie stosunku pracy w służbie cywilnej* [in:] ed. W. Sanetra, *Stosunki pracy w służbie cywilnej i samorządzie terytorialnym*, Białystok 2001, p. 173.

49 Journal of Laws 2022, item 1467 unified text, as amended.

Małgorzata Wróblewska

Government Legislation Center in the Public Service

The purpose of this article is to introduce the institution of the Government Legislation Center (RCL), which will celebrate the 25th anniversary of its establishment in 2025. In view of this anniversary, it seems that the is the time when it would be appropriate to take stock of its activities. Hence, the following has been done, in the first part of the article, a synthetic presentation of the genesis of the creation of the RCL, the evolution of the of the tasks entrusted to it. In turn, the subsequent part analyzes the implementation of the tasks entrusted to it tasks.

Genesis of the Establishment of the Government Legislation Center The Government Legislation

Center was established on the basis of Article 8 item 2 of the Act of July 24, 1999 on amendments to the Act on Departments of Government Administration and certain other acts[1]. This institution is a state organizational unit, subordinate to the President of the Council of Ministers Council of Ministers[2]. One of the reasons for its establishment was the political transformation. The other the prospect of the Republic of Poland's accession to the European Union. At that time Prime Minister was additionally burdened with the tasks of direct supervision of most central offices. Thus, the Prime Minister Ministers needed a strong substantive background. The creation of the RCL was intended to complement the systemic reform of the government[3]. Admittedly, within the Prime Minister's Office (Chancellery of the Prime Minister) there was a unit providing substantive support for the activities of the Council of Ministers.

1 Journal of Laws of the Republic of Poland No. 70, item 778.

2 See also in the literature on the subject e.g.: M. Berek, *Rada Ministrów jako organ inicjujący postępowanie ustawodawcze*, Warszawa 2017.

3 R. Mojak, *Skład, organizacja wewnętrzna oraz zasady funkcjonowania Rady Ministrów*, in: ed. A. Bałaban, *Rada Ministrów, organizacja i funkcjonowanie*, p. 236.

Ministers, which was the Government Legislative Center[4] but, as *K. Barczyk*, the initiator of the of the creation of the RCL, who in 1997 was Secretary of State at the Chancellery and Secretary of the Socio-Political Committee of the Council of Ministers, there was no "adequate apparatus of legal professionals"[5]. Certainly, one cannot speak of the inexperience of the legislators[6] who are employees of the employees of this Center, but rather the lack of an adequate number of legislators for the tasks entrusted to them. Therefore, the premise of the establishment of the RCL was to create such an institution, which was to have several hundred people, as mentioned[7] by the initiator of the RCL.

With the political transformation, both representatives of doctrine and practitioners working to improve lawmaking in Poland, basically as early as the 1970s, have alleged a number of irregularities in the lawmaking process, as was written about in an article[8] devoted to the role of the RCL. *S. Wronkowska* pointed out that. "state bodies issue too many legal acts, which, in view of the insufficiently precise repeal of existing legal acts makes it difficult to orient oneself in the legal state no longer not only for citizens, but even for law-making bodies. It was emphasized that the number of The applicable acts are excessive in relation to the possibility of their effective application by state bodies.

At the same time, it was pointed out that the legal system is not stable enough; existing acts are frequently and hastily amended or repealed and replaced by new norms, which was not always associated with a justified statement of inefficiency of the of the law in some respect and not always, it should be emphasized, based on duly justified assumptions as to the greater effectiveness of the newly introduced norms"[9].

---

4 Regulation of the Prime Minister of June 23, 1999, on granting the statute of the Chancellery of the Prime Minister Prime Minister's Office (Journal of Laws No. 56, item 590).

5 *Rządowe Centrum Legislacji 15 lat w historii tworzenia i ogłaszania prawa*, Warszawa, 2015, p. 17.

6 See more: R. Iłowiecki, *Statut legislatora w organach władzy publicznej. Zawód legislator*, Przegląd Sejmowy, No. 6 (2010), pp. 27–48.

7 *Rządowe Centrum Legislacji 15 lat w historii...* , p. 19.

8 M. Wróblewska, *Rola Rządowego Centrum Legislacji w procesie tworzenia prawa*, Folia Iuridica Universitatis Wratislaviensis, 5, No. 1 (2016), p. 52. https://repozytorium.uni.wroc.pl/Content/79294/PDF/01_03_M_Wroblewska_Rola_Rzadowego_Centrum_Legislacji_w_procesie_tworzenia_prawa.pdf (accessed: 24.08.2024).

9 S. Wronkowska, *Problem racjonalnego tworzenia prawa*, Poznań 1982, Chapter IV.

Therefore, when creating this institution, it was believed that it would improve lawmaking, by moving away from departmental[10] lawmaking. Above all, attention was drawn to over-regulation, instability of the law and lack of transparency in the legal system, inconsistency of norms, lack of planning of the Government's work or treatment of public consultations public consultations merely as a formality.

It should be noted that at that time, not all participants in the law-making process of the law-making process believed that the creation of the RCL was justified. Despite the indicated premises in favor of creation of the RCL there were opponents[11] of this "idea" who feared the weakening of power in the ministries.

Government Legislation Center Activities – Selected Issues

1. Despite these concerns, as of January 1, 2000, the RCL was successfully established, entrusting the coordination of the legislative activities of the Council of Ministers, the Prime Minister and other government administration bodies. It should be noted that the RCL does not have its own separate law, example as the Committee for European Affairs[12].

On the organizational side, the management of the RCL is entrusted to the President of the RCL, with the assistance of vice presidents and directors of organizational units. The first president of the RCL was appointed by *A. Proksa* appointed by the Prime Minister. What seems important to emphasize is that President of the RCL was also appointed as Secretary of the Council of Ministers. The combination of these functions undoubtedly has a positive effect in cooperation with the Prime Minister and its members. This does not mean that the RCL controls the work of ministers, as legislative plans are adopted by the Council of Ministers.

The substantive employees who received employment at the RCL were, for the most part. mostly employees of the Legislative Center. To date, ten of these legislators, performing various functions. RCL employees are not part of the civil service civil service[13].

10 See more: M. Wróblewska, *Pilny projekt ustawy – założenia konstytucyjnoprawne a praktyka ustrojowa*, Warszawa, 2024, part I, Chapter III, § 4.

11 Letter marked: GPM64/98/dated 2.07.1997 in *Rządowe Centrum Legislacji 15 lat w historii ...* , p. 24.

12 Law of August 27, 2009 on the Committee for European Affairs (Journal of Laws of the Republic of Poland of 2024, item 562).

13 Law of November 21, 2028 on the Civil Service (Journal of Laws of the Republic of Poland of 2024, item 409).

The tasks originally assigned to the RCL were primarily to provide legal services to the legal service to the Council of Ministers consisting, in particular, of:

1. developing legal-legislative positions for government draft legislation;
2. coordinating the course of arrangements for government drafts of legal acts;
3. preparing in legislative terms government drafts of legal acts directed for consideration by the Council of Ministers;
4. developing government drafts of legal acts within the scope established by the Chairman of the Council of Ministers;
5. editing the Official Gazette of the Republic of Poland and the Official Gazette of the Republic of Poland & quot; Monitor Polski"
6. cooperating with the Committee for European Integration on harmonization of Polish law Polish law with the requirements of the law of the European Communities;
7. cooperation with the Legislative Council in the field of giving opinions on government drafts of normative acts normative acts in terms of their compliance with the Constitution of the Republic of Poland and consistency with the system of law consistency with the system of law;
8. controlling the issuance by government administration bodies of executive regulations to laws;
9. carrying out other task specified in separate regulations or indicated by the Prime Minister Chairman of the Council of Ministers.

In addition, the RCL is entrusted with cooperation with the Polish Academy of Sciences, universities and other scientific institutions.

Over time, as a result primarily of the constant criticism, evident in numerous publications[14], directed at the government over the manner in which laws are

---

14 See more: S. Wronkowska, *Tworzenie prawa w Polsce – ocena i poprawne kierunki zmian.* Raport Rady Legislacyjnej przy Prezesie Rady Ministrów, „Przegląd Legislacyjny", nr 1, 2006; raporty z realizacji projektów: *Społeczny monitoring procesu stanowienia prawa*, Fundacja im. Stefana Batorego, Warszawa 2008; *Obserwatorium demokracji Instytut Spraw Publicznych, Demokracja w Polsce 2007–2009*, Warszawa 2009, *System stanowienia prawa w Polsce – Zielona Księga*, Kancelaria Prezydenta Rzeczypospolitej Polskiej, Warszawa 2013; raport K. H. Goetza i R. Zubka, *Stanowienie prawa w Polsce. Reguły legislacyjne a jakość ustawodawstwa*, opracowanie wydane w ramach programu Ernst & Young „Sprawne Państwo", maj 2005; E. Balcerowicz (ed.), *Reforma procesu stanowienia prawa*, Centrum Analiz Społeczno-Ekonomicznych, Warszawa 2004 i publikacja W. Staśkiewicza, *Stanowienie prawa*, in: ed. L. Kolarska-Bobińska, *Co warto, co należy zmienić. Poprawa jakości demokracji w Polsce*, Instytut Spraw Publicznych, Warszawa 2008.

made, the tasks assigned to the RCL to provide legal services to the Council of Ministers has evolved.

In criticizing the manner of lawmaking, it was mainly alleged that the RCL was not equipped with competencies allowing it to co-determine the course of the government's legislative process legislative process.

"Unfortunately, neither the reform of the government administration system nor the creation of the RCL brought the expected changes. Subsequent evaluations of the law-making process. There was still no entity responsible for all government legislation. W. Staśkiewicz believed that "these entities are neither individual ministries, nor the Ministry of Justice, nor the Government Legislation Center, nor – naturally – the Council of Ministers. natural – the Council of Ministers. None of these entities has a reasonably comprehensive knowledge of functioning legislation." In his opinion, the current model of legislation can be called a spontaneous model, which does not tolerate planning of lawmaking and destroys its elements. Even more widely referred to this state of affairs by K.H. Goetz and R. Zubek: "Decentralization of lawmaking is the main cause of some serious problems of Polish legislation, especially its sprawl, instability and excessive detail, and the tendency to create laws that realize benefits for narrow social groups at the expense of the collective good."[15].

2. A consequence of this criticism was the lawmaking reform introduced by the Law of January 23, 2009 on amending the Law on the Council of Ministers and certain other laws[16], which came into force on April 1, 2009, and introduced changes in the creation of government bills, which also affected the amendment of the Regulations on the Work of the Council of Ministers Council of Ministers[17], hereinafter referred to as the RpRM. The amended RpRM introduced a "new"[18] government model for drafting laws on the basis of assumptions, in which the RCL played a key role in their creation. This model was in effect from April 1, 2009 to June 21 June 2016.

Prior to the entry into force of the Law of January 23, 2009 amending the Law on the Council of Council of Ministers and some other laws and the RpRM, the RCL and legislators from the legal departments of the legal departments of ministries participated in numerous conferences, discussions and workshops,

---

15 M. Wróblewska, *Rola Rządowego Centrum Legislacji* ..., pp. 56–57.

16 Journal of Laws of the Republic of Poland No. 42, item 337.

17 Resolution No. 38 of the Council of Ministers of March 31, 2009. – Amending the Resolution – RpRM (M.P. No. 20, item 246).

18 See more: M. Wróblewska, *Pilny project ustawy* ..., Part I, Chapter III, § 3.

organized by the RCL, dedicated to the new model. They were also co-participants in the development of this model. For the RCL, additional support for carrying out the new task was an increase in FTEs[19], particularly for legislators.

The essence of this model is to move away from resor[20] lawmaking, by giving the RCL the statutory task (Article 14c (1) of the law) of drafting laws on the basis of assumptions. Undoubtedly, entrusting the RCL with this task was an attempt to response to the objections directed at the government in terms of departmental lawmaking. The initiator of this model was *M. Berek* – acting, in one person, as the President of the RCL and the Secretary of the Council of Ministers.

It should be noted that also during this work on moving away from departmental lawmaking, the proposed concept raised concerns about limiting the power of ministers and slowing down the law-making process. The ministries, or at least part of it saw this as a threat[21]. The explanation of the *retio legis* of the proposed regulation that the development of projects by the RCL on the basis of assumptions prepared by ministries would speed up the lawmaking process was intended to mitigate these concerns. Undoubtedly, an additional impact on reducing the concerns of ministers were the bylaw regulations, which introduced exceptions to the application of the principle that the on the drafting of laws by the RCL. The first exception concerned the situation when, in justified cases, the Prime Minister or the Secretary of the Council of Ministers, acting under his authority Secretary of the Council of Ministers, at the request of the requesting body or the President of the RCL, decides to entrust the drafting of a bill on the basis of assumptions adopted by the Council of Ministers to the requesting body Ministers to the requesting body. The second exception covered situations in which the drafting of a law by an entity other than the RCL resulted from separate regulations. It should be note, as has already been written about[22], such exceptions, already at the stage of drafting these regulations aroused concern of the Bureau of Analysis of the Sejm. According to the opinion of this office, it was

19 The RCL initially had 78 employees, and in 2015 the number of employees rose to 179, with employed legislators was 84. The data comes from: *Rządowe Centrum Legislacji 15 lat w historii* ..., p. 55, and from: *Księga XV-lecia rządowego Centrum Legislacji* "*Lege sab omnibus intellegi debent*," Wydawnictwo Sejmowe, Warszawa 2015, p. 33).

20 See more: M. Wróblewska, *Pilny projekt ustawy* ..., Warszawa, 2024, Part I, Chapter III, § 2.

21 *Rządowe Centrum Legislacji 15 lat w historii* ... , p. 61.

22 M. Wróblewska, *Rola Rządowego Centrum Legislacji* ... , pp. 59–62.

believed that they could pose a danger of squandering the hope of eliminating the defects of the existing system[23].

With the entry into force on April 1, 2009 of the aforementioned law and the RpRM departmental lawmaking has ended. The Government Legislation Center is carrying out, as part of the provision of legal services, new tasks[24] which have since been specified in Article 14c of the Law of August 8, 1996 on the Council of Ministers[25].

First, the RCL drafts[26] bills on the basis of assumptions adopted by the Council of Ministers (according to the principles and procedure set forth in the RpRM unless, under separate regulations, the development of certain types of draft laws is the responsibility of jurisdiction of other entities). To complete this task, the RpRM specified procedures for drafting laws on the basis of assumptions (this model was in effect from 2009 – 2016). The drafting of these laws was to involve cooperation between the RCL and the body proposing body, which in particular was to provide RCL with detailed proposals for the solutions necessary for the drafting of the bill, and provide information and explanations on the draft law. Also, members of the Council of Ministers, the Head of the Chancellery of the Prime Minister, as well as central government administration bodies, governors, government plenipotentiaries, and other entities authorized to draft normative acts, within the scope of their jurisdiction, were required to cooperate with the RCL and the requesting body in matters of drafting the bill, including the provision of necessary information and explanations (§ 112 of the RpRM)[27].

Second, the RCL analyzes the jurisprudence of the Constitutional Court (TK), the Supreme Court Supreme Court and Supreme Administrative Court, as well as the Court of Justice of the European Union European Court of Justice and the Court of First Instance, particularly with regard to the impact on the Polish legal system law.

---

23 A. Szmyt, Opinion to the draft amendment of the law on the Council of Ministers (print no. 1344), Biuro Analiz Sejmowych, Warsaw, December 19, 2008, p. 3, http://orka.sejm.gov.pl/proc6.nsf, [access 1.06.2015].

24 M. Wróblewska, *Rola Rządowego Centrum Legislacji ...*, pp. 59–62.

25 Journal of Laws of the Republic of Poland of 2024, item 1050.

26 Since the RCL was entrusted with the task of drafting government bills on the basis of assumptions 147 such bills have been drafted, of which 125 have been adopted by the Council of Ministers, and 112 have been published in the Official Gazette, 1 bill is in the pipeline, and 4 bills have been dropped from further work (as of October 30, 2015), M. Wróblewska, *Rola Rządowego Centrum Legislacji ...*, pp. 56–57.

27 M.P. of 2013, item 979.

Third, not only – as was the case before the law was amended – edits the Dziennik Ustaw of the Republic of Poland and the Official Journal of the Republic of Poland Polish "Monitor Polski," but also publishes these journals in electronic form. In addition to editing of these dailies as of January 1, 2016, the RCL, under the amended Act of July 20, 2000 on the promulgation of normative acts and some other legal acts, is also responsible for cooperating with the Speaker of the Sejm in the preparation of unified texts of laws (Article 16(2))[28].

In addition to the statutory tasks indicated, during the government's model of drafting of laws between 2009 and 2016, the RCL was entrusted with another task, under the based on the law of June 25, 2015 on the Constitutional Court[29], which entered into force on August 30, 2015. This was just before the parliamentary elections. It consists of ensuring the participation of the Council of Ministers and the Prime Minister in the proceedings before the Constitutional Court (Article 131 of the law).

In addition, during the course of the government model of lawmaking from 2009 to 2016 RCL carried out the tasks that the RpRM defined. It should be noted that during the duration of this model (2009 – 2016) the RpRM was repeatedly amended. One of the statutory tasks, was to develop for information purposes and make available in the Bulletin of Information Public Information Bulletin on the RCL's subject page and updating the description of the procedures for adopting draft government documents. Another statutory task – in connection with obligation of public authorities and other entities performing public tasks, in particular, in terms of drafting normative acts in accordance with the provisions of the Law of September 6, 2001 on access to public information[30]- is the creation by the RCL of the service "Government Legislative Process" (RPL). Access to the RPL is provided for draft laws and draft regulations, until June 21, 2016 assumptions to draft laws were also published.

Relatively recently, further tasks have been imposed on RCL as specified in RpRM[31]. At particularly noteworthy, the obligation that the President of RCL also develop and makes available in the Public Information Bulletin on the RCL's subject page and updates the recommendations on procedures for conducting public consultations (§ 23 of the RpRM).

28 Journal of Laws of the Republic of Poland of 2017, item 1523.

29 Journal of Laws of the Republic of Poland item 1064.

30 Journal of Laws of 2014, item 782, as amended.

31 M.P. of 2024, item 757.

The government's lawmaking model, in which the principle was that the RCL would draft laws on the basis of assumptions was maintained only until June 21, 2016, despite the fact that the In its reports, the Legislative Council recognized the "higher legislative standard"[32] of the bills drafted by the RCL.

3. On June 22, 2016, the new government returned to departmental lawmaking, which remains in effect to this day.

The reasons for the departure from the government model of lawmaking between 2009 and 2016, as written[33] were the allegations directed at the government by various circles. Practitioners who participated in the drafting of laws, firstly alleged that many draft laws were not drafted on the basis of assumptions (ministers used unusually RCL's ability to refrain from drafting laws on the basis of assumptions). Second, they believed that drafting bills on the basis of assumptions did not contributed to reducing the total time to carry out the government legislative process legislative process, as was pointed out when this government model was introduced in 2009. J. Rusiniak – who was in office during the period of changes to this model (moving away from the mandatory drafting of the draft laws on the basis of assumptions) President of the RCL and Secretary of the Council of Ministers, in one person from 16.12.2015 to 4.06.2019, after which she served as the only the President of the RCL – claimed that the writing of laws by the RCL prolongs the entire legislative process legislative process and dilutes responsibility[34]. Referring to these allegations, it should be noted at the outset point out that none of them can apply to the RCL, as it has no jurisdiction in this regard.

Admittedly, one should agree with the allegation indicated above regarding the fact that many projects were not developed on the basis of assumptions[35] is the allegation regarding, in particular that the project's procedure prolongs the process is incomprehensible. First because **in a democratic state of law, where there should be an effort to reduce the "overproduction" of the law – which**

32 Report on the activities of the Legislative Council of the 11th Legislature.

33 See more: M. Wroblewska, *Pilny project ustawy ...*, Part I, ch. III, § 4.

34 Interview with J. Rusiniak – President of RCL A. Dąbrowska, G. Rzeczkowski, *Źle lub jeszcze gorzej, czyli jak się tworzy w Polsce prawo*, Polityka, 7.3.2012.

35 For example: when conducting research on government bills (15 bills), which the government has given an urgency clause under Article 123 of the 1997 Constitution of the Republic of Poland in the seventh term of the Sejm and the eighth term of the Senate, when the government's lawmaking model of moving away from departmental lawmaking was in effect then only 1 project was drafted by the RCL on the basis of assumptions.

results in instability of the law and lack of transparency of the legal system, inconsistency of regulations – the essence of lawmaking is not is quick creation (blandness), but proper planning of its creation and preparation of assumptions based on an impact assessment[36]. Secondly, in the case of real need to urgently proceed with the law, it is possible to abandon the development of a draft on the basis of assumptions or proceed on the basis of the assumptions or proceed separately after meeting the prerequisites of the regulations.

Representatives of the doctrine, also had doubts. For example, *K. Skotnicki* was not was not convinced of the rightness of drafting bills on the basis of assumptions by the RCL legislators. He claimed that "Legislators are also necessary in individual ministries, since by working there they better understand the specifics of the ministry in which they are employed, and thus it is easier for them to include in a legal provision the proposed solution. It is also easy to predict that in practice individual legislators from the RCL will be more or less formally responsible for cooperation with a particular ministry, and thus a kind of specialization of them will develop. (...) RCL legislators should cooperate with legislators in individual ministries – not There should be a further procedure for draft legislation without its approval at the Center in legal terms."[37].

Referring to this, it cannot be faulted in any way. First ministries will always need skilled departmental legislators. Secondly it should be emphasized that whether RCL drafts on the basis of assumptions or not, there is cooperation between RCL legislators and legislators from legal departments and staff from substantive departments, individual ministries. It often happens RCL legislators collaborate with staff from substantive departments of ministries, as they have greater expertise than legislators employed in the laundry departments of ministries. As K. Skotnicki notes, in some departments of the legal departments of ministries "lack officials with such qualifications"[38]. When creating legislation, whether on the basis of assumptions, or in drafting, during the Law Commission conducted by the RCL, the RCL legislator usually draws on the expertise of a primarily expert (usually a substantive employee of the ministry). Thus, RCL

---

36 For example: Report of the Legislative Council conference held on 14.12.2005, compiled by. S. Wronkowska, PL 2006, No. 1; W. Szpringer, W. Rogowski, *Ocena skutków regulacji,* in R. Zubek (ed.), Analysis of the Polish practice of assessing the effects of regulation in 2001–2005, Warsaw 2007, p. 31; M. Wróblewska, *Pilny project ustawy* ..., p. 63 et seq.

37 K. Skotnicki, *Rządowe Centrum Legislacji,* https://dspace.uni.lodz.pl/bitstream/handle/11089/40606/229-241-skotnicki.pdf?seque (access:20.08.2024).

38 K. Skotnicki, *Rządowe Centrum* ..., p. 235.

legislators acquire the knowledge of an expert knowledge, which has a positive impact on lawmaking.

It should be noted that the statutory tasks referred to in Article 14 c of the Law of 8 August 1996 on the Council of Ministers entrusted to the RCL in the provision of legal services legal services, during the binding of the previous government's lawmaking model from 2009 – 2016, are still in effect – except that, as a result of the amendment of RpRM[39] as of June 22 2016, the development of government bills by the RCL on the basis of assumptions is no longer an exception to the rule of departmental drafting of laws.

In addition, based on the law of August 11, 2021 amending the Law on Public Finance and Certain Other Laws[40], in addition to coordinating the legislative activities of the legislative activities of the Council of Ministers, the Prime Minister and other government administration bodies government, the RCL was entrusted with conducting educational and training activities consisting of dissemination and popularization of knowledge about legislation, as well as unification of legislative practice legislative practice. It should be noted that prior to being entrusted with this activity, the RCL conducted a legislative application[41] , and continues to do so. At this point, RCL has conducted 24 editions of the legislative application. In addition, work is underway to widely promote legislation, including on various platforms. Therefore, the Prime Minister has established the E-team. Legislation. Originally, work on publicly accessible information and education tool on legislation and jurisprudence. To this end, RCL President *K. Szczucki* formed a team to develop assumptions for the system entitled "Publicly available information and educational tools on legislation and case law". As a result of this work legislators who are members of the team developed the assumptions.

The Government Legislation Center, as of January 1, 2022, also operates the Council of Legislative Council[42], and is also the publisher of the journal Legislative Review. It should be mentioned that the RCL also interacts with the entities referred to in Art. 7(1)(1), (2) and (4) to (8) of the Law of July 20,

39 Resolution No. 62 of 1.6.2016. Council of Ministers amending the RpRM.

40 Article 4 item 3 of the Act of August 11, 2021 on amending the Law on Public Finance and certain other laws (Journal of Laws of the Republic of Poland item 1535).

41 Regulation of the Prime Minister of April 28, 2015 on legislative application (Journal of Laws of the Republic of Poland of 2021 item 1229, as amended).

42 There is a Legislative Council attached to the Prime Minister. It is a consultative and advisory body of the Council of Ministers of the Council of Ministers and the Prime Minister in matters relating to the legal system.

2018. – Law on higher education and science (Journal of Laws of 2024, item 124, as amended), and other organizational units conducting activities related to the and other tasks of the RCL.

4. Summarizing the activities of the RCL, before the anniversary day of the 25th anniversary of the RCL, referring to the RCL's performance of the aforementioned tasks, first of all, the RCL should be appreciated for its service. The time of the pandemic caused by COVID-19 proved, the great commitment of all RCL employees in the law-making process. Every day, legislators as well as RCL editors performed the assigned tasks.

In light of all the tasks entrusted to the RCL, it is currently employed in seven departments[43] and one office[44] about 163 employees. In the substantive departments substantive departments there are about 86 legislators, counting directors, deputy directors and chiefs. The Government Legislation Center is headed by the President of the RCL, assisted by two presidents. The RCL also employs a Director General[45], who heads the Office of the Director General.

It can be noted that the tasks entrusted to the RCL are evolving almost all the time, along with the changing governments. Despite the numerous tasks entrusted to the RCL, at no time of its operation, the RCL has not employed the number of legislators mentioned by mentioned by K. Barczyk, the initiator of the establishment of the RCL. The RCL seems to have been up to all the

---

43 In accordance with Order No. 79 of January 29, 2024 of the Prime Minister on granting the statute of the Government Legislation Center (M.P. of 2024, item 83) the Department of Administrative Law, the Department of Economic and Financial Law, Department of Social Law, Department of Environmental Law and Infrastructure, the Department of Legal Affairs and Education, and the Department of Information Technology and Legal Information Systems. Law.

44 Pursuant to Order No. 79 of January 29, 2024 of the Prime Minister's Office on Establishing the Statute of the Government Legislation Center (M.P. of 2024, item 83) the Office of the Director General.

45 In the Ordinance of February 14, 2024 of the Prime Minister amending the Ordinance on the principles of remuneration and qualification requirements for employees of the Government Legislation Center (Journal of Laws of the Republic of Poland, item 185), § 1 amends the table of the appendix to the Ordinance of the Prime Minister on the principles of remuneration and qualification requirements for employees of the Government Legislation Center. remuneration and qualification requirements for employees of the Government Legislation Center, adding a director general. In turn, by the order of January 29, 2024, No. 79 of the Prime Minister's Council on the on granting the statute of the Government Legislation Center (M.P. of 2024, item 83), the RCL also includes the Office of the Director General.

tasks, especially the most demanding and extremely important for correct lawmaking – the development of draft laws on the basis of assumptions. The Legislative Council in its reports indicated that "it was possible to observe a general rule that higher legislative standard was presented by acts drafted by the Government Legislation Center Legislation."[46]. Unfortunately, despite such an assessment, the RCL's drafting of laws was withdrawn draft laws on the basis of assumptions, making this an exception to the rule.

It should be noted that despite the demands of representatives of the doctrine[47], no attempt has been made to attempt to improve this model. *M. Berka*, argued that imperfections in the government legislative procedure legislative procedure should be overcome by implementing appropriate corrections, primarily by defining the scope of permissible exceptions to the statutory rule of development of assumptions, and by exercising due supervision over the process of legislative process.

The Government Legislation Center has also been up to the task of publishing dailies in electronic form, which allows widespread and immediate accessibility to them, even during the COVID-19 pandemic. These tasks are carried out at the RCL by the Department of Official Journals and Uniform Texts. It should be recalled that the preparation and distribution of the paper version sometimes took quite a long time, and at the present time both every office, as well as the citizen, has almost instant access to the published regulations. This form also contributes to the transparency and transparency of the legal system[48], which is an undoubtedly a success for the RCL.

It should also be appreciated that the RCL is carrying out the task of analyzing the case law of the Constitutional Court, the Supreme Court and the Supreme Administrative Court Administrative Court and the Court of Justice of the European Union, particularly in in terms of impact on the Polish legal system. As *K. Skotnicki* notes, the activities carried out by the RCL "also bring the expected changes in the law"[49].

The educational activities of the RCL deserve special recognition. Not only in terms of the legislative application carried out, but also in terms of those conducted for the employees of ministries and local government units workshops

---

46 Report on the Activities of the Legislative Council of the 11th Legislature

47 M. Berek, *Założenia do projektów ustaw – proceduralne superfluum czy obowiązek demokratycznego projektodawcy?*, p. 26.

48 M. Wróblewska, *Rola Rządowego Centrum Legislacji ...*, p. 61.

49 K. Skotnicki, *Rządowe Centrum ...*, p. 237.

and training courses, in particular on the principles of lawmaking, the principles of proper legislation, as well as the governmental law-making procedure. Since recently, RCL has been conducting for employees of various units also webinars in online and on-site forms.

In turn, referring to the tasks arising from the RpRM, it should be noted that RCL maintains an RPL service on its entity website, and the RCL President also develops and makes available in the Public Information Bulletin on RCL's entity website and updates the descriptions of procedures for the adoption of draft government documents[50] and recommendations on the on procedures for conducting public consultations – after consulting the subject.

Conclusions

To sum up the activities of the RCL in light of the tasks performed, the RCL is concerned with transparency and clarity of the legal system, the proper conduct of the legislative process and the development of legal education, (for example, on the law-making process or the principles of legislative technique). It should be noted that despite such important tasks for government lawmaking, the RCL does not have "its own" law, which would regulate comprehensively its activities and government lawmaking (for example, the RCL's bodies, tasks, employees, method of hiring legislators, including the legislative profession, legislative application, financing of the body, legislative planning, impact assessment, consultations public consultation, or public hearing[51]).

It should be noted that the RCL, in shaping the rules of lawmaking, has no real influence on departmental drafting of laws. Despite the fact that the goal[52] was to preparation of all government bills at the RCL this amendment to the RpRM in June 2016 halted the direction of change in lawmaking reform, and thus reduced the RCL's real influence on departmental bill drafting. While the tasks carried out RCL's tasks positively affect the transparency of the legal system, allegations of over-regulation, instability of the law and inconsistency of norms, or the treatment of public consultations merely as a formality are still valid. It seems It seems that the dispersion of tasks in coordinating the impact assessment or

50 Provision of § 19 of the RpRM (M.P. of 2022, item 347, as amended).

51 B. Przywora. M. Wróblewska, *On the Institution of Public Hearing – An Analysis from the Theoretical Point of View and the Perspective of the State's Political Practice (Fifth to Ninth Term of the Sejm of the Republic of Poland).* file:///C:/Users/gosia/Downloads/Criticism%20Law%202_2024%20Przywora%20EN.pdf (accessed: 30.08.2024).

52 *Rządowe Centrum Legislacji 15 lat w historii* ..., p. 95.

giving an opinion on draft laws in the field of European Union law by entrusting them to organizational units in the Chancellery and not the RCL may affect this state of affairs.

Poland lacks an institution that is responsible for the way government bills are created draft laws. It would have a comprehensive knowledge of both functioning national acts domestic legal acts, as well as those of the European Union, would deal with the analysis of the of the law in practice, including evaluating the effects of regulations, would conduct post-legislative studies post-legislative, would analyze the jurisprudence of the Constitutional Tribunal, the Court of Justice of the European Court of Justice of the European Union, the Supreme Administrative Court and the Supreme Court Supreme Court, together with the development of legislative solutions.

Such an institution, in principle, could be the RCL, with an appropriate base of substantive resources, which would include, in addition to legislators, editors, substantive employees substantive staff, as well as scientists who are experts in various fields of law. This would mean that the number of RCL employees should be, at least twice as high than the current one. Only, an institution shaped in this way, conducting a proper personnel policy[53], combined with the tasks carried out by the RCL, can promote the ordering and stabilization of the legal system. Perhaps the fact that in 2024 the RCL employed, for the first time in the RCL's history, a Director General, in such a small organizational unit, where the employees are not in the civil service, is the beginning of a larger reorganization.

53 See more: K. Skotnicki, *Rządowe Centrum* ..., p. 237.

Tomasz Barankiewicz, Bogusław Przywora

Conclusion: Prospects for the Polish Public and Civil Service

The 100th anniversary of the Polish Civil Service invites us to reflect on the condition not only of the Polish Civil Service, but of the entire Public Service in the face of the many threats it faces (including, in particular, pandemics), or in the face of a crisis: an economic one on the one hand, and a military (armed) threat on the other. The question is, in what direction should the civil service evolve to meet contemporary challenges in an optimal way? What changes are necessary to strengthen the implementation of the standards set out in the Constitution of the Republic of Poland of 2 April 1997 (professionalism, reliability, impartiality, and political neutrality)?

Firstly, changes are necessary in the direction of restoring the authority (significance) of the Civil Service from the period of the 2nd Republic of Poland, formed on the norms of the Act of 1922 on the State Civil Service. The social expectation is that the civil service should employ people with the highest qualifications (both professional and moral). To achieve this goal, efforts should be made in particular to strengthen the professionalisation and political neutrality of the Polish civil service.

Secondly, this should be followed by changes to make the process of selecting officials and working time more flexible, to indicate paths of promotion and professional development, and to change the principles of remuneration. The issue of appropriate remuneration in the public sphere is a frequently discussed topic both in discussions with officials and in the daily and professional press.

Thirdly, the editors would like to conclude with the thought that in the presented studies, a number of regularities can be noticed, which ultimately create a common picture of the process of reforms in the 20th and 21st centuries, which emerges as the so-called the Neo-Weberian model of public and civil service. We should be aware that in Europe, under the influence of M. Weber's thought, subsequent distinguishable models of public administration are sometimes based on very strong criticism of earlier models, but in practice they do not radically break with earlier approaches. Therefore, in the visible process of change, development involves moving from simple ideas of the rule of law and bureaucracy to complex concepts. However, under the influence of the current criticism of the concepts of Management and Governance, there is a return to the original thought of M. Weber, but it is not a simple renewal of his thought, but its connection with the experiences of the 20th and 21st centuries.

The new interpretation of M. Weber's thought would be based on the reaffirmation of four basic assumptions: (1) reaffirmation of the special role of the state, (2) maintaining the system of representative democracy, (3) restoring the role and importance of administrative law, (4) maintaining and implementing the idea of public service.

References

Agopszowicz A., Gilowska Z., *Ustawa o gminnym samorządzie terytorialnym. Komentarz*, Warsaw 1999.

Andrzejczuk G., *Godność i wolność w nauczaniu Jana Pawła II [in:] Dziecko w historii – między godnością a zniewoleniem. vol. 1. Dziecko jako fundament praw człowieka,* collective work edited by Elwira J. Kryńska, Łukasz Kalisz and Agnieszka Suplicka, Białystok 2021.

Balcerowicz E. (ed.), *Reforma procesu stanowienia prawa*, Centrum Analiz Społeczno-Ekonomicznych, Warszawa 2004.

Balicki R., Komentarz do art. 153, in *Konstytucja Rzeczypospolitej Polskiej. Komentarz,* red. M. Haczkowska Warszawa 2014.

Banaszak B., *Konstytucja Rzeczypospolitej Polskiej – komentarz,* Warsaw 2012.

Banaszak B., *Konstytucja Rzeczypospolitej Polskiej. Komentarz*, Warsaw 2009.

Banaszak B., Jabłoński M., Commentary to Article 65 of the Constitution of the Republic of Poland, in: J. Boć (ed.), *Konstytucje Rzeczypospolitej Polskiej oraz komentarz do Konstytucji RP z 1997 r.*, Wrocław 1998.

Banaszkiewicz A., Nowelizacja ustawy o służbie cywilnej z dnia 30 grudnia 2015 r. w kontekście wymogu neutralności politycznej członków korpusu służby cywilnej, *Studia Iuridica Lublinensia* XXV (4) 2016.

Baran K.W., Commentary to Article 9 u.s.c., in: *Ustawa o służbie cywilnej. Komentarz,* Baran K.W. (ed.), Dubowik A., Duraj T., Grześków M., Książek D., Lekston M., Perdeus W., Pisarczyk Ł., Płażek S., Przywora B., Tomaszewska M., Ura E., Walczak K., Witoszko W., Wujczyk M., published: JPC 2021, www.sip.lex.pl (accessed 10.11.2022).

Barankiewicz T., *Neoweberyzm. Etos służby publicznej. Analiza krytyczna i perspektywy*, Lublin 2020.

Barankiewicz T., *Etyka urzędnicza – funkcje, zasady, postawy [in:] Metryka. Studia z zakresu prawa osobowego i rejestracji stanu cywilnego No* 3, Cracow 2014.

Barankiewicz T., Przywora B., Kształtowanie się etosu służby cywilnej w Polsce – analiza historyczna i systematyczna, *Studia Iuridica* 92, 2022.

Baranowski K., *Inteligencja łódzka w latach II RP.* Ed. Technical University of Lodz, Łódź 1996.

Barszcz T., VI Otwarte Seminarium Naukowe „100-lecie polskiej służby cywilnej", Lublin–Częstochowa, 17 lutego 2022 r., „Studia Prawnicze" *KUL* 1 (93) 2023.

Budzanowska A., Radziewski M., The constitutional principle of common welfare at a time of a pandemic in Poland, *Horyzonty Polityki*, 13 (45) 2022, DOI: 10.35765/HP.2389

Bukowski Z., Jędrzejewski T., Rączka P., *Ustrój samorządu terytorialnego*, Toruń 2003.

Boć J., Commentary to Article 45 of the Constitution of the Republic of Poland, in: Boć J. (ed.), *Konstytucje Rzeczypospolitej Polskiej oraz komentarz do Konstytucji RP z 1997 r.*, Wrocław 1998.

Borowicz J., Wolność pracy, w: Banaszak B., Preisner A. (eds.), *Prawa i wolności obywatelskie w Konstytucji RP*, Warsaw 2002.

Bossaert D., Demmke Ch., *Służba cywilna w państwach akcesyjnych. Tendencje i wpływ procesów integracyjnych*, Łódź 2003

Brzozowski W., Rec.: A. Łukaszczuk, Kształtowanie się modelu ustrojowego służby cywilnej w Polsce, Warszawa 2014, *Państwo i Prawo* (4) 2015.

Ceglarska-Piłat P., Pojęcie i cechy charakterystyczne odpowiedzialności dyscyplinarnej w prawie polskim, in: *Studia Prawnicze* z. 2, Warsaw 2015.

Cudowski B., Zmiany regulacji prawnej dodatkowego zatrudnienia, *Studia Iuridica Lublinensia*, XXIV (3) 2015.

Cudowski B., *Dodatkowe zatrudnienie*, Warsaw 2007.

Cudowski B., Dodatkowe zatrudnienie pracowników samorządowych i radnych (zarys problematyki), in: *Prawo pracy, zabezpieczenie społeczne (z aktualnych zagadnień)*, Ćwiertniak B.M. (ed.), Opole 2001.

Cudowski B., Ograniczenia swobody zatrudnienia pracowników samorządowych i członków korpusu służby cywilnej, in: *Stosunki pracy w służbie cywilnej i samorządzie terytorialnym*, Sanetra W. (ed.), Białystok 2001.

Chmaj M., *Prawo samorządu terytorialnego*, Warsaw 2013.

Chojniak Ł., [w:] *System Prawa Karnego Procesowego. Tom VI. Strony i inni uczestnicy postępowania karnego*, Hofmański, P. Kulesza C. (eds.), Warszawa 2016, LEX/el.

Cieślik Z. (red.), *Nauka administracji*, LexisNexis, Warsaw 2012.

Corte-Real I., Administracja publiczna a Unia Europejska, *Służba cywilna* (1) 2000.

Ćwiertniak B.M., O zasadach prawa urzędniczego (podstawowe problemy), *Studia Iuridica Lublinensia* 24 (3) 2015.

Czapliński W., Wyrozumska A., *Prawo międzynarodowe publiczne*. Zagadnienie systemowe, Warszawa 1999.

Czaputowicz J., Modele administracji publicznej i ich przydatność dla konceptualizacji administracji publicznej w państwach Europy Środkowej, in: *Misja publiczna, wspólnota, państwo. Studia z prawa i administracji. Księga dedykowana pamięci profesora Michała Kuleszy*, Mednis, A. (ed.), Wrocław 2016, t. 2.

Czaputowicz J., Implikacje integracji z Unią Europejską dla polskiej służby cywilnej, *Służba Cywilna* (1) 2000.

Czarny P., Komentarz do art. 153, in: *Konstytucja Rzeczypospolitej Polskiej. Komentarz*, Tuleja P. (ed.), Warszawa 2023.

Czerw J. *Wynagrodzenie pracowników samorządowych zatrudnionych na kierowniczych stanowiskach pracowniczych – wnioski de lege ferenda, Samorząd Terytorialny*, 2020.

Czerw J., Recruitment as a Way of Employing Self-Government Employees in Clerical Positions in Poland, *International Journal of Legal Studies* 1(3) 2018.

Czerw J., *Ustrój i funkcjonowanie rad i zarządów powiatów. Stan aktualny i postulaty zmian (w wybranych obszarach)*, Lublin 2014.

Czerw J., Wybór organów wykonawczych jednostek samorządu terytorialnego – analiza aktualnego stanu prawnego i propozycje zmian w wybranych obszarach, *Przegląd Prawa Publicznego* 2014, 7–8.

Czerw J., Liżewski B., Influence of Hybrid Legal Institutions on the Management in Local Government on the Example of the Institution of Public-Private Partnership, *LEX LOCALIS – Journal of Local Self-Government*, 19(3) 2021.

Deryng-Dziuk Anna, Dyskryminacja pracownika jako naruszenie konstytucyjnych praw i wolności człowieka, Malczyńska-Biały M. (ed.), *Bezpieczeństwo. Prawa człowieka. Stosunki międzynarodowe*, Rzeszów 2021.

Deryng A., *Rzecznik Praw Obywatelskich jako wnioskodawca w postępowaniu przed Trybunałem Konstytucyjnym*, Warsaw 2014.

Deryng A., Sąd polubowny a realizacja konstytucyjnej zasady prawa do sądu, w: *ADR. Arbitraż i Mediacja* (1) 2009. *"Perspektywy rozwoju sądownictwa arbitrażowego", Katowice, 20–21.11.2008 r. – materiały pokonferencyjne (part 1).*

Dębiński A., Misztal-Konecka J., Wójcik M., *Prawo rzymskie publiczne*, Warszawa 2010.

Drechsler W., Max Weber (1864–1920) and Public Administration Today, *The Estonian Journal of Administrative Culture and Digital Governance* 1, 2020.

Dobosz P., Dylematy konstrukcyjne samorządności terytorialnej w Polsce w kontekście przestrzegania w przez państwo wymogów Europejskiej Karty Samorządu Lokalnego, in: Ofiarska M. (ed.), *Europejska Karta Samorządu Lokalnego a prawo samorządu terytorialnego*, Szczecin 2015.

Drobny W., *Kierunki zmian tożsamości polskiego prawa urzędniczego*, „Annales Universitatis Mariae Curie-Skłodowska", *Sectio G*, 64, z. 2. 2017.

Drobny W., *Przekształcenia pragmatyk urzędniczych członków korpusu służby cywilnej i pracowników samorządowych w prawie polskim po 1989 r.*, Warszawa 2015.

Drobny W., [w:] W. Drobny, M. Mazuryk, P. Zuzankiewicz, *Ustawa o służbie cywilnej. Komentarz*, Warszawa 2012.

Dubowik A., Dodatkowe zatrudnienie i inne zajęcia pracowników służby publicznej, *Praca i Zabezpieczenie Społeczne* (10) 2005.

Dubowik A., Pisarczyk Ł., *Prawo urzędnicze*, Warszawa 2011.

Dudek D., Komentarz do art. 153, in: *Konstytucja RP. Tom II. Komentarz do art. 87–243*, Safjan, M. Bosek, L. (eds.), Warszawa 2016.

Dudek D., Zasada bezstronności władz publicznych w sprawach przekonań i wolność ich wyrażania w życiu publicznym, in: *Katolickie zasady relacji Państwo-Kościół a prawo polskie*, Krukowski, J. Sitarz, M. Stawniak, H. (eds.), Lublin 2015.

Duniewska Z., Hauser R., Jaśkowska M., Matczak M., Niewiadomski Z., Wróbel Z., Instytucje prawa administracyjnego (w:) Hauser R., Niewiadomski Z., Wróbel A., *System prawa administracyjnego*. Tom 1.

Działocha K., Łukaszczuk A., *Nowa ustawa o służbie cywilnej (aspekt prawno-konstytucyjny), Państwo i Prawo* (11) 2006.

Florek L., Chapter 3. Swoboda umów w stosunku pracy, in: *System prawa pracy. Tom II. Indywidualne prawo pracy. Część ogólna*, Baran K.W. (ed. nauk.), Goździewicz G.(red.nauk.), Warsaw 2017.

Florek L., *Powszechne a szczególne prawo pracy*, WK 2016, LEX.

Frederickson H.G., *Whatever Happened to Public Administration? Governance, Governance Everywhere,* 'Working Paper. Queen's University Belfast' 2004, Vol. 3, p. 3, https://citeseerx.ist.psu.edu/viewdoc/download?doi=10.1.1.537.8624&rep=rep1 &type=pdf. (accessed 20.12.2022).

Gamian-Wilk M., *Mobbing w miejscu pracy. Uwarunkowania i konsekwencje bycia poddawanym mobbingowi*, Warsaw 2018.

Glumińska- Pawlic J. Zacharko L., Wybrane aspekty funkcjonowania służby cywilnej we Francji i w Polsce [in:] *Państwo, Administracja i prawo administracyjne w europejskiej kulturze prawnej. Księga jubileuszowa dedykowana Janowi Andrzejowi Jeżewskiemu z okazji osiemdziesiątej rocznicy urodzin*, Warsaw 2018.

Gołaczyński J., Krzywonos A., Prawo do sądu, in: Banaszak B., Preisner A. (eds.), *Prawa i wolności obywatelskie w Konstytucji RP*, Warsaw 2002.

Góral Z., Artykuł 1 ustawy o służbie cywilnej, in: *Prawo urzędnicze. Komentarz*, Baran K. W. (ed.), Warszawa 2014.

Górski, P., *Profesjonalizacja administracji państwowej w Polsce 1918–1939. Uwarunkowania społeczne i kulturowe*, Kraków 2011.

Górzyńska T., *Polskie prawo urzędnicze – kryzys tożsamości?*, Drobny, W. (ed.), Warszawa 2016.

Górzyńska T., Konstytucyjne podstawy służby cywilnej, in: *System Prawa Administracyjnego. Tom 2. Konstytucyjne podstawy funkcjonowania administracji publicznej*, red. Hauser R., Niewiadomski Z., Wróbel A. (eds.), Warszawa 2012.

Górzyńska T., *Standardy europejskie dotyczące pracowników administracji publicznej*, Studia Prawnicze, Warszawa 2001.

Gręzicki D., Służba cywilna w Polsce- rys historyczny, in: *Współczesna administracja publiczna w Polsce. Wybrane zagadnienia prawne, polityczne i ekonomiczne*, Bruski, R. Joachimowski, J. Koczur, T. (eds.), Toruń 2010.

Grzegorczyk T., *[w:] System Prawa Karnego Procesowego. Tom IV. Dopuszczalność procesu*, Hofmański, P. Jeż-Ludwichowska, M. Lach A. (red.), Warszawa 2015, LEX/el.

Grzybowski M., *Krajowe organy regulacyjne w sektorach infrastrukturalnych w świetle polskich ustaw sektorowych*, Białystok 2021.

Hauriou M., *Precis de droit administratif*, Paris 1927.

Hauser R., Konstytucyjna zasada niezawisłości sędziowskiej, in: *Zeszyty Naukowe Sądownictwa Administracyjnego* (1) 2015.

Hass L., *Pracownicze organizacje związkowe w Polsce 1918–1939, Roczniki Dziejów Społecznych i Gospodarczych*, XXV, 1963.

Iłowiecki R., *Statut legislatora w organach władzy publicznej. Zawód legislator* [in] Przegląd Sejmowy, No. 6, Warszawa 2010.

Itrich-Drabarek J. *Służba cywilna w Europie Środkowo-Wschodniej. Implementacja norm, procedur i wartości europejskiej służby cywilnej*, Warszawa 2013.

Itrich-Drabarek J., *Uwarunkowania, standardy i kierunki zmian funkcjonowania służby cywilnej w Polsce na tle europejskim*, Warszawa 2011.

Itrich-Drabarek J., *Uwarunkowania standardy i kierunki zmian funkcjonowania służby cywilnej w Polsce na tle europejskim*, Warszawa 2010.

Itrich-Drabarek J., The Evolution of the Polish Civil Service since 1989, *Studia Politologiczne* (57) 2006.

Izdebski H., *Komentarz do Konstytucji RP. Art. 149, 152, 153*, Warszawa 2023, 122 et sqq.

Izdebski H., *Wpływ rozwiązań prawnych i tradycji służby cywilnej RP na obecny model służby cywilnej*, „Studia Iuridica" 92/2022Izdebski H., *Fundamenty współczesnych państw,* Warsaw 2007.

Izdebski H., *Historia administracji,* Warsaw 2001.

Izdebski H., *Współczesne modele administracji*, Urząd Rady Ministrów, Pełnomocnik Rządu do spraw Reformy Administracji Publicznej, Wydawnictwo Urząd Rady Ministrów, Warszawa 1993.

Izdebski H., Kulesza M., *Administracja publiczna. Zagadnienia ogólne*, Warsaw 2004.

Jackiewicz A. I., *Prawo do dobrej administracji jako standard europejski*, Toruń 2008.

Jagielski J., [w:] Rączka K., Jagielski J., *Ustawa o służbie cywilnej. Komentarz*, Warszawa 2010.

Jagielski J., *Komentarz do ustawy o służbie cywilnej*, Warszawa 2001.

Jagielski J., Przepisy ogólne, in: *Komentarz do ustawy o służbie cywilnej,* Cieślak, Z. Jagielski, J. Rączka K. (eds.), Warsaw 1998.

Jaroszyński M., Zimmermann M., *Polskie prawo administracyjne, część ogólna*, Warszawa 1956.

Jaśkowski K., Maniewska E., Commentary to Article 10 of the Labour Code, in: *Komentarz aktualizowany do Kodeksu pracy*, Jaśkowski K., Maniewska E., (eds.), published: LEX/el.2022, www.sip.lex.pl (accessed 21.10.2022).

Jasudowicz T., *Kilka uwag o europejskich standardach administracyjnych – ze szczególnym uwzględnieniem służby cywilnej – w świetle europejskich standardów praw człowieka* [w:] Księga pamiątkowa profesora Eugeniusza Ochendowskiego, Toruń 1999.

Jezierska-Markocka A., [w:] A. Jezierska-Markocka, M. Markocki, *Służba cywilna. Stosunek pracy. Zarządzanie zasobami ludzkimi*, Warszawa 2016, Legalis/el.

Karwowska-Sokołowska A., Stawicka A., Stawicki P., Woźniczko J., *Kształtowanie wynagrodzeń w państwowej sferze budżetowej. Cz. II. Wynagrodzenia urzędników w II RP,* Warszawa 2021.

Kettel D.F., *The Global Public Management Revolution,* Washington 2005.

Kisiel W., *Ustrój samorządu terytorialnego w Polsce*, Warsaw 2002.

Klink B., Podejmowanie dodatkowego zatrudnienia przez pracowników administracji publicznej – problematyka prawna, *Radca Prawny* (6), 1999.

Kopczyński J., *Przepisy normujące stosunek państwowej służby cywilnej*, Warszawa 1925.

Korczak J., Refleksje nad polską służbą cywilną z perspektywy setnej rocznicy uchwalenia ustawy o państwowej służbie cywilnej, in: *Pro Opere Perfecto Gratias Agimus. Księga jubileuszowa dedykowana Profesorowi Tadeuszowi Kuczyńskiemu*, ed. Górnicz-Mulcahy A., Lewandowicz-Machnikowka M., Tomanek A. (eds.), Wrocław 2022.

Krąpiec M., *Powszechna Encyklopedia Filozofii vol.* III, collective work edited by Krąpiec M. A., Lublin 2002.

Krzyżanowska-Mierzewska M., *Dobra administracja a orzecznictwo Europejskiego Trybunału Praw Człowieka*, Warszawa 2007.

Kubiak A., *Konstytucyjna zasada prawa do sądu w świetle orzecznictwa Trybunału Konstytucyjnego*, Łódź 2006

Kubot Z., Kuczyński T., Masternak Z., Szurgacz H., *Prawo pracy. Zarys wykładu*, Warsaw 2008.

Kuczyński T., Mazurczak-Jasińska E., Stelina J., Stosunek służbowy [w:] *System prawa administracyjnego*, Hauser R., Niewiadomski Z., Wróbel A. (eds.), Tom 11, Warszawa 2011.

Kulesza C., [w:] *Kodeks postępowania karnego. Komentarz*, K. Dudka (ed.), Warszawa 2020,

Kulesza M., Niziołek M., *Etyka służby publicznej*, Warsaw 2010

Kurzyna-Chmiel D., Samorząd terytorialny – teraźniejszość i wnioski na przyszłość, *Samorząd Terytorialny* (9) 2020.

Kwiatkowski Z., Prawo do sądu w demokratycznym państwie prawnym, *Ius Novum* (2) 2019.

Lang J., [w:] *Prawo geodezyjne i kartograficzne. Komentarz*, Maćkowiak J., Myśliński T., Stefańska E. (red.), Warszawa 2018, LEX/el.

Lekston M. Komentarz do *art. 3 i 6*, in: *Ustawa o służbie cywilnej. Komentarz*, Baran K. W. (ed.), Warszawa 2021.

Leoński Z., *Zarys prawa administracyjnego*, Warszawa 2006.

Lewandowski T., *Samodzielność jednostek samorządu terytorialnego*, LEX/el. 2011, LEX.

Lipowicz I., Prawo obywatela do dobrej administracji, in: *Księga Jubileuszowa Jerzego Świątkiewicza. Państwo w służbie obywateli*, Hauser R., Nawacki L. (eds.), Warszawa 2005.

Lis-Staranowicz D., Chapter VIII Konstytucyjne środki ochrony wolności i praw, in: *Wolności i prawa człowieka w Konstytucji Rzeczypospolitej Polskiej*, Chmaj M. (ed.), Cracow 2006.

Lisowska-Krakowiak S., *Instytucje kuratorów a realizacja prawa do sądu w cywilnym postępowaniu rozpoznawczym*, Warsaw 2018.

Liszcz T. (ed.), *Prawo urzędnicze*, Lublin 2010.

Logchamps F., O pojęciu stosunku prawnego w prawie administracyjnym, *AUWr*, Prawo XII (19) 1964.

Łętowski J., *Pracownicy administracji w PRL,* Wrocław 1994.

Łukaszczuk A., Służba cywilna II Rzeczypospolitej, *Acta Universitatis Wratislaviensis. Przegląd Prawa i Administracji* 83, 2010.

Mądrzak H., Prawo do sądu jako gwarancja ochrony praw człowieka (studium na tle polskiego prawa konstytucyjnego, prawa cywilnego materialnego i procesowego), in: *Podstawowe prawa jednostki i ich sądowa ochrona*, Wiśniewski L. (ed.), Warsaw 1997.

Maniewska E., Commentary to Article 16 of the Labour Code, in: *Komentarz aktualizowany do Kodeksu pracy*, Jaśkowski K., Maniewska E. (eds.), published: LEX/wl. 2022, www.sip.lex.pl (accessed 10.11.2022).

Marciniak J., *Mobbing, dyskryminacja, molestowanie przeciwdziałanie w praktyce*, Warsaw 2020.

Mazur S., Możdżeń M., Oramus M., The Instrumental and Ideological Politicisation of Senior Positions, *Poland's Civil Service and Its Selected Consequences. The NISPAcee Journal of Public Administration and Policy* 11 (1) 2018.

Mazuryk M., Zuzankiewicz P., Drobny W., *Ustawa o służbie cywilnej. Komentarz*, Warszawa 2012.

Mojak R., *Skład, organizacja wewnętrzna oraz zasady funkcjonowania Rady Ministrów* [in] *Rada Ministrów, organizacja i funkcjonowanie* (ed.) A. Bałaban,2002.

Moroń D., Wynagradzanie członków korpusu służby cywilnej, *Studia Iuridica* (92) 2022.

Mroczka K., Służba cywilna w orzecznictwie Trybunału Konstytucyjnego, *Przegląd Prawa Konstytucyjnego* (3) 2021.

Mroczka K., Prawne i organizacyjne uwarunkowania systemu odpowiedzialności członków korpusu służby cywilnej w Polsce, in: *Polska Polityka i Historia. Politeja No.* 4, Cracow 2016.

Mroczka K., Samorządowa służba cywilna – szansa dla obywateli czy zagrożenie dla samorządności? Wnioski z badania jakościowego, in: *Sprawne państwo. Systemowe zmiany w funkcjonowaniu polskiego samorządu terytorialnego*, Ćwiklicki M. (red.), Kraków 2015.

Mróz B., Chudzicka-Czupała A., Kuśpit M., *Kompetencje osobowościowe i twórcze. Psychologiczne uwarunkowania kreatywności pracowników*, Warsaw 2017.

Niewiadomski Z., Prawo do dobrej administracji – aspekty procesowe, ustrojowe i materialne, in: *Prawo do dobrej administracji*, Warszawa 2003.

Olejniczak-Szałowska E., Problematyka determinantów wyboru monokratycznego lub kolegialnego modelu organu wykonawczego na poszczególnych szczeblach jednostek samorządu terytorialnego, in: *Pozycja ustrojowa organów wykonawczych jednostek samorządu terytorialnego*, Małysa-Sulińska K., Stec M. (eds.), LEX 2014.

Oleksy, K. *Etyka w służbie cywilnej [in:] Studia z zakresu nauk prawnoustrojowych Miscellanea No.* 5, Bydgoszcz 2015.

Olszówka M., Komentarz do art. 25, in: *Konstytucja RP. Komentarz, T. I*, Safajan M., Bosek L., (eds.), Warszawa 2016.

Paczocha J., *Raport Partia w Państwie. Bezprecedensowa wymiana kadr w administracji rządowej i jej legislacyjne podstawy*, FOR, Warsaw 2018.

Piotrowski R., Polityka zagraniczna a dobro wspólne. Uwagi o zgodności z Konstytucją RP projektu ustawowej regulacji służby zagranicznej, *Gdańskie Studia Prawnicze* (2) 2018.

Pisarczyk Ł., *Model zatrudnienia w administracji publicznej, [in:] Prawo administracyjne wobec współczesnych wyzwań. Księga jubileuszowa dedykowana Profesorowi Markowi Wierzbowskiemu*, Warsaw 2018.

Płażek S., Commentary to Article 80 of the Civil Service Act, in: *Ustawa o służbie cywilnej. Komentarz*, Baran K.(ed.), published: JPC 2021, www.sip.lex.pl (accessed 22.10.2022).

Pollitt Ch., Bouckaert G., *Public Management Reform. A comparative Analysis*, Oxford-New York 2000.

Potoczek A., Model współczesnego urzędnika administracji publicznej, in: *Urzędnik w administracji publicznej*, Sprengel B., Strzelecki A. (eds.), WSH-E in Wloclawek, Włocławek 2005.

Przygodzka R., Efektywność sektora publicznego, *Optimum – Studia Ekonomiczne* 4 (40) 2008.

Przywora B., Problematyka zgodności z Konstytucją RP alternatywnego trybu obsadzania stanowisk urzędniczych w administracji samorządowej (tzw. awansu wewnętrznego), *Samorząd Terytorialny* (7–8) 2014.

Przywora B., *Transformacje ustrojowe polskiej służby cywilnej*, Kraków 2012.

Przywora B., Kształtowanie kadr administracji publicznej, in: *Etyka urzędnicza i etyka służby publicznej. System prawa administracyjnego*, Vol. XIII, Hauser R., Niewiadomski Z., Wróbel A. (eds.), Warszawa 2016.

Rączka K., Jagielski J., *Ustawa o służbie cywilnej. Komentarz*, Warszawa 2010.

Romer M. T. (w:) *Prawo pracy. Komentarz, wyd. V*, Warszawa 2012.

Romer M. T., *Dodatkowe zatrudnienie a uprawnienia pracownicze*, Warsaw 1995.

Rożek K., Prawo do dobrej administracji w orzecznictwie Europejskiego Trybunału Praw Człowieka, *Roczniki Administracji i Prawa* XVIII (1).

Rydlewski G., *Służba cywilna w Polsce*, Warszawa 2001.

Rydlewski G., *Służba cywilna w Polsce. Przegląd rozwiązań na tle doświadczeń innych państw i podstawowe akty prawne*, Warszawa 2001.

Rzetecka-Gil A., *Glosa do wyroku SN z dnia 28 czerwca 2013 r.*, I PK 27/13, LEX/el. 2014.

Sala-Szczypiński M., *Zasadność zmiany klauzuli zasady współżycia społecznego [in:] Studia Prawnicze. Rozprawy i materiały No* 1, Cracow 2007.

Sala-Szczypiński M., *Znaczenie zasad współżycia społecznego w prawie polskim* [in:] *Państwo i Prawo No.* 1, Warsaw 2005.

Sanetra W. (ed.), *Stosunki pracy w służbie cywilnej i samorządzie terytorialnym*, Białystok 2001

Sienkiewicz M.W., *Samorząd powiatowy w Polsce. Założenia i realizacja*, Lublin 2011.

Sikora K., Samorząd województwa, in: *Administracja publiczna*, Tom III, *Ustrój administracji samorządowej. Komentarz*, Szmulik B., Miaskowska – Daszkiewicz K. (eds.), Warsaw 2012.

Sinkowska L., *Status prawny członka korpusu służby cywilnej*, Toruń 2002.

Skuczyński P., *Granice odpowiedzialności dyscyplinarnej [in:] Odpowiedzialność dyscyplinarna. Podstawy, procedura i orzecznictwo w sprawach studentów Uniwersytetu Warszawskiego 2000–2005*, collective work edited by Skuczyński P., Zawadzki P., Warsaw 2008.

Skrzydło W., Komentarz do art. 15 Konstytucji RP, in: *Konstytucja Rzeczypospolitej Polskiej. Komentarz*, issue VII, Warsaw 2013, LEX.

Skrzydło W., *Konstytucja Rzeczypospolitej Polskiej. Komentarz, 4th edition*, Cracow 2005.

Skrzydlewski P., *Osoba w przestrzeni publicznej. Wybrane zagadnienia z filozofii człowieka i polityki*, Cracow 2016.

Sługocki J., *Prawo administracyjne. Zagadnienia ustrojowe*, Warsaw 2012.

Sokolewicz W., Komentarz do art. 153, [in:] *Konstytucja Rzeczypospolitej Polskiej. Komentarz*, Garlicki L., red. Warszawa 2005.

Sokolewicz W., Komentarz do art. 153, in: *Konstytucja Rzeczypospolitej Polskiej, Komentarz*, t.II. L. Garlicki (ed.), Parliamentary issue, Warsaw 2001.

Springer B., Przesłanki i uwarunkowania tworzenia nowoczesnego korpusu służby cywilnej w Polsce po 1989 roku, in: *Stulecie polskiej administracji. Doświadczenia i perspektywy*, KSAP, Warsaw 2018.

Staśkiewicz W. *Stanowienie prawa*, [in:] L. Kolarska-Bobińska (ed.), *Co warto, co należy zmienić. Poprawa jakości demokracji w Polsce*, Instytut Spraw Publicznych, Warszawa 2008

Środa M., *Etyka dla nauczycieli*, Warsaw 2015.

Stelina J., *Stosunki pracy osób pełniących funkcje organów państwa*, Warszawa 2016.

Stelina J., Komentarz do art. 22 ustawy o pracownikach samorządowych, in: Rycak A. et al., (eds.), *Ustawa o pracownikach samorządowych. Komentarz*, issue II, WK 2016, LEX.

Stelina J. *Prawo urzędnicze*, Warszawa 2013.

Stelina J., *Prawo urzędnicze*, Warsaw 2009.

Szczerski K., Demokracja, nowoczesne państwo i korpus urzędniczy, *Służba Cywilna* (15) 2006.

Szewc A., Komentarz do art. 11 ustawy o samorządzie województwa [in] Szewc A., Ustawa o samorządzie województwa. Komentarz, *ABC* 2008, LEX.

Szewczyk H., Glosa do wyroku SN z dnia 12 czerwca 2013 r., I PK 2/13, *Judicature of Polish Courts* (1) 2015, item 6.

Szewczyk H., Modele służby publicznej i ich przydatność dla polskiego porządku prawnego, in: *Służba publiczna. Stan obecny, wyzwania i oczekiwania*, Stec M., Płażek S. (red.), Warszawa 2013.

Szewczyk H., *Mobbing w stosunkach pracy. Zagadnienia prawne*, Warsaw 2012.

Szewczyk H., *Stosunki pracy w służbie cywilnej*, Warszawa 2010.

Szewczyk H., *Opinia prawna do rządowego projektu nowelizacji ustawy o zmianie ustawy o służbie cywilnej 15.09.2008*, Biuro Analiz Sejmowych./H. Szewczyk, Legal opinion on the government's draft amendment to the Act amending the Civil Service Act 15 Sept. 2008, Sejm Analyses Office.

Szmit J., Pojęcie pracownika samorządowego (uwagi de lege lata), *Samorząd Terytorialny* (3) 2011.

Szydło M., *Regulacja sektorów infrastrukturalnych jako rodzaj funkcji państwa wobec gospodarki*, Warszawa 2005.

Tuleja P., Komentarz do art. 15 Konstytucji RP, in: *Konstytucja Rzeczypospolitej Polskiej. Komentarz*, Tuleja P. (ed.), WKP 2019, LEX.

Tymiński M., *PZPR i przedsiębiorstwo. Nadzór partyjny nad zakładami przemysłowymi*, Warszawa 2001.

Tykwińska-Rutkowska D., [in:] *Leksykon prawa administracyjnego*, Bojanowski E., Żukowski K. (eds.), Warszawa 2009.

Ura E., *Prawo administracyjne*, Warsaw 2009.

Ura E., *Pozycja prawna pracowników terenowej administracji rządowej i samorządu terytorialnego*, Lublin 1995.

Wachowiak J., *Dysfunkcjonalne zachowania pracowników*, Warsaw 2011.

Warecki W., Warecki M., *Słowo o mobbingu, czyli jak sobie radzić z dręczycielem*, Warsaw 2005.

Wieleba I., Umowne ograniczenie podejmowania dodatkowego zatrudnienia jako przejaw lojalności pracowniczej. Wybrane zagadnienia, in: *Annales Universitatis Mariae Curie-Skłodowska. Lublin-Polonia*, LXV (2) 2018.

Wiliński P., *Proces karny w świetle Konstytucji*, Warsaw 2011.

Winczorek P., *Komentarz do Konstytucji Rzeczypospolitej Polskiej z dnia 2 kwietnia 1997 r.*, Warsaw 2000.

Witoszko W., [w:] *Ustawa o służbie cywilnej. Komentarz*, K. W. Baran (red.), Warszawa 2021.

Włodkowska E., Wygaśnięcie stosunku pracy w służbie cywilnej [w:] *Stosunki pracy w służbie cywilnej i samorządzie terytorialnym*, W. Sanetra (red.), Białystok 2001.

Wojtyła K., *Miłość i odpowiedzialność*, Lublin 1960.

Wróbel A., Przedawnienie przestępstw funkcjonariuszy publicznych nieściganych z przyczyn politycznych (art. 44 Konstytucji Rzeczypospolitej Polskiej) [w:] *Z prawem ustrojowym porównawczym przez ponad półwiecze. Księga Jubileuszowa dedykowana Profesorowi Marianowi Grzybowskiemu z okazji 55-lecia pracy naukowej*, B. Przywora, A. Rogacka-Łukasik, K. Skotnicki (red.), Częstochowa 2022.

Wróblewska M., *Pilny projekt ustawy – założenia konstytucyjnoprawne a praktyka ustrojowa*, Warszawa 2024.

Wróblewska M., Rola Rządowego Centrum Legislacji w procesie tworzenia prawa, *Folia Iuridica Universitatis Wratislaviensis* 5(1) 2016.

Wronkowska S., *Problem racjonalnego tworzenia prawa*, Poznań 1982.

Wujczyk M., Komentarz do art. 2 ustawy o pracownikach samorządowych, in: *Komentarz do ustawy o pracownikach samorządowych*, in: *Prawo urzędnicze. Komentarz*, Baran K. W. (ed.), LEX 2014.

Wujczyk M., Commentary to Article 2, in: *Ustawa o służbie cywilnej. Komentarz*, ed. K. W. Baran, Warszawa 2021.

Wytrążek W., *Samorząd terytorialny w XX wieku w Polsce*, Lublin 2009.

Zacharko L., Janik M., *Nauka administracji. Paradygmaty współczesnego zarządzania w administracji publicznej*, L. Zacharko (ed.), Racibórz 2016.

Załucki M., *Kodeks cywilny – komentarz*, Warsaw 2022.

Zdyb M., *Standardy służby publicznej. Uwagi ogólne [in:] Annales Universitatis Mariae Curiae-Sklodowska* VOL. LXIV, 2, Lublin 2017.

Zonn-Pastemak K.(red.), *Państwowa służba cywilna*, Warszawa 1993.

Żurawik A., *Dobre obyczaje a zwyczaje, zasady współżycia społecznego i dobra wiara: ujęcie teoretyczne [in:] Kwartalnik Prawa Publicznego No. 7/4*, Warsaw 2007.

Zuzankiewicz P., Commentary to Article 80 u.s.c., in: *Ustawa o służbie cywilnej. Komentarz*, Drobny W., Mazuryk M., Zuzankiewicz P. (eds.), published: LEX 2012, www.sip.lex.pl (accessed 09.11.2022).

Zuzankiewicz P., Komentarz do art. 22 ustawy o pracownikach samorządowych, in: *Ustawa o pracownikach samorządowych. Komentarz*, Drobny W., Mazuryk M., Zuzankiewicz P. (eds.), Warsaw 2010.

Żuradzki P., Prawo do dobrej administracji w polskim porządku prawnym na tle Europejskiego kodeksu dobrej administracji, in: *Duch praw w krajach Europy Środkowo-Wschodniej*, Kępa M., Marszał M. (eds.), Wrocław 2016.

Others Publications.

- Odpowiedź na interpelację nr 29299 z dnia 27 kwietnia 2019 r. (Sejm VIII kadencji) MNISW.
- K.H. Goetza K. H. i Zubka Z., *Stanowienie prawa w Polsce. Reguły legislacyjne a jakość ustawodawstwa*, opracowanie wydane w ramach programu Ernst & Young „Sprawne Państwo", maj 2005.
  - Wronkowska S., *Tworzenie prawa w Polsce – ocena i poprawne kierunki zmian*. Raport Rady Legislacyjnej przy Prezesie Rady Ministrów, „Przegląd Legislacyjny" 2006, nr 1.
  - Szpringer W., Rogowski W., *Ocena skutków regulacji*, in R. Zubek (ed.), Analysis of the Polish practice of assessing the effects of regulation in 2001-2005, Warsaw 2007.
  - raporty z realizacji projektów: *Społeczny monitoring procesu stanowienia prawa*, Fundacja im. Stefana Batorego, Warszawa 2008.
  - Szmyt A., Opinion to the draft amendment of the law on the Council of Ministers (print no. 1344), Biuro Analiz Sejmowych, Warsaw 2008.
  - *Obserwatorium demokracji Instytut Spraw Publicznych, Demokracja w Polsce 2007–2009*, Warszawa 2009.
  - Dąbrowska A., Rzeczkowski G., *Źle lub jeszcze gorzej, czyli jak się tworzy w Polsce prawo*, Polityka, 7.3.2012.

System stanowienia prawa w Polsce – Zielona Księga, Kancelaria Prezydenta Rzeczypospolitej Polskiej, Warszawa 2013.

Rządowe Centrum Legislacji 15 lat w historii tworzenia i ogłaszania prawa, Warszawa, 2015.

- Report of the Head of the Civil Service on the state of the civil service and on the implementation of the tasks of the civil service for 2021. (accessed: https://www.bing.com/search?q=sprawozdanie+szefa+służby+cywilnej+za+2021&cvid=e7f8074fd2714d1193c660abb932e9f7&aqs=edge.0.69i59i450l8...8.704212j0j4&FORM=ANAB01&PC=DCTS, 19.10.2022 r.).
- Report of the Head of the Civil Service on the state of the civil service and on the implementation of the tasks of the civil service for 2021.
- Sprawozdanie Szefa Służby Cywilnej o stanie służby cywilnej i realizacji zadań tej służby za rok 1999, Kancelaria Prezesa Rady Ministrów, Warsaw 2000.
- Skotnicki K, Rządowe Centrum Legislacji, https://dspace.uni.lodz.pl/bitstream/handle/11089/40606/229-241-skotnicki.pdf?seque (access:20.08.2024).

Translation

Constitution of the Kingdom of Sweden Grundlagarna. Form of Government Act (Regeringsformen); Translation: Krzysztof Dembiński, Marian Grzybowski https://biblioteka.sejm.gov.pl/wp-content/uploads/2016/04/Szwecja_pol_010711.pdf (accessed 15.10.2022).

Constitution of Spain of 27 December 1978. translated by Tadeusz Mołdawa: https://biblioteka.sejm.gov.pl/wp-content/uploads/2015/10/Hiszpania_pol_300612.pdf (accessed 15.10.2022).

Constitution of the Portuguese Republic of 2 April 1976 Translation: Agnieszka Wojtyczek-Bonnand; https://biblioteka.sejm.gov.pl/wp-content/uploads/2016/03/Portugalia_pol_010116.pdf (accessed 15.10.2022).

Constitution of the Italian Republic of 27 December 1947, source: Constitution of Italy, transl. Z. Witkowski, Warsaw 2004, http://libr.sejm.gov.pl/tek01/txt/konst/wlochy.html (accessed 15.10.2022).

Costituzione Italiana. Testo vigente aggiornato alla legge costituzionale 11 febbraio 2022, n. 1. [Italian Constitution. Text of the current Fundamental Law updated to Constitutional Law No. 1 of 11 February 2022], https://www.senato.it/sites/default/files/media-documents/Costituzione.pdf (accessed 15.10.2022).

Przywora B. Wróblewska M., *On the Institution of Public Hearing - An Analysis from the Theoretical Point of View and the Perspective of the State's Political Practice (Fifth to Ninth Term of the Sejm of the Republic of Poland)*. file:///C:/Users/gosia/Downloads/Criticism%20Law%202_2024%20Przywora%20EN.pdf [access: 30.08.2024].

Normative Acts

Act of 23 December 1988 on economic activity, Journal of Laws 1988 no. 41 item 324.

Act of 5 July 1996 on civil service, Journal of Laws 1996, No. 89, item 402 (as amended).

Act of 10 April 1997. – Energy Law, Journal of Laws 1997 No. 54 item 348 as amended.

Act of 24 July 1999 on amendments to the Act on Departments of Government Administration and certain other acts Poland No. 70, item 778.

Act of 3 July 2002. Aviation Law, Journal of Laws 2002 No. 130 item 1112 (as amended).

Act of 28 March 2003 on railway transport, Journal of Laws 2003 No. 86 item 789 (as amended).

Act of 24 August 2006 on state human resources and high state positions, Journal of Laws 2006 No. 170 item 1217 (as amended).

Act of 21 November 2008 on civil service, Journal of Laws 2008 No. 227 item 1505 (as amended).

Act of 27 August 2009 on the Committee for European Affairs (Journal of Laws of the Republic of Poland of 2024, item 562).

Act of 23 July 2021 amending the Railway Transport Act, Journal of Laws 2021 item 1556.

Constitution of the Republic of Poland of 2nd April 1997 (Journal of Laws, item 483, as amended).

The Act of 8 March 1990 amending the Constitution of the Republic of Poland (Journal of Laws of 1990 No. 16, item 94).

The Act of 26 June 1974 - the Labour Code (uniform text, Journal of Laws of 2020, item 920, as amended).

The Act of 8 March 1990 on Local Government (Journal of Laws of 1990 No. 16, item 95).

The Act of 8 March 1990 on Commune Government (uniform text, Journal of Laws of 2022, item 559).

The Act of 8 March 1990 on Direct Elections to Commune Councils (Journal of Laws of 1990 No. 16, item 96).

The Act of 5 June 1998 on District Government (uniform text, Journal of Laws of 2022, item 528).

The Act of 5 June 1998 on Province Government (uniform text, Journal of Laws of 2022, item 547).

The Act of 21 November 2008 on Local Government Employees (uniform text, Journal of Laws of 2022, item 530).

The Act of 5 January 2011 - the Election Code (uniform text, Journal of Laws of 2020, item 1319 as amended).

The Act of 11 August 2021 on amending the Law on Public Finance and certain other laws (Journal of Laws of the Republic of Poland item 1535).

The European Charter of Local Self-Government drawn up by Members States of the Council of Europe in Strasbourg on 15 October 1985, ratified by Poland on 26 April 1993 (Journal of Laws of 1994 No. 124, item 607, as amended).

The Regulation of 25 October 2021 on Remuneration of Local Government Employees (Journal of Laws of 2021, item 1960).

Regulation of the Prime Minister of 23 June 1999 on granting the statute of the Chancellery of the Prime Minister Prime Minister's Office (Journal of Laws No. 56, item 590),

Resolution No. 38 of the Council of Ministers of March 31, 2009. – Amending the Resolution (M.P. No. 20, item 246),

Regulation of the Prime Minister of April 28, 2015 on legislative application (Journal of Laws of the Republic of Poland of 2021 item 1229, as amended).

Statute of 21 November 2008 on the civil service, Journal of Laws 2021, item 1233 unified text, as amended.

Statute of 21 January 2021 on the Foreign Service, Journal of Laws 2022, item 1076 unified text, as amended.

Statute of 17 December 2020 on strategic reserves, Journal of Laws 2022, item 637 unified text, as amended.

Statute of 8 December 2017 on the State Protection Service, Journal of Laws 2021, item 575 unified text, as amended.

Statute of 10 July 2015 on the Military Property Agency, Journal of Laws 2021, item 303 unified text, as amended.

Statute of 26 September 2014 on the Polish Space Agency, Journal of Laws of 2020, 1957 unified text.

Statute of 9 June 2011, Geological and Mining Law, Journal of Laws of 2022, item 1072 unified text, as amended

Statute of 9 May 2008 on the Agency for the Restructuring and Modernisation of Agriculture, Journal of Laws of 2019, item 1505 unified text, as amended.

Statute of 12 September 2002 on standardisation, Journal of Laws 2015, item 1483 unified text.

Statute of 3 July 2002, Aviation Law, Journal of Laws of 2022, item 1235 unified text.

Statute of 6 September 2001, Pharmaceutical Law, Journal of Laws of 2021, item 1977 unified text, as amended.

Statute of 27 April 2001, Environmental Protection Law, Journal of Laws 2021, item 1973 unified text, as amended.

Statute of 21 December 2000 on technical supervision, Journal of Laws 2021, item 272 unified text as amended.

Statute of 29 November 2000, Atomic Law, Journal of Laws 2021, item 1941 unified text, as amended.

Statute of 15 September 2000, Commercial Companies Code, Journal of Laws of 2022, item 1467 unified text, as amended.

Statute of 6 June 1997, Code of Criminal Procedure, Journal of Laws 2022, item 1375 unified text, as amended.

Statute of 10 September 1999, Fiscal Criminal Code, Journal of Laws 2022, item 859 unified text, as amended (sometimes helpfully: translation of the Criminal Code of June 6, 1997,).

Statute of 6 June 1997, Criminal Code, Journal of Laws 2022, item 1138 unified text, as amended.

Statute of 8 August 1996 on the Council of Ministers, Journal of Laws 2022, item 1188 unified text.

Statute of 20 July 1991 on Environmental Protection Inspection, Journal of Laws of 2020, item 995 unified text, as amended.

Statute of 7 December 1989 on amnesty, Journal of Laws of 1989, No. 64, item 390.

Statute of 14 March 1985 on the State Sanitary Inspectorate, Journal of Laws 2021, item 195 unified text, as amended.

Statute of 21 July 1984 on amnesty, Journal of Laws of 1984, No. 36, item 192.

Statute of 21 July 1983 on amnesty, Journal of Laws of 1983, No. 39, item 177.

Statute of 26 June 1974, Labour Code, Journal of Laws 2022, item 1510 unified text, as amended.

Case Law of the Constitutional Court

The judgment of Constitutional Tribunal of 17 July 2018. K 9/17, LEX No. 2518248.

The judgement of the Constitutional Tribunal of 26 September 2013, K 22/12, OTK-A 2013, No. 7, item 95.

The judgment of the of the Constitutional Tribunal of 15.06.2011, K 2/09, OTK-A 2011, no. 5, item 42.

The judgment of the of the Constitutional Tribunal of 14.06.2011, Kp 1/11, OTK-A 2011, no. 5, item 41.

The judgment of the Constitutional Tribunal of 15 November 2010, ref. P 32/09, OTK ZU No. 9/A/2010, item 100.

The judgment of the Constitutional Tribunal of 18 December 2007, ref. SK 54/05, OTK ZU No. 11/A/2007, item 158.

The judgment of the Constitutional Tribunal of 30 May 2007, ref. SK 68/06, OTK ZU No. 6/A/2007, item 53.

The judgment of the of the Constitutional Tribunal of 13.11.2003, K 51/02, OTK-A 2003, no. 8, item 86.

The judgment of the Constitutional Tribunal of 15 April 2003, ref. SK 4/02, OTK ZU No. 4/A/2003, item 31.

The judgment of the of the Constitutional Tribunal of 12.12.2002, K 9/02, OTK-A 2002, no. 7, item 94.

The judgment of the Constitutional Tribunal of 12 December 2002, ref. K 9/02, OTK ZU No. 7/A/2002, item 94.

The judgment of the Constitutional Tribunal of 10 April 2002, ref. K 26/00, OTK ZU No. 2/A/2002, item 18.

The judgment of the of the Constitutional Tribunal of 28.04.1999, K 3/99, OTK 1999, no. 4, item 73.

The judgment of the Constitutional Tribunal of 28 April 1999, ref. K 3/99, OTK ZU No. 4/1999, item 73.

The judgment of the Constitutional Tribunal of 17 November 1998, ref. K 42/97, OTK No. 7/1998, item 113.

Judicature of the Supreme Court

Order of the Supreme Court of 2 February 2022, I CSK 1036/22, Portal of Judgments of Common Courts.

The Judgment of the Supreme Court of 29 January 2019, ref: III PK 6/18, LEX no. 2619173, www.sip.lex.pl (accessed 05.12.2022).

The judgment of the Supreme Court of 18 December 2018, ref: II PK 243/17, published: OSNP 2019/8/97, www.sip.lex.pl (accessed 05.12.2022).

The judgment of the Supreme Court of 25 May 2016. II PK 185/15, LEX No. 2069441.

Judicature of the Supreme Court, Labour Chamber of 2014, No. 3, item 38.

The judgement of the Supreme Court of 12 June 2013, I PK 2/13,

Judgment of the Supreme Court of 15 March 2011. I PK 192/10, LEX No. 1162172.

Judgment of the Supreme Court of 18 May 2006, II UK 164/05, LEX No. 192462.

Judgment of the Supreme Court of 18 December 2003 I PK 157/03, LEX No. 127823.

Judgment of the Supreme Court of 6 January 1999, ref: III RN 180/98, http://www.sn.pl/sites/orzecznictwo/orzeczenia1/iii%20rn%20180-98.pdf (accessed 09.11.2022).

Judgement of The

Judgment of the Supreme Administrative Court of 13 March 2007, I OSK 630/06, LEX No. 330453.

Judgement of the Provincial Administrative Court

The judgement of the Provincial Administrative Court in Warsaw of 7 March 2012, VIII SA/Wa 110/12, LEX No. 1139883.

The judgement of the Provincial Administrative Court in Warsaw of 20 May 2016, I OSK 1996/14, LEX No. 2064205.

The judgement of the Provincial Administrative Court in Kraków of 24 October 2017, III SA/Kr 397/17, LEX No. 2381414.

The judgement of the Provincial Administrative Court in Gliwice of 15 May 2018, IV SA/Gl 1133/17, LEX No. 2505669.

The judgement of the Provincial Administrative Court in Wrocław of 3 March 2020, IV SA/Wr 412/19, LEX No. 2973907.

Others Courts

The judgment of the Court of Appeals in Łódź of 3 September 2014, III AUa 2070/13, LEX No. 1511671.

The judgment of the Court of Appeals in Warsaw of 19 December 2014, II AKa 441/14, LEX No. 1621228.

The judgment of the Świdnica Regional Court of 28 February 2013, II Ca 1000/12, Świdnica Regional Court Judgments Portal.

Ius, Lex et Res Publica
Studies in Law, Philosophy and Political Cultures

Edited by
Barbara Janusz-Pohl
Anna Jaron

Vol. 1 Anna Jaron: Socio-Economic Constitutional Rights in Democratisation Processes. An Account of the Constitutional Dialogue Theory. 2012.

Vol. 2 Stanisław Filipowicz: Democracy – The Power of Illusion. 2013.

Vol. 3 Teresa Dukiet-Nagórska (ed.): The Postulates of Restorative Justice and the Continental Model of Criminal Law. As Illustrated by Polish Criminal Law 2014.

Vol. 4 Agnieszka Kupzok: Enforcement of Patents on Geographically Divisible Inventions. An Inquiry into the Standard of Substantive Patent Law Infringement in Cross-Border Constellations. 2015.

Vol. 5 Alicja Jagielska-Burduk / Wojciech Szafrański: Legal Issues in Cultural Heritage Management. A Polish Perspective. 2016.

Vol. 6 Maciej Mataczyński (ed.): The Takeover of Public Companies as a Mode of Exercising EU Treaty Freedoms. 2017.

Vol. 7 Maciej Barczewski (ed.): Value of Information. Intellectual Property, Privacy and Big Data. 2018.

Vol. 8 Pawel Smoleń, Marcin Burzec: Introduction to Polish Tax Law. 2018.

Vol. 9 Łukasz Pohl, Konrad Burdziak: Judicial Interpretation of the 1997 Criminal Code Provisions on Self-Defence. 2019.

Vol. 10 Adam Szot: Judicial Review of Administrative Discretion. The Influence of Court Decisions on Administrative Actions. 2019.

Vol. 11 Michał Peno / Konrad Burdziak (eds.): The Concept of Modern Law. Polish and Central European Tradition. 2019.

Vol. 12 Leszek Leszczyński / Bartosz Liżewski / Adam Szot (eds.): Potential of Precedent in the Statutory Legal Order. 2019.

Vol. 13 Łukasz Bolesta: In Search of a Model for the Legal Protection of a Whistleblower in the Workplace in Poland. A legal and comparative study. 2020.

Vol. 14 Paweł Chmielnicki / Adam Sulikowski (eds.): New Perspectives on Legislation. A Comparative Approach. 2020.

Vol. 15 Marcin Burzec / Beata Kucia-Guściora / Paweł Smoleń: Agricultural Activity in Poland: A Fiscal and Legal Study. 2020.

Vol. 16 Magdalena Półtorak / Ilona Topa (eds.): Women, Children and (Other) Vulnerable Groups. Standards of Protection and Challenges for International Law. 2021.

Vol. 17 Josef Albert Fox: Die polnische Verfassung vom 3. Mai 1791. Hintergründe der Entstehung und der Außerkraftsetzung. Stellung Polens im Zeitalter der Aufklärung. 2021.

Vol. 18 Barbara Janusz-Pohl (ed.): Juvenile Justice Systems: Poland-Brazil-Portugal. 2021.

Vol. 19 Leszek Leszczyński: General Reference Clauses in the Judicial Process. Context of Legislative Intentions Interpretative Discretion. 2021.

Vol. 20 Francisco J. Campos Zamora: Das Problem der Begründung richterlicher Entscheidungen. Eine Analyse auf der Grundlage der Theorie der juristischen Argumentation. 2021.

Vol. 21 Aneta Skorupa-Wulczyńska: Language Rights of the Citizen of the European Union. 2022.

Vol. 22 Mateusz Osiecki: International Legal Aspects of Aerial Terrorism. Methods of Law Enforcement in Aviation. 2022.

Vol. 23 Vladimír Sharp / Gabriela Blahoudková / Jakub Handrlica (eds.): Law, Pandemics and Ownership Restrictions. 2022.

Vol. 24 Piotr Kasprzyk / Anna Konert: Drones – Future of Aviation Law? Interference of Public Law in Private Law. 2023.

Vol. 25 Szymon Pawelec (ed.): Consensual Procedures in Criminal Law – Comparative Perspective. 2023.

Vol. 26 Dorota Pudzianowska: The Statelessness in Public Law. 2023.

Vol. 27 Bogusław Przywora / Aleksander Wróbel: Formalised Access to Pre-jurisdictional Free Legal Aid. Analysis based on Example of Ukraine, Poland, Great Britain and Sweden. 2023.

Vol. 28 Ewa Dawidziuk / Patricia Panero / Anna Tarwacka (eds.): Family, Law, and Society: from Roman Law to the Present Day. 2023.

Vol. 29 Marian Grzybowski / Bogusław Przywora / Aleksandra Syryt (eds.): Free Legal Aid, Theory, Legal Basis and Practice. European Standards. 2023.

Vol. 30 Karolina Gmerek: Trial as a Social Communication Occurrence. Interactions Between Professional and Non-professional Participants of a Trial. 2023.

Vol. 31 Paweł Wiliński (ed.): Effective Legal Remedies in Criminal Justice System. European Perspective. 2024.

Vol. 32 Olga Sitarz / Anna Jaworska-Wieloch / Jakub Hanc : On the (Non)existence of the Right to Religious Freedom of Persons Deprived of Liberty. A Reconstruction of the Normative Standard Based on Polish and German Regulations in Comparison With Empirical Studies. 2024.

Vol. 33 Marian Grzybowski / Bogusław Przywora / Aleksandra Syryt (eds.) : Free Legal Aid – A Comparative Approach. Volume 2. 2024.

Vol. 34 Dominik J. Gajewski (ed.) : Functioning of Administrative Judiciary in the Context of Economic Changes. 2024.

Vol. 35 Barbara Mikołajczyk : Older Migrants – Vulnerable and Excluded. Searching for Visibility in Universal and European Laws. 2024.

Vol. 36 Maciej Świder: The Exercise of the Right to a Fair Trial in Light of Changes in Civil Procedure in the Era of the COVID-19 Pandemic. 2024.

Vol. 37 Tomasz Barankiewicz / Bogusław Przywora (eds.): Public and Civil Service in Poland. 2025.

www.peterlang.com

www.ingramcontent.com/pod-product-compliance
Ingram Content Group UK Ltd.
Pitfield, Milton Keynes, MK11 3LW, UK
UKHW020836290926
15470UKWH00004B/1375

9 783631 905647